DEACONS:

MALE AND FEMALE?

A Study for Churches of Christ

J. Stephen Sandifer

Copyright 1989

Additional copies may be ordered from:

J. Stephen Sandifer, P.O. Box 35296, Houston, TX 77235-5296

Library of Congress Catalog Card Number 88-92783
ISBN 0-9621965-0-9

Cover Design, Bob Nutt

Third Printing
by
Brentwood Christian Press
4000 Beallwood Ave.
Columbus, GA 31904-7217

All quotations are from the *New International Version of the Bible*, copyright 1978, New York International Bible Society.

Table of Contents

PART THREE
The Restoration Movement

PART FOUR
Contemporary Implications

Appendices

Preface

This study began in the fall of 1986. The elders of the Southwest Central Church of Christ in Houston were concerned about the status of deacons within the congregation. Like many congregations of the 80's, this church had a ministry system which organized much of the ministry of the church and a group of male deacons. Most members of the congregation would have difficulty naming the deacons. The elders were considering the relationship of deacons to the teams, what to do with elderly or non-functioning deacons, and the participation of women in the diaconate or ministry system.

I gave myself the assignment of preparing some thoughts for the elders' consideration. By the time of the designated elders' discussion, a twenty-five page paper had been delivered. But I could not let the study rest. Bits and pieces of material kept surfacing, and the word processor file grew longer and longer, taking on different formats.

Many of our concepts of the work of the deacon are based on tradition, not text. This study seeks to uncover the original concept of the diaconate and then trace its evolution. Most restoration readers are suprised at the variety of interpretations of the work and qualifications that are voiced in the short history of the Stone-Campbell movement.

The female deacon consumes a disproportionate part of this study. Most readers from Churches of Christ assume the validity of the male role, although I try to trace the historical development in detail. The female diaconate is generally denied among Churches of Christ; therefore, the materials concerning female involvement are presented at great length.

I do not expect this paper to radically change church polity. What I do expect is for readers to think. My purpose is to assemble in one location a volume of materials that most readers would not have the advantage of reading. Whatever conclusions are reached by the reader should be based on information, not ignorance or emotion. One of the largest segments of this publication is the bibliography. The works by Barnett, Echlin, Martimort and Gryson should be required reading for anyone interested in a detailed historical development of the subject. The works by Harrell and Bailey are especially helpful to understanding Disciples' development.

When one considers the feasibility of female deacons or a substantial change in the traditional male diaconate, he must also consider the unity of the local body. To correct one possible omission at the cost of disunity is highly questionable. To hold back the cause of Christ for the sake of a small minority or to please the brotherhood is also questionable. We should never be afraid to seek and test truth. Wisdom in applying truth is a gift from God.

The usefulness of this study will probably be found in open discussion and teaching over a period of years. That openness may create an atmosphere of increased acceptance of divergent viewpoints which will eventually allow for adaptations without biblical compromise.

Thanks are in order to all of those scholars who through the past 2000 years have written, compiled, translated and commented on the activities of the Christian church. Special thanks are due to: the elders of the Southwest Central church in Houston who encouraged me to study and publish this work; to Lynn Mitchell who was a constant encouragement and resource; to the libraries of the Rice University, Abilene Christian University, and St. Mary's Seminary (Houston); to the research staff of the Disciples of Christ Historical Society; and to numerous scholars who through correspondence provided council, research, and reference for this study. Thanks are also due to my proofreaders who gently guided me: Martha Haun, Robert R. Marshall, Lynn Mitchell, and Tom Olbricht.

Most of all, I thank Jo, Kenneth, and Cody who allowed me to spend so much time on this project.

J. Stephen Sandifer
February, 1989

Abbreviations

Ac.	*Acts*	Ju.	*Jude*
Am.	*Amos*	1Ki.	*1 Kings*
1Ch.	*1 Chronicles*	2Ki.	*2 Kings*
2Ch.	*2 Chronicles*	La.	*Lamentations*
1Co.	*1 Corinthians*	Lk.	*Luke*
2Co.	*2 Corinthians*	Lev.	*Leviticus*
Col.	*Colossians*	Mal.	*Malachi*
Da.	*Daniel*	Mic.	*Micah*
Du.	*Deuteronomy*	Mk.	*Mark*
Ec.	*Ecclesiastes*	Mt.	*Matthew*
Ep.	*Ephesians*	Na.	*Nahum*
Es.	*Esther*	Ne.	*Nehemiah*
Ex.	*Exodus*	Nu.	*Numbers*
Eze.	*Ezekial*	Ob.	*Obadiah*
Ezr.	*Ezra*	Phl.	*Philippians*
Ga.	*Galatians*	Phm.	*Philemon*
Gn.	*Genesis*	Prv.	*Proverbs*
Ha.	*Habakkuk*	Ps.	*Psalms*
Hg.	*Haggai*	1Pt.	*1 Peter*
Hb.	*Hebrews*	2Pt.	*2 Peter*
Ho.	*Hosea*	Ro.	*Romans*
Is.	*Isaiah*	Rv.	*Revelation*
Js.	*James*	Ru.	*Ruth*
Jer.	*Jeremiah*	1Sa.	*1 Samuel*
Job	*Job*	2Sa.	*2 Samuel*
Joel	*Joel*	Sol.	*Song of Solomon*
Jn.	*John*	1Th.	*1 Thessalonians*
Jos.	*Joshua*	2Th.	*2 Thessalonians*
1Jn.	*1 John*	1Tm.	*1 Timothy*
2Jn.	*2 John*	2Tm.	*2 Timothy*
3Jn.	*3 John*	Tit.	*Titus*
Jon.	*Jonah*	Zec.	*Zechariah*
Jud.	*Judges*	Zep.	*Zephaniah*

CHAPTER 1

Introduction

Members of Churches of Christ during the second half of the Twentieth Century no doubt heard deacons described in a way mirrored by J. D. Bales: "Although there were temporary offices in the church, such as apostles and prophets, the permanent offices in the church are two: the eldership and the deaconship," and "to function at its maximum capacity, the church needs to have elders and deacons" (7+).

However, this understanding was not the only one held by restoration authors during the brief period from Campbell to the present. Although Campbell held that elders and deacons were a biblical pattern, he did express reserve, stating that all we know about them is "purely incidental" and the result of human induction. He also added a third permanent office, that of the evangelist.

The most radical view from the Nineteenth Century came from Tolbert Fanning who served as editor of the *Gospel Advocate*. He denied that there were any offices in the church, finding the terms "elder" and "deacon" descriptive of work in progress, not names of appointed positions.

Contemporary writings echo some of Fanning's concepts. The concern today is about function, not office. As James Thompson puts it, "Their [deacons'] legitimacy is not derived specifically from ordination or appointment, but from their commitment to a task and the church's recognition of their work" (28).

Concerning Phoebe and deaconesses in general, the church of this century has denied any biblical basis for female deacons. Yet this understanding is neither universal nor historical within the Restoration Movement.

The pages to follow ask many questions and reproduce many documents from the past in an attempt to examine the diaconate from pre-Christian times to the present. The emphasis is on churches of Christ, but the development of the diaconate cannot be seen in a vacuum. Campbell, Fanning, Bales and Thompson are all products of education and culture. Their understandings differ because they are different, not because any one of them is more dedicated to Jesus or any better educated.

Part one will look at the biblical text. Chapter two will demonstrate that the diaconate was not a creation of the church but existed in society hundreds of years before it was adapted to church needs. The chapter will examine the deacons' work in pagan culture and will seek Old Testament models for the diaconate.

Chapters three and four will define the biblical term "deacon" and investigate passages that use it. The reader will immediately be impressed by the lack of texts available to define the work of deacons in the New Testament. A number of other words will be mentioned which flesh out the diaconal picture.

Much has been written about the qualifications of deacons. Chapter five reviews that material with an emphasis on the debated phrase, "husband of one wife." Many restoration fathers did not see marriage as a requirement for the deacon or elder.

The second section of four chapters will cover the seventeen hundred years between the close of the New Testament and the work of Campbell and Stone. Two chapters will discuss the development of the deaconate during the first four hundred years, the period in which the work evolves into clearly definable tasks and in which authority questions are framed and processed. The other two chapters examine the redefinition of the male diaconate and the rediscovery of the female diaconate beginning with the Protestant Reformation.

Part three takes a close look at the Churches of Christ. As culture and technology have changed, so have the church and the definition of its leaders. The work of the male deacon moves from treasurer to team leader. The work of the female deacon moves from being valued, to denied, and back to questioned. Discussions of considerable import are the effects of culture on the split between the Disciples of Christ and the Churches of Christ and how women were affected by cultural differences.

The last section may be the most hotly contested, as that is where conclusions will be drawn and implications presented. However, that section may also be the least significant in this book. The conclusions of the author are not as significant as those of the reader. The first three sections seek to present a volume of material on which reasoned conclusions can be based. Readers may have conclusions as varied as those of Campbell, Fanning, Bales and Thompson, but hopefully those conclusions are based on a prayerful consideration of the available information and the reader is understanding of others who have examined the same information with a different set of conclusions.

Finally, three appendixes are included to assist the serious student. The first lists all of the occurrences of διακονος in the New Testament in context. This collection emphasizes the complexity of the translation process. The second appendix is a compilation of quotations from early church writers concerning deacons, male and female. Many readers may not have access to extensive patristic libraries and will find this information interesting. Finally, a chart is included which compares the Greek words used for the qualifications of elders and deacons and groups those words into similar concepts.

To talk of deacons is to talk of service. The service of a deacon to a critically ill person two thousand years ago is vastly different from hospital ministry today. The complex mega-church with its multiplied specialized ministries requires a different set of duties for its servants than did the simple "mom and pop" church of the first century. An understanding of both the simplicity and the complexity of ministry frees the church for more meaningful service in the twenty-first century.

PART ONE

TEXTUAL CONSIDERATIONS

CHAPTER 2

Deacons Before Christianity

Men and women were designated as special servants in religions long before the development of Christianity. Some of these were referred to by the Greek διακονος. Early Christian churches were not creating a new ministry term when using that word; they were adapting one familiar in Greek society to the Christian situation.

Pre-Christian Judaism

Synagogue Organization

The concept of elders and deacons in the Jewish church may have had some precedence in the synagogue. The direction of the synagogue was in the hands of Jewish elders. In smaller and predominately Jewish communities, the leadership of the city and the synagogue would have been the same. Larger communities would have had several different groups of elders for city and synagogue organization as required by the circumstances. The elders had ultimate rule in the congregation. No trace has been found of congregational meetings to decide administration or discipline (Schurer 431).

A significant responsibility of the elders was the discipline of the synagogue members, including excommunication (Schurer 431). Jewish elders saw that the Law was observed, and they represented their community in dealing with the Roman authorities - judicial and administrative functions. Later Christian elders developed much wider functions which included pastoring the people and leading the corporate worship (Carpenter 149).

Individual officials within the synagogue were the "ruler of the synagogue" (αρχισυναγωγος), a "minister" (υπηρετης), and an almoner (Lk. 4:16; Schurer 428). The αρχισυναγωγος (president) was to ensure that nothing improper took place in the synagogue and probably was in charge of the synagogue building. He was responsible for the educational function of the synagogue and collected monies (Brooten 27+). Though he did not conduct the worship, he was in charge of supervising the arrangements and generally oversaw the business of the community (Schurer 433+).

The same word, αρχισυναγωγος, is found in pagan cults and guilds. This person was the president who convened and led the assembly. Sometimes he is also the founder of the society. Whether the Jewish synagogue borrowed the title from the Greeks or the Greeks borrowed it from the synagogue is uncertain (Schrage 845, Schurer 2.512 n. 38), but there is evidence that the Greeks originated the term (Horsley 113 219+).

In later times, the word is extended as a title for children and women. Schurer states that this use occurs especially in honorific situations (Schurer 433+). His interpretation has been questioned by Brooten who sees female αρχισυναγωγος as being entrusted with the actual charge of an office (5+). Brooten also has a lengthy excursus on the meaning of honorific titles, concluding that, ". . . there is no indication in the ancient sources that any of the titles of synagogue leadership were honorific at any period" (10). She does show that the title could have been given to the widow or child of an αρχισυναγωγος and that there may have been cases, especially with children, where the title would have been honorific until the child grew mature enough to provide the required leadership.

A recently published manuscript from Smyrna, written in the third century, speaks of a female αρχισυναγωγος. This woman is also the head of a household. Scholars debate whether this was an official position, merely honorific, or the recognition of the ruler's wife (Hemer 52).

Horsley feels that Brooten may have overstated her case but agrees that the function is no more to be denied for women than for men. If the title were merely honorific, he suggests that we should expect to see a greater number of females called by the term. The rarity of occurance supports the functional role just as it does female οικονομοι, προσταται, and asiarchs (113 219).

A synagogue could have had more than one "head of the synagogue" (αρχισυναγωγος). They were selected in a number of ways including inheritance and election. Female "heads" may have been part of a team of several αρχισυναγωγοι working together, with the female primarily responsible for the care of females and children (Brooten 32). Brooten also looked at manuscript evidence for women as elders (πρεσβυτεραι) and priests (ιερειαι), however, she never mentioned female διακονοι.

Schaff saw the activity of the synagogue in selecting two or three officers to care for the poor as a precedent pattern for deacons ("Deacon" 370). These officers were in charge of two collections: the weekly money chest from which the local poor were supported and the plate from which any needy person, especially strangers, could obtain a daily portion (Schurer 437). These almoners were not called διακονοι.

Although υπηρετης and διακονος were used interchangeably in Greek writings, it has been questioned whether διακονος ever appeared specifically of the synagogue helper (Hebrew *hazzan*). Beyer said "no" (92) while Schurer said "yes" (438). In Temple and talmudic times he was the only permanent synagogue official, presumably paid for his services (Kaploun 15). His job was to bring out and put away the Scriptures (Lk. 4:16 +), to announce the beginning and end of the service with a trumpet call, to execute punishment by scourging, and to teach the children to read. There appeared to have been only one of these ministers in a given synagogue. Schurer stated, "No one was nominated to conduct worship proper: the reading of the Scriptures, preaching, and public prayer.... These were still performed by the members of the congregation" (434 +). Υπηρετης and διακονος were not used together in the New Testament, but Ignatius did refer to the diaconate as the υπηρεται of God's Church in *Trallians* 2.3.

In later centuries, the roles of deacons and deaconesses are paralleled to the Levites (Apostolic Constitutions 2:25). When one thinks of the broad spectrum of duties assigned to the Levites (Nu. 3:5 +; 8:14 +, 18:3 +), the parallel is of interest. Roman Catholic scholars put a great emphasis on this parallel, seeing deacons, like Levites, as primarily concerned with assisting the priests in the service of worship (Biskupek 1 +).

The Levites were seen primarily as assistants to the temple priests. They served God's people as doorkeepers, administrators, chanters, and custodians of vessels and loaves. They were supported by the people; they taught and served (Echlin 4). Such a pattern may have served for the first century deacons and definitely parallels the deacons of the third and fourth century.

Lightfoot does not see the Levitical parallels:

It would appear... that the institution [diaconate] was not merely new within the Christian Church, but novel absolutely. There is no reason for connecting it with any prototype existing in the Jewish community. The narrative offers no hint that it was either a continuation of the order of Levites or an adaptation of an office in the synagogue. The philanthropic purpose for which it was established presents no direct point of contact with the known duties of either. The Levite, whose function it was to keep the beasts for slaughter, to cleanse away the blood and offal of the sacrifices, to serve as porter at the temple gates, and to swell the chorus of sacred psalmody, bears no strong resemblance to the Christian deacon, whose ministrations lay among the widows and orphans, and whose time was almost wholly spent in works of charity. And again, the Chazan or attendant in the synagogue, whose duties were confined to the care of the building; and the preparation of the service, has more in common with the modern parish clerk than with the deacon in the infant Church of Christ. ("Fresh Revision" 189+)

Female Servants

Exodus 38:8 mentions a group of "women who served at the entrance to the tent of meeting." There are two schools of thought about this tent. Those who take Exodus as a unified chronological writing see this "tent of meeting" predating the tabernacle and being the tent mentioned in Ex. 33:7. Moses pitches this tent outside of the camp and goes there to "inquire of the Lord:" "As Moses went into the tent, the pillar of cloud would come down and stay at the entrance, while the Lord spoke with Moses. . . . The Lord would speak to Moses face to face, as a man speaks with his friend." The literary-critical school sees Ex. 33:7-11 as a fragment of an older and different tradition which has been added for a literary purpose (Childs 590+).

More significant to our study is the organized work of women in connection with this tent. Driver states that the Hebrew verb for serving is used peculiarly in the ritual legislation of the Priest's Code of the service of the Levites about the tent of meeting. Here it expresses the performance of duties by women (33). Childs calls their service "organized service like the professional Levites." Nothing is known of the origin of this tent or of the service of the women, though suggestions include cleaning, making repairs, singing, and dancing (Childs 636).

1 Samuel 2:22 speaks of women who "served at the entrance to the tent of meeting" and tells that Eli's sons committed adultery with them. This "tent of meeting" is the tabernacle after it was established at Shiloh. This is probably a different tent from the tent mentioned in Exodus. In Eze. 8:14, Ezekiel describes idolatry in the Temple. He speaks of women sitting at the gate of the house of the Lord, "mourning for Tammuz," the Sumerian diety of spring vegetation. This reference may be to an adaptation by Israel of the Canaanite practice of temple prostitution connected with fertility and worship. We are uncertain what the women who served in the temple and early synagogues were called, but there was some type of organized service by females.

A first century inscription mentions a synagogue which contained "a hospice and chambers and water installations for lodging needy strangers." The Talmud talks of "visitors and wayfarers who eat, drink and sleep in the synagogue." Synagogues are used as hospices for Jews from abroad, especially in Jerusalem during the great feasts (Schrage 826). Considering the sexual division of labor during that period, women would perform such a ministry. This may be helpful in understanding the work of enrolled widows in 1Tm. 5.

Luke 2:36 + speaks of Anna who was a prophetess in the Temple. This suggests that she was a recognized teacher with the sanction of the Jewish leaders. Geldenhuys says: "It is possible, but not certain, that a room was given to her in one of the buildings on the temple-hill to live in. In any case, she was exceptionally faithful in attending all services in the temple and spent much time in fasting and prayer (121)." There is no specific connection between Anna and διακονος.

Some of the above examples were of servants connected with the worship of the Jews. In examining Christian deacons in the New Testament, no mention was made of liturgical functions. By the third century that function developed and was the primary role of deacons. Deacons in the Roman church and its derivatives have been concerned primarily with worship order, the Eucharist, and other sacraments since the third century. Only the most recent revival in the Catholic and Episcopal church has redirected their diaconate toward a lay ministry.

Pre-Christian Gentile World

Many examples of διακονος can be found in pre-Christian writings, mainly of one who waits at table. Other uses include: "servant," "messenger," "steward," "assistant helmsman," "baker," "cook," "wine-steward," "statesman," and (female) "maid." The word is also used of pagan religious servants. Diogenes was the διακονος of Zeus. In listing titles of those in a sacral union, διακονος is frequently found. These lists date from the first, second and third centuries B.C. (Beyer 92+).

Moulton and Milligan report, "There is now abundant evidence that the way had been prepared for the Christian usage of this word διακονος by its technical application to the holders of various offices." They list an inscription concerning the dedicators of a statue of Hermes, first century B.C., as including "heralders and διακονος." A list of temple officials dating 100 B.C. includes "wise men and διακονος." A third century B.C. inscription includes a "college of deacons" overseen by a priest who are in the service of the Egyptian deities Serapis and Isis. Some of these deacons are female (149). "The Greek word undoubtedly achieves its Christian significations (though not, of course, its significance) through its special use to name 'attendants' who were officials of religious guilds or societies in Hellenistic times" (Skemp 17). Little is known about the service of these pagan deacons and deaconesses. "Because of the importance of cultic meals in many of the pagan cults, this office may have been that of the sacred 'waiter' who served the religious meals" (Oster).

In a fascinating chapter comparing bishops and deacons to officers in ancient Roman associations, Hatch pointed out that the Romans had organizations for everything: trade guilds, dramatic guilds, athletic clubs, burial clubs, and literary and financial societies. Almost all of these had religious elements and patron gods. These associations were called by Greek terms known to Bible students: εκκλησια (assembly, church), συναγωγη (assembly, synagogue), συνοδια (sojourners, companions), and κοινωνια (association, communion, fellowship). The associations had treasuries and some shared common meals, activities with parallels in Christianity (28 +).

The officers in the Christian communities had the same names as those in the municipal senate or the controlling committee of the association and were known by other names common to a non-Christian society: συνεδρια (council, Sanhedrin), γερουσιαι (council of elders), πρεσβυτεροι (elders) and επισκοποι (overseers, bishops). In these associations, the chief administrative and financial officers were generally known by two names: επιμελετες (care taker) and επισκοπος (overseer, bishop) (Hatch 39).

The citizens of the first century composed a broad economic spectrum, making philanthropy very significant. Finance became a central focus in many associations. The funds were brought to one man, the επισκοπος, and he then gave them to servants known as οικονομοι (managers, stewards) or διακονοι (servants, deacons) to distribute. The benevolent need was even greater in Christianity because perpetual virginity and perpetual widowhood were encouraged, thus increasing the proportion of single women requiring financial assistance (Hatch 41 +).

The διακονοι were those who commonly served tables, especially in distributing the meat of sacrifice among the festival company in pagan religious associations. It was natural for them to become responsible for the Eucharist in the Christian association (Hatch 50).

Although not mentioning deacons, Porter comments at length on the pre-Christian use of επισκοπος, with some applications to the diaconate. He states that passive citizenship is unfamiliar to Greeks; they join societies and expect to assume responsibilities. Greek Christians take the titles of societal functions and apply them to the Christian church. They also seek to identify the titles with Old Testament patterns. Chapter Six discusses this further with Clement. Porter sees in the church the indefinite function and the official title combined in men. For instance, the overseers, επισκοποι, are both administers in an official sense and supervisors of spiritual matters in the indefinite sense. Their "authority" is centered in their care. They are not legislators or governors (103+).

The Christian Distinction

The difference between the pre-Christian and Christian usage of διακονος is centered in the message of Jesus. Jesus speaks of service as the opposite of authority or power. His message is best seen in the story of Lk. 22:24 + :

> Also a dispute arose among them as to which of them was considered to be greatest. Jesus said to them, "The kings of the Gentiles lord it over them; and those who exercise authority over them call themselves benefactors. But you are not to be like that. Instead, the greatest among you should be like the youngest, and the one who rules like the one who serves. For who is greater, the one who is at the table or the one who serves? Is it not the one who is at the table? But I am among you as one who serves."

Jesus illustrates his ministry by comparing himself with the table servant, the διακονος, although only the verb form appears in the passage. This service is sacramental in nature only as every Christian is a priest (1Pt. 2:5) having presented his body as a living sacrifice (Ro. 12:1). This is in sharp contrast to the Levitical priesthood and the sacerdotal diaconate of the third century A.D. It appears that the lesson of Jesus is quickly lost as the post-New Testament church reverts to the authoritarian structures of its Jewish and Gentile backgrounds.

The evidence is abundantly clear that there were deacons in both secular and religious circles prior to the church, and that the church adopted this terminology within its circles. However, the emphasis was changed to center on the service of Jesus as opposed to authority. "Thus we have in the Jewish community many points of initiation for the Christian offices of bishop and deacon, but neither here nor in paganism are there any exact models which are simply copied" (Beyer 91).

CHAPTER 3

Deacons in the New Testament

Nowhere but in a Christian context do we find the English word "deacon." The Greek word from which it originates, διακονος, appears in masses of Greek literature with a variety of servant applications of religious and secular import, but "deacon" is a product of Christian translators.

Probably no word more clearly defines the ministry of the church than διακονια or "service." The Christian is repeatedly called to service, and the noun, adjective, and verb forms appear over one hundred times in the New Testament.

Carpenter put it well: "In the Christian community, any conspicuous position, office or work was essentially a "ministry," a "service" to God and to the brethren, which might culminate in a total sacrifice like that of the Lord himself" (146).

Christian service - Christian deaconship - derives its essential nature directly from the person and work of Jesus Christ.

New Testament Words for Servants

The derivation of διακονος is uncertain. Διακονος is possibly cognate with the Latin *conari*, "to give oneself trouble", "to hasten" (Reicke "Deacons" 9). It is not linked with κονισ, "dust," and therefore does not mean "to go through the dust" (Hess 545). It has also been suggested that it is derived from διεκ–, "to reach from one place to another." The root meaning would be for someone to reach out with diligence to render service on behalf of others (Liddell and Scott 369). We can only conclude that the derivation is uncertain.

The verb form, διακονεω, is used thirty-six times to talk of someone serving another, such as Martha serving Jesus while Mary anointed His feet (Mt. 26:6+; Mk. 14:3+; Jn. 12:1+). The noun διακονια appears thirty-five times and is usually translated "service" or "ministry." The noun διακονος is used thirty times for the one doing the serving, that is, the "servant" or "minister." It is this last word which became the Latin *diaconus* and has been Anglicized as "deacon."

Various Greek words are used for servants with differing shades of meaning and emphasis. The diversity of meanings can be seen in the *LXX* translations of the Hebrew *ebed*: παις, servant, menial, 340 times; δουλος, slave, 327 times; Θεραπων, servant, attendant, forty-six times; οικετης, household slave, thirty-six times; υιος, son, once; and υπηρετης, servant, helper, once (Michel "Son" 609).

The most common word was δουλος, meaning "a slave, a bond servant." This person was owned by another and was obligated to whatever the master desired, stressing subjection, bondage, and limitation. The early church adopted the term to stress the Christian's total submission to his heavenly Lord (Hiebert 151, Rengstorf "δουλος" 261 +). Epaphras was called συνδουλος (fellow-slave) and διακονος (minister) in Col. 1:7, δουλος (slave) of Christ in Col. 4:12, and συναιχμαλωτος (fellow-captive) in Phm. 23.

The term οικετης was a practical equivalent, but was slightly more personal or intimate. The household slave, the one who personally waited on his master, was an οικετης in contrast to the slave in the field who was a δουλος (Hiebert 152).

The μισΘιος and μισΘωτος (Mk. 1:20) were hired servants or employees. They were not owned, but worked for a price. Jesus contrasts the good shepherd with the hireling (μισΘωτος) in Jn 10:12 +.

A servant who willingly served out of respect or concern was a Θεραπων. Personal tenderness was present in this term, and the English word "therapy" was derived from the Greek. In the technical sense, it was applied to the service of healing (Hiebert 152).

Sometimes the word for child, παις is used for slaves (Lk. 7:7). This, too, is a term of endearment. The centurion's servant (Mt. 8:6 +; Lk. 7:7) and Herod's servants (Mt. 14:2) are παις. Παις Θεου is a common translation for the Hebrew "servant of God" passages, although it is rare in the New Testament. Of the eight occurrences, five are to Jesus, two to David, and one to Israel (Jeremias "παις" 700).

Λειτουργος refers to ministry in various senses: Ro. 13:6 refers to civil servants; Paul refers to himself as a minister with the priestly duty of proclamation (Ro. 15:16); angels are God's ministers (Hb. 1:7); and Jesus is a minister of the sanctuary (Hb. 8:2). Epaphroditus is described as συνεργος (fellow-worker), συστρατιωτης (fellow-soldier), αποστολος (messenger), and λειτουργος (minister) in Phl. 2:25. From the Greek, the English word "liturgy" was developed to refer to the sacral functions of worship. In its later use the term largely takes on a clerical and sacral nuance and is found referring to deacons (Strathmann 231). In Ro. 15 and 2Co. 8 and 9 the λειτουργεω and διακονεω word groups stand parallel (Hess 553).

The υπηρετης was a subordinate and was bound to obey, but as a freeman and not as a slave. Contrary to some older commentators, it is highly questionable if the term originally meant "under-rower." This slave possibly had a very specific duty in a system of integrated functions. Staff officers of the high priest (Jn. 7:32+; 18:3+; 19:6; Ac. 5:22+), the synagogue assistant (Lk. 4:20), John Mark in relation to Paul and Barnabas (Ac. 13:5), and disciples of Christ were called υπηρετης. In the patristic period, especially in Ignatius, the word is closely associated with the diaconate (Rengstorf "υπερετες" 533+).

The "steward" was the οικονομος. He was usually entrusted with some possession of his master and was to manage that possession and give account for it (Michel "οικονομος" 149). In five of the ten occurrences in the New Testament, the position was used of the treasurer for the master or municipality (Lk. 12:42; 16:1+; Ro. 16:23). The word for household administration was οικονομια and occurs eight times.

In some areas, οικονομος became a title for a church official. Several manuscripts have been found which refer to females, οικονομεισσα, within the church setting. One second century epitaph from Bithynia is discussed by Horsley. He states that women did function of their own right, but is undecided whether the term was the title of a female officer or simply refers to the wife of an οικονομος (69 161).

Although not translated "servant," the word συνεργος, "fellow-worker, colleague, assistant," should be included in our list, as there is evidence that it was used interchangeable with διακονος in the first century. It is frequently used in the missionary situation to describe the disciple as a cooperating servant of God, not merely an inactive instrument in the proclaiming the word (Hahn "Work" 1152).

The word of primary concern to our study is διακονος. It refers to a servant in relationship to his service, his activity:

> The difference between διακονος and δουλος (slave) is important for our understanding of διακονος. Δουλος stresses almost exclusively the Christian's complete subjection to the Lord; διακονος is concerned with his service for the church, his brothers and fellow-men, for the fellowship, whether this is done by serving at table, with the word, or in some other way. The διακονος is always one who serves on Christ's behalf and continues Christ's service for the outer and inner man; he is concerned with the salvation of men. (Hess 548)

Διακονος communicates a feeling of voluntary or cheerful service.

Of all the servant words, this is the one which most closely expresses a love motivated service (Hiebert 155).

Determining the meaning of a word must frequently be based on its context. The word διακονος used in 1Tm. 3:8, "διακονους likewise are to be men worthy of respect, sincere, . . . " is the same word that appears in Jn. 2:5, "His mother said to the διακονος, 'Do whatever he tells you.'" It is only the context that reveals that the servants of Jn. 2 are household servants at a wedding feast while the servants of 1Tm. 3 are a special group within the church. In classical Greek the word describes one who waits at tables, a messenger, servant, steward, assistant helmsman, baker, cook, wine-steward, statesman, and maid (Beyer 91). The "table servant" seems to be the primary use and is so used later in reference to cultic meals (Hess 545). The idea of table servant seems to be retained in Acts 6 for the verb form.

The word primarily is non-religious in the Greek and nearly always denotes something of inferior value (Schweizer 21c). "For a Greek or Roman citizen, consideration for service to those in need was limited to weaker fellow citizens; outsiders - slaves or resident aliens - were not generally included" (Hennessey 62).

One cannot look to the Old Testament for an understanding of διακονος. The *LXX* (Greek Old Testament) does not use διακονεω; διακονος is used seven times exclusively for court servants; and διακονια is used in two unimportant cases. Instead, the word groups of δουλευω (slave) and λατρευω (servant) are used (Hess 545).

Deacon in the New Testament

The translators had a difficulty. How were they to translate διακονος? Their solution in three passages was not to translate it at all. The Latin Vulgate was one of the first to use the loan word *diaconus* in Phl. 1 and 1Tm. 3. It was peculiar to Christian Latin (Easton 181). English writers simply coined an English word - deacon - with a variety of spellings. Jack Lewis gave a succinct explanation:

> That it is not translated "minister" or "servant" in these cases is due to the translators following the pattern Jerome set in Latin and likely a reflection of high churchmanship on the part of the K. J. V. translators who consciously or unconsciously wanted to preserve established church organization. (2)

Appendix A gives every use of the noun διακονος in the New Testament. It is used of a special church servant, of Christ, of Paul, and of other individuals (Phoebe, Apollos, Epaphras, Tychicus, and Timothy), as a model for all Christians, and of general servants.

Turner puts it well:

> We should represent to ourselves more effectually the meaning of the New Testament if instead of talking of "deacons" we talked of "servants," - "men-servants" and "women-servants." Moreover, the duties performed by these "servants" of the Church of Cenchreae or of Philippi or whatever Church it might be, were, if not menial, at any rate humble, and such as really corresponded to the name. (330)

Philippians 1:1

Only three times, in two passages, is διακονος consistently translated in a technical sense as the special group of servants of the church that we call "deacons." In Phl. 1, Paul writes "to all the saints in Christ Jesus at Philippi, together with the overseers and servants." The Philippian letter was probably written between A.D. 53 and 58.

Grammatically, there are two ways to translate Phl. 1:1. It can refer to two distinct groups, "overseers (bishops) and servants (deacons)," or it may refer to a single group of people, "bishops who are deacons (overseers who are servants or who serve)." Almost all scholars prefer the first interpretation. Hawthorne argues for the later (9+). But Hardy says: "One must remain uncertain whether this refers to two definite orders, or simply to those who guided and served the church, which might indeed mean the same individuals in different capacities" (14).

Most commentators see επισκοπος and διακονος as two functioning groups within the church. Lightfoot holds that the Philippians sent financial aid to Jerusalem in the name of its church officers; hence the address to that group (Philippians 82). Not all would accept this passage as addressing established office holders in the church, suggesting that the leaders and servants of the church are addressed without a technical identity.

Hennessey suggests that the bishops and deacons of Gentile Philippi parallel those administrative offices of Hellenistic cults and clubs (see Chapter Two). These offices could also parallel the prophets and teachers of the Jewish church in Antioch (72; Didache 15).

1 Timothy 3

Most writers interpret the mention in 1Tm. 3 as specific offices. Some of these writers also see 1Tm. as non-Pauline and written at a much later date, usually in the first half of the second century. They would, therefore, view Phl. 1 as the seed which is developed into an office a century later in 1Tm. 3. One of several difficulties with the late dating of 1Tm. is that the words "elder" and "bishop" are apparently used synonymously in 1Tm. without any mention of a monarchial bishop. The monarchial bishop is known at a date earlier than the date most of these scholars would ascribe to the Pastorals. The conservative dating of 1Tm. in the A.D. 60's does not allow as much time for the devolopment of ecclesiastical polity.

It is generally agreed that Philippians was written early in Paul's ministry, and 1 Timothy at the end, so some development is expected. Frend finds in the development of the church an emphasis on sound doctrine and the development of a canon of literature. He states, "There was also a striving towards what may best be called a 'normative Christianity.' This was perhaps not wholly uninfluenced by the emergence of a rival normative Judaism" (134). Part of this canon can be seen in Timothy as Paul emphasizes doctrine (1Tm. 4:16), "sound words" (2Tm. 1:13), and discipline of those who are in opposition (1Tm. 1:19+). The goal is a single faith with an ordered church government (Frend 134).

1 Timothy 3 begins by saying, "If anyone sets his heart on being an overseer (bishop), he desires a noble task." Seven verses later, Paul writes, "Servants (deacons), likewise, are to be men worthy of respect, sincere. . . ." In light of the context, the "servants" should be seen as a recognized group within the church. The third appearance of διακονος is near the end of the same passage in vs. 12.

Hort emphasizes that bishops and deacons are not merely two different offices, "[but] two contrasting offices, or (to speak more correctly) two contrasting functions. . . . The community of the saints was indeed an organized body, needing and possessing government on the one side and service on the other" (212+).

Many translations use the word "deacon" another time in 1Tm. 3. The N. I. V. translates the entire passage as follows:

> Deacons, likewise, are to be men worthy of respect, sincere, not indulging in much wine, and not pursuing dishonest gain. They must keep hold of the deep truths of the faith with a clear conscience. They must first be tested; and then if there is nothing against them, let them serve *as deacons*. In the same way, their wives are to be women worthy of respect, not malicious talkers but temperate and trustworthy in everything. A deacon must be the husband of but one wife and must manage his children and his household well. Those who have served well gain an excellent standing and great assurance in their faith in Christ Jesus. (1Tm. 3:8+)

"As deacons" in vs. 10 does not appear in the Greek text. The text simply reads, "let them serve." Some translations also insert the word "office" at this point. Considerable discussion exists among scholars whether "elder" and "deacon" are office titles or just recognition of service. Reicke states, "Bishops and deacons do not appear here as church dignitaries or officials, but as brethren of the church who carried out tasks of leadership and of unity" ("Deacons" 10). Schweizer argues against the work as an office by examining the various words normally used for political offices and rulers. He finds these words used in the New Testament of: Roman authorities, the Jewish priestly service, the service rendered by Jesus himself, and the service rendered by the church as a whole, but never of individual Christians toward the community (171). Hort also remarks:

> In reality he is probably thinking less of the men coming under either head than of the Ecclesia as a whole. . . . It would matter little how many offices there were. . . . That was a matter of external arrangement, which might vary endlessly according to circumstances. The essential thing was to recognize the need of the two fundamental types of function. (212+)

While examining this passage, another translator liberty should be noted which will be examined at greater length in the next chapter. Verse eleven literally says, "similarly women grave, not slanderers, sober, faithful in all things." All other words in the verse must be seen as interpretation by the translators.

The other twenty-seven uses of διακονος in the New Testament are less clear in their meaning. Jesus Christ is the model servant for all Christians. The men and women in Appendix A, section D, may be interpreted as functionaries, or in a few cases, as set apart servants.

Acts 6

Many writers use Ac. 6 in defining the role of a deacon. This passage is extremely important, for it is the only supposed scriptural authority for deacons leading in the financial and benevolent concerns of the church in contrast to the elders/bishops who care for the spiritual and pastoral concerns. This is the only passage which gives any example of the work of deacons, if one interprets the Seven as deacons.

Although the verb form "to serve" appears in the passage, the noun form does not. Certainly the Seven are special servants of the Jerusalem church. The question that remains unanswered is whether or not they are a special recognized class of worker in the same sense that "deacons" are designated later in the development of church order. Dana suggests that since the Jerusalem church used Aramaic, the Seven would not have been known officially by a Greek title (257). Many current scholars are less certain as to what language was spoken by Jesus and the Palestinian church. C. F. D. Moule states, "it seems impossible to treat this passage as evidence of the diaconate" (407). Lightfoot counters, "I do not see how the identity of the two can reasonably be called in question" ("Philippians" 188). The view that the Seven are deacons appears first in Irenaeus (A.D. 200) and is the traditional view of the Roman church (Against Heresies, 1:26:3, 3:12:10). Clement, a contemporary of Irenaeus, makes no such identification (Stromata 2:20; 3:4).

While *Didascalia* and *Constitutions* both stated that the number of deacons was determined by the needs of the church, it was not uncommon in the early church to find seven deacons in a city. The practice of seven deacons per city became a law in the fifteenth canon of the Council of Neo-Caesarea (A.D. 315): "In even the largest towns there must be, according to the rule, no more than seven deacons. This may be proved from the Acts of the Apostles" (Hefele 1.230). The *Testament of our Lord* (A.D. 450) mentioned a church which had a bishop, twelve presbyters, seven deacons, fourteen sub-deacons, and thirteen widows who had precedence (1.34 cited in Martimort 50). Prudentius in his *Peristephanon* refered to Lawrence as the chief of the seven deacons at Rome (2.37) and named Vincent as one of the seven deacons of Saragossa in the days of Diocletian (5.32) (Symonds 408).

Eusebius, writing about a challenger to the Roman authority, stated that the church in Rome had seven deacons, although it had forty-six presbyters (6.43). Fabian, Bishop of Rome (A.D. 236-250), divided the city into seven districts, each assigned to a deacon for care of the poor (Symonds 409). Sozomen (A.D. 425) reported that Rome had seven deacons, but other churches found the number of no significance (7.19). Justinian (A.D. 535) stated that the number of deacons in the metropolitan church of Constantinople should be no more than one hundred (Novelle 3.3.1 cited in Martimort 109). In the acts of the Council of Chalcedon, it is reported that the Church of Edessa had fifteen priests and thirty-eight deacons (Actio 10). In Rome, the Seven Cardinal Deacons remained until the eleventh century when the number was increased to fourteen (Neo-Caesarea 15). Since there were only seven deacons, they would be closer to the bishop and would need power to delegate their immense work to a larger number of sub-deacons and deaconesses under their care.

Ancient tradition is not unanimous on the identification of the Seven as deacons. Chrysostom denies it (Homily on Acts 14). The Council of Trullo (A.D. 692) quotes and approves his arguments against the identification (16). We also see that the work of the Seven is primarily the financial concern of the poor in Jerusalem, while the deacons of the later church were servants and assistants of the bishops. The bishop, not the deacons, is often in charge of the funds in the later church. Relief for the Jerusalem poor is delivered to the elders (Ac. 11:30). If financial concerns are a primary work of these men, οικονομος, "steward," would be a more exacting word to use.

There are other options to the identification of the Seven. First, they may be a temporary committee. Conybeare describes them as "ministering servants...who were elected to supply a temporary emergency" (466). Against the idea of a temporary committee is the suggestion that, in a growing church, the number of people needing service does not decline. It appears that the need for benevolent care for the widows would continue and increase. If anything, the committee needs to expand as time passes.

Others see the Seven as forerunners to the elders. This theory advocates that the Seven were the leaders of the Hellenistic Church. Elders do appear in the Jerusalem church quite early. The first mention is Ac. 11:30 where a contribution for the poor is sent to the elders. These elders were doing the same thing that the Seven had done - caring for the poor. The next mention of elders in Acts is chapter fifteen where the elders and the apostles discuss the question of binding the Jewish legal requirements on Gentile converts. The apostles and elders in Jerusalem appear to be the Christian Sanhedrin, the doctrinal council to decide the issue (15:2); the elders with the apostles and church welcome Paul and Barnabas and others (15:4); the apostles and elders meet to discuss the issues (15:6); the apostles, elders, and whole church choose their emissaries to send back to Antioch (15:22); and the apostles and elders sign the letter describing their recommendations (15:23). The distinction of elders being spiritual overseers working independently of apostles does not appear until Ac. 20:17 + with Paul's charge to the Ephesian elders.

Raymond Brown views the Seven as carrying out the overseeing tasks exercised by the presbyters/bishops later in the first century. They lead the Gentile church, while, at a later time, the apostles also set up a corresponding set of administrators (elders) for the Hebrew community. Those Hebrew presbyters are pictured as also being responsible for food distribution in Ac. 11:30 (326).

In the Jewish structure of the first century we see a twin set of authorities: the rulers of the people and the elders (Ac. 4:5, 8) or the high priests and the elders (Ac. 23:14; 25:15). The similarity between this and the Christian structure of the Apostles and the elders (Ac. 15) is not surprising. At times the Jewish high priest is singled out for emphasis, such as Annas or Ananias, just as James is singled out in Ac. 15 (Brown "επισχοπη" 326+).

If Philippians was a prison epistle, then the first evidence of deacons in the church occurs much later, parallel in time with the end of Acts. Remember that at least two of the Seven, Stephen and Philip, are also evangelists. The ability to handle the Word of God is later a qualification for elders, not deacons (1Tm. 3:2; Tit. 1:9+). Considering the implications of holding "the mystery of the faith with a clear conscience" (1Tm. 3:9), the Seven more nearly fit the work of elders as models for the ministries of oversight and of the word.

There are parallels between the number seven in Acts 6 and the seven judges appointed by Josephus in every city of Galilee to adjudicate petty disputes (113):

> And being conscious to himself that if he communicated part of his power to the great men, he should make them his fast friends; and that he should gain the same favor from the multitude if he executed his commands by persons of their own country, and with whom they were well acquainted; he chose out seventy of the most prudent men, and those elders in age, and appointed them to be rulers of all Galilee, as he chose seven judges in every city to hear the lesser quarrels; for as to the greater causes, and those wherein life and death were concerned, he enjoined they should be brought to him and the seventy elders. (Wars 2:20:5)

His citation may point out that a seven man council to handle minor disputes simply makes sense, be it in civil or spiritual matters.

One needs to realize that the Seven of Ac. 6 were not the first ones chosen to look after the needs of the Jerusalem widows. The Seven were chosen because the former administrators, whoever they were, were not being equitable to the Greek widows. Some system was already in place and functioning, although not to everyone's approval. The Seven all bore Greek names, significant to their ministry to the Greek widows, and may have been added to an existing benevolent body instead of being a totally new arrangement.

Acts 6 begins a distinction between the Jewish and Gentile churches of Jerusalem. Stephen's attack of the Jewish system, not his faith in Jesus, resulted in his death. Persecution occurred in Jerusalem, but somehow the Apostles and Jewish Christians remained in relative peace while Hellenistic church leaders, like Philip, had to leave. The Ac. 6 incident is the beginning of tension between the Hebrew Christians who wanted to keep the cultic aspects of the Law and the Hellenistic Christians who sought freedom from it.

If the above is an accurate interpretation, then, in many ways, the Seven should be seen as the leaders of the Hellenistic church while the Apostles are leaders of the Hebrew church. The Seven work side by side with the Apostles and on their own initiative. They are seen preaching and teaching with boldness, a role many scholars would deny to later deacons. Acts tells us nothing of their service to widows after their selection but instead concentrates on the ministry of the word as demonstrated by Stephen and Philip. This may explain why they were never called deacons. Although leading the Hellenistic church, they are not called Apostles either. It took an outsider, Saul of Tarsus, to become the first Hellenistic Christian recognized with Apostolic authority.

Schaff states: "the diaconate, like the presbytero-episcopate, grew out of the apostolic office, which at first embraced all the functions and duties of the ministry - the ministry (διακονια) of tables and of the word." It was left to the apostles to divide labor and form offices as times and circumstances required (Schaff "Deacon" 370).

While denying that the Seven in Ac. 6 were deacons, Conybeare says that even though the title "deacon" does not occur until later, the office seems to have existed from the beginning of the Jerusalem church. He uses the "young men" of Ac. 5:6, 10, as proof for this. He goes on to say, "In fact, the office of the Seven was one of much higher importance than that held by the subsequent deacons" (467+).

Perhaps Echlin is closest to the truth when he says, "It is more accurate to see here the church structuring its ministry but not the ordination of officers clearly differentiated from other community leaders" (7).

Young Men and Old Men

Raymond Brown examines the use of "young men," and states that each church office has two designations: the πρεσβυτερος (elder) or επισκοπος (bishop) and the νεωτερος (younger) or deacon. He cites 1Pt. 5:1, 5 as one example of νεωτερος for the subordinate office:

> The fact that νεωτερος, "younger," is not simply an age bracket (any more than is πρεσβυτερος, "elder") but another name for the subordinate office has frequently been missed, resulting in strange combinations, e.g., while the reference in 1Pt. 5:1-4 to πρεσβυτεροι has rightly been understood as a designation not simply for elderly men but for the holders of presbyterial office, the next verse (5:5) is thought to shift with its νεωτεροι to the theme of youth!

Brown also cites the parallelism of Lk. 22:26: "Let the great one among you become as a νεωτερος; let the one who rules become as a διακονος." In these passages, νεωτερος and διακονος are interchangeable terms (333).

An extensive and fascinating study of 1Pt. 5 comes from the pen of John Elliott. His conclusion is that the νεωτερος are "recently baptized persons, neophytes in the faith" (390). Eight *hapax legomena* appear in 5:2-5, and this can only be explained by contributing the section to an oral tradition that predates Peter's writing (373). Further parallels are drawn between the elder/younger contrast of 1Tm. 5 and 1Pt. 5 and the rank dispute that appears in Mk. 10:35 +, Mt. 20:20 +, and Lk. 22:24 +. Although his conclusion concerning the νεωτερος is unique, many commentators agree with him that there is "a specific group within the community, a group which involves more than their merely being young men" (377). The young men mentioned in Ac. 5:6 with the burial of Ananias and Saphira illustrate this conclusion.

The Greek νεοτερος is used comparatively in several places: 1Tm. 5:1 +; Tit. 2:4 +; 1Pt. 5:5. In two of these passages, 1Tm. 5 and 1Pt. 5, πρεσβυτερος is probably used of church leaders in the near context (1Tm. 5:17; 1Pt 5:1). There are several options with these passages: 1) The πρεσβυτερος in one passage are office holders while in the comparative sense are old men. The νεοτερος are young men. 2) The πρεσβυτερος are office holders throughout the contexts and the νεωτερος are deacons. 3) Both terms refer to age distinctions without reference to church offices. Most commentators hold to the second option above. Jeremias supports it ("Losegeld"), while Bigg (I. C. C.) denies that the young men were "the germ of the later deacon" and sees the contrast as one of age (190).

Some scholars have seen four classes of workers in the text of 1Tm. 5:1: elders, deacons, deaconesses, and virgins. The passage reads: "Do not rebuke an older man [elder] harshly, but exhort him as if he were your father. Treat younger men [deacons] as brothers, older women [deaconesses] as mothers, and younger women [virgins] as sisters, with absolute piety." The passage continues with a discussion of who is a real widow, followed by a charge to support the elders who serve well. Paul closes the section by saying, "Do not be hasty in the laying on of hands" (5:22). This is a possible reference to the ordination of the four groups. Problems exist with this interpretation, however it does deserve examination.

Office or Function

The same problem exists with διακονος that occurs with another

Anglicized word, αποστολος (apostle, one sent). Not only is this word applied to the Twelve (fourteen including Matthias and Paul), but it is used of Titus (2Co. 8:23), Andronicus (male) and Junias (female) (Ro. 16:7), Epaphroditus (Phl. 2:25), Jesus (Hb. 3:1), James (Ga. 1:19, 1Co. 15:7), and Barnabas (Ac 14:14). The use of the term in 1Co. 15:7 seems to imply more than the twelve spoken of in 1Co. 15:5. The word has several meanings, depending on the context.

Similar is the use of the Greek terms for elder (πρεσβυτερος), bishop or overseer (επισχοπος), and shepherd (ποιμην). All of these words were common descriptive terms. The words primarily describe the activity or age of individuals; rarely are they titles. The thing that makes an apostle an apostle is that someone sent him. An overseer was a bishop because he already led others and cared for their souls. The elder did not become an elder because of his appointment; he was already a family patriarch respected for his leadership. The deacon was one who served the church, and the church recognized that service.

Vincent, in the I. C. C., has an "Excursus" on bishops and deacons. He states:

> We find within this circle an entire lack of uniformity in the terms applied to church officials, and a marked vagueness in their use. The terms do not wholly explain themselves. Most of them are capable of a functional meaning; and in most, if not all, cases of their occurrence, they may be explained as indicating the peculiar function of an official instead of his official title. This is the case in Ac. 20:28, which is so often cited as decisive of the original identity of presbyter and bishop. (38)

He cites the functions or offices in 1Co. 12:28 + which lists apostles, prophets, teachers, miracle workers, healers, helpers, administrators, tongue speakers, and interpreters. Ephesians 4:11 + cites another group: apostles, prophets, evangelists, pastors, and teachers. Neither list includes "elders and deacons" as some traditions might anticipate. Vincent observes:

> This unsettled state of the nomenclature corresponds with the fact that the primitive church was not a homogeneous body throughout Christendom. While the Jewish-Christian church assumed the connection of all local congregations with the mother-church at Jerusalem, there was no similar bond among the Gentile churches. (I. C. C. 38)

Lightfoot includes a dissertation on "The Christian Ministry" in his commentary on Philippians. He sees the ideal Christian church having, "no sacerdotal system. It interposes no sacrificial tribe or class between God and man, by whose intervention alone God is reconciled and man forgiven. Each individual member holds personal communion with the Divine Head" (181).

However, he also states that the ideal can not be reached. He reasons:

> It must be evident that no society of men could hold together without officers, without rules, without institutions of any kind. . . . The church could not fulfill the purposes for which she exists without rulers and teachers, without an order of men who may in some sense be designated a priesthood. (182)

> For communicating instruction and for preserving public order, for conducting religious worship and for dispensing social charities, it became necessary to appoint special officers. But the priestly functions and privileges of the Christian people are never regarded as transferred or even delegated to these officers. They are called stewards or messengers of God, servants or ministers of the church, and the like: but the sacerdotal title is never once conferred upon them. (184)

Lightfoot goes on to demonstrate the evolution of church polity. He holds that the lists of 1Co. 12:28 and Ep. 4:11 reflect the natural development of leadership in two different communities. Neither list is intended to be exhaustive nor to give titles to offices. Rather, they reflect the work of the Spirit within the community. The diaconate, in his reasoning, originated in Ac. 6 to care for the needs of widows and orphans, though it was not a universal phenomenon as indicated in Titus. The work of presbyters developed early and universally. It started as government and developed to include teaching (185+). Thus is seen a gradual development of functionaries to meet specific needs within the early community. Lightfoot continues by examining the developments of the office of bishop for several hundred years. The question that is posed by this development is when, if ever, does structure become negative?

Moule, in editing a series on the diaconate in *Theology*, remarks on the origin of elders and deacons:

> If certain persons within the community are distinguished as διακονοι, it is only because they are rendering, in some representative form, the service of "ministry" which it is the vocation of every member of the whole church to render to all who need it. And if, again, there are further distinctions within this more specialized diaconate or "ministry," that is only another example of the principle of specialization. If there are waiters, there must be head-waiters or foremen; and such men will naturally be drawn from the more experienced members of the community: they are elders, or elder-overseers. ("Deacons" 405).

Carpenter points out that Paul did not mean to enumerate ecclesiastical offices, but to describe the various functions and services performed by the church body. He states that passages such as Ro. 12, 1Co. 12, and Ep. 4 tell us nothing about the organized ministry of the early church but do tell us about the types of activities in which the membership was engaged (147).

Vincent further stated:

Paul is a sower of ideas, not a methodical administrator; a despiser of ecclesiastical forms and ritualism; a mighty idealist filled with Christian enthusiasm, and who knew no other church government than that of Christ himself inspiring his disciples with the knowledge of what they ought to say and do. (Philippians 39)

There can be no doubt that discussions of this subject have too often been unduly influenced by ecclesiastical preconceptions, and conclusions reached in which the wish was father to the thought. To be able successfully to vindicate for any system of ecclesiastical polity an apostolic origin and sanction is to put into the hands of its representatives a tremendous lever. Investigation of this subject, if it is to lead to the truth, must be conducted on purely historical grounds apart from all dogmatic or ecclesiastical prepossessions. In the conduct of such investigations we shall do well to heed the caution conveyed in the words of Reville: "The prolonged and minute analysis of the smallest texts, in which one thinks to find an echo of the first Christians ecclesiastical organization, tends to a forcing of the meaning and to an exaggeration of the value of each trace that we discover; because we cannot be satisfied without reconstructing a complete organism, in which all the parts are logically related and mutually adjusted like the wheels of a perfect machine. Not only is the mechanism not complete, but properly speaking, there is yet no regular mechanism. . . . The functions, the dignities, the spiritual magistrates of primitive Christianity emerge little by little by organic growth." ("Les Origines de l'Epicopat" 330 quoted in Vincent 50).

Schweizer agrees stating:

The very choice of the word [deacon], which still clearly involves the idea of humble activity, proves that the Church wishes to denote the attitude of one who is at the service of God and his fellow-man, not a position carrying with it rights and powers. (21e)

It is nowhere forgotten that such renunciation of titles, honors, and offices testifies to the Church's newness in contrast to the old religious or secular order (Mt. 23:8 +; Mk. 10:42 +; 12:39; Lk. 11:43; 14:7 +; 16:15; 1Co.4:7 +; 2Co. 10 +). Of course, this does not mean that the ministry carried out in Jesus' name required no obedience. Ministry and authority are certainly not mutually exclusive opposites, either in the teaching of Jesus himself or in his Church. But it is not an obedience that is demanded on the ground of position or dignity, but an obedience that is given because a person is overcome by the ministry that is performed, and in particular by the word that is preached. (21f)

Conclusions

Based on the three accepted appearances of "deacon" in the New Testament, it is difficult to say much about the diaconate. The two passages seem to indicate that two classes of members were recognized as special servants in Philippi and Ephesus: 1) bishops/elders and 2) deacons. Bishops (επισκοπος in both cases) are listed first and have the stricter qualifications. It is assumed that deacons are under their direction, are their assistants and are juniors in leadership. 1Tm. 3 gives guidelines for their character.

All that can be said of their work is determined by translating the description, "servant". If the Seven of Acts 6 were not deacons, and the stronger evidence supports such an interpretation, then there is no biblical support for deacons being almoners or men in charge of benevolence. Exactly what they did, whether the work was an office or a function, how they were selected, and the tenure of their service is not revealed.

Cranfield adds an important statement:

> That the diaconate did not free either the congregation as a whole or the individual members severally from their responsibility for διακονια (ministry) is clear from evidence already considered. Rather it must have served to stimulate and to organize, to lead and to focus, the διακονια of the whole Christian community. ("Διακονια" 46)

In Ac. 14:23, Paul and Barnabas appoint elders in every church. Evidently this was not done in every virgin church, because Titus was instructed to "amend what was defective, and appoint elders in every town" (Tit. 1:5). Paul then gives instructions on the selection of elders. The absence of the mention of bishops/elders in the Corinthian correspondence is a significant exception to what otherwise appears to be standard polity in Pauline churches.

However, deacons are not mentioned in Acts or Titus. Timothy serves the church at Ephesus, therefore deacons are present or anticipated in Ephesus. Philippi also may have formal deacons, but there is no biblical evidence for deacons in any other congregation unless Phoebe, Apollos, Epaphras, Tychicus, or Timothy (Appendix A, Section D) are formal "deacons." If every complete assembly has deacons, it is strange that so little biblical evidence supports that structure.

Other lists of church officers are made in the New Testament, but not as the paired expressions "bishops and deacons." 1 Corinthians 12:28 mentions apostles, prophets, teachers, workers of miracles, those with the gift of healing, those who help, those who administer (κυβερνησις), and those who speak in tongues. Ephesians 4:11 lists apostles, prophets, evangelists, pastors (ποιμην) and teachers. Jerusalem had its Apostles and elders while Antioch had prophets and teachers. It appears that the early church had no unified internal structure. Each congregation was organized as it saw fit adapting the leadership forms of its cultural and religious background. The formal hierarchy of bishop - elder - deacon would not be seen until the second century.

An understanding of deacons in the first century church can only be derived from "reading between the lines." A more complete picture comes from examining the development of διακονος in the centuries before and after the formation of the Christian community.

CHAPTER 4

Female Deacons
in the New Testament

A much more debated and usually rejected concept in the churches of Christ is the position of a female deacon in the church.

Gryson, in his excellent study of the role of women states: "The conscientious historian, accustomed to affirm nothing except through strict investigation, must protest the naive self-confidence of those for whom all these matters are simple and evident at first sight" (xvi).

Martimort agrees:

What is most evident about the history of deaconesses. . . is the complexity of the whole subject. Even the Latin and Greek names, *diakona* and *diakonissa*, designated institutions that, in the history of the Church, were very different depending upon the era as well as upon the region concerned. (9)

A close look at the New Testament reveals primary passages that probably apply to female deacons and other texts which may be related.

Romans 16:1 - Phoebe

In Ro. 16:1 Phoebe is described as "a servant of the church in Cenchrea" (N. I. V.). The use of the masculine form διακονος in this quotation can be translated as "servant" or "deacon." Διακονος in Ro. 16:1 is the same word used in Phl. 1 and 1Tm. 3 of men. As with these passages, only the context can determine if an official status is being indicated. The Greek διακονισσα, "deaconess," and its Latin equivalent *ministrae* occur only in later ecclesiastical Greek (Vincent "Word Studies" 3:176), with the main use of διακονισσα coming at the beginning of the third century. Since the word "deaconess" never appears in biblical Greek, it would seem more correct to speak of a female deacon/servant than a deaconess. Josephus also uses the masculine διακονος of a female - of Rachel as a minister to Jacob (Antiquities 1:19:4).

Some translations of Ro. 16:1 include: "deaconess" - Revised Standard Version, J. B. Phillips, and Williams translations; "dear Christian woman" - The Living Bible; "a fellow Christian who holds office in the church" - New English Bible; "our sister, Phoebe, who serves the church" - Today's English Version; "servant" - King James, New International and Conybeare and Howson.

A second word that describes Phoebe is also extremely significant. Προστατις (Ro. 16:2) is translated as "protectress, patroness, helper;" and this is the only place the word occurs in the New Testament (Arndt & Gingrich 726). It is a noun form of the verb προιστεμι which is the Greek word for leadership through service.

Reicke points out: "in most cases προιστημι seems to have a sense a. 'to lead' but the context shows in each case that one must also take into account sense b. 'to care for.'" He continues of Ro. 12:8:

> Here the second expression is plainly analogous to the other two, which both refer to works of love. The meaning, then, is somewhat as follows: "He who gives let him do so with simplicity, he who cares with zeal, he who does good with cheerfulness.". . . The position is the same in 1Th. 5:12 . . . [where] the task of the προισταμενοι is in large measure that of pastoral care, and the emphasis is not on their rank or authority but on their efforts for the eternal salvation of believers. . . . 1 Timothy 3:12 describes good deacons as those who care well for their own households. . . . His attention is primarily directed, not to the exercise of power, but to the discretion and care to be shown therein. . . . The context [1Tm. 5:17] shows that the reference is not merely to elders who rule well but especially to those who exercise a sincere care of souls. The second half of the verse makes their diligence in pastoral care the criterion. ("προιστημι" 701 +)

The verb is also used in Tit. 3:8, 14, where it is clearly associated with the care of good works. It is in the post-apostolic fathers that the use comes to refer to administrative functions with no reference to care (Reicke "προιστημι" 703).

Scholars have debated at what point προστατις came to signify an office and not just a service. Horsley points out that by the end of the second century it had become an office and he cites statuary inscriptions which make that distinction. Although the application of the term to women is more limited than to men, he concludes that there were women of wealth who did provide patronage while holding a civil position. In Macedonia, the senior civil official beside the king was the *prostates*, and Olympias, widow of Philip II, served in that position in 334 B.C. Horsley concludes: "We can say that there is an entirely reasonable case for considering that the word could be used of women no less than men" (Horsley 122 243).

Porter in examining επισκοπος states, "Protection rather than direction or management was regarded as the principal attribute of the gods as επισκοποι." This leadership through loving care parallels that of the deacon. He summarizes that the επισκοπος was a custodian whose primary duty was to see to it that society functioned. He was not a legislator or governor, but an inspector and facilitator (106+). The *LXX* uses the word in that way in 2Ki. 12:11 and 1Ch. 34:12, 17.

Προστατις used of Phoebe means protectress or patroness. Her care is extended to many and to Paul himself. She is a model of servant leadership, just as elders and deacons are called to be. Be it deacon or servant, Phoebe was recognized as a special servant of the church in Cenchrea. She was so recognized by the church, by Paul, and by others. That is the work of a deacon with or without the title. She evidently had opened her home to Paul on his trips and was now entrusted with what may be considered his greatest work, the book of Romans, which she is delivering for him (Gibson "Phoebe" 281).

It is suggested that Phoebe was a widow because she should not by Greek manners have been mentioned independent of her husband had he been alive. The same applies to Tryphaena, Tryphosa, and Persis (Ro. 16:12). This may lend support to the interpretation that these women were either deacons or a special class of widow as mentioned in 1Tm. 5 (Schaff "Deaconess" 3:374).

Prohl suggests that prior to her conversion by Paul, Phoebe may have been one of the female philosophers of Athens, the εταιραι. If so, she would be permitted to travel freely and to preach to men and women (70).

Romans 16:1 may have a bearing on how Philippians 1:1 is interpreted. Since Ro. 16:1 clearly demonstrates that a female could be called διακονος (the masculine word), one can argue on linguistic grounds that the διακονος of Phl. 1 could be male or female. In Ro. 16, the masculine διακονος is used in conjunction with the feminine προστατις. Διακονος need not be limited to males in any passage on linguistic ground unless the context indicates that only males are implied.

1 Timothy 3:11 - Wives or Female Deacons

A second passage is 1Tm. 3:11: "In the same way, their wives are to be women worthy of respect, not malicious talkers but temperate and trustworthy in everything" (N. I. V.). The issue at question is whether the word γυνη should be translated as "women" or "wives," and more specifically if they are female deacons, the wives of deacons, or possibly the wives of other church officials. The passage literally states, "women similarly grave, not slanderers, sober, faithful in all things."

"Wives" is the translation of W. J. Conybeare, J. B. Phillips, the New International, New English, King James (in italics), Living Bible, and Berkeley version. "Women" appears in the American Standard, New American Standard, Revised Standard, Amplified, Weymouth, and Basic English translations. "Deaconess" is the rendering in the Williams and Centenary Translations.

Are the women of 1Tm. 3 wives of deacons or female deacons? Although the answer is uncertain, female deacons are strongly suggested. 1.) Note the first seven verses of the passage which speak of bishops. The only mention of a wife is that the bishop is "husband of one wife." It seems unusual that the wife of a deacon would be regulated while the wife of an elder is not. 2.) If the description were being given for the deacon's wife, it would also seem more logical to provide her description after the instruction concerning the deacon's marital status, not before. 3.) If these are the deacons' wives, why doesn't Paul use the genitive pronoun "their wives" or the article "the wives?" 4.) Notice also the form with which Paul begins his discussion of deacons, "Likewise... (vs. 8)." He uses the same formula at the beginning of vs. 11 as if beginning yet another type of church leader (see Chapter Five). 5.) In New Testament times, the word "deacon" has no feminine form, the masculine word is used of women. Paul was obliged to use another word, such as "women," to distinguish females from their male counterparts.

Brown summarizes the majority position of scholarship:

Paul's use of the masculine term διακονος not only suggests the existence of an order of women deacons, but also that the women were included in the same order as male deacons. This explanation would make the best sense of the injunction to women in 1Tm. 3:11 which occurs in a discussion of the qualities required in deacons. ... The use of διακονος for Phoebe and the fact that Paul is talking about διακονοι both before and after v. 11 suggests that he is also talking here about women deacons, and that men and women alike could be deacons. ("Woman" 1065)

The following parallel illustrates this interpretation:

Likewise must the deacons	Likewise must women
be worthy of respect,	be worthy of respect,
sincere,	not malicious talkers,
not indulging in much wine,	temperate,
not pursuing dishonest gain,	- - - - - - -
holding the deep truths of the faith with a clear conscience.	Trustworthy in everything.

In favor of "wives" as the meaning of 1Tm. 3:11 are the following:

1.) Verses 8 and 12 deal with male deacons; it is unlikely that a reference to deaconesses would be introduced in between them. 2.) If the women are church officers, the qualifications should be more detailed. 3) A more specific term for "women" would have been used for female deacons. 4) Having this verse wedged into the discourse seems to indicate that the women are related to the men. 5) The work of women is discussed in 5:3 + while 3:1 + is a discussion of men. It is inconceivable that two distinct classes of women existed - "deaconesses" and "enrolled widows" - whose duties would be precisely the same.

In countering the previous objection that the wives of elders are not mentioned, some suggest that deacons' wives could assist deacons in their duties, while elders' wives could not because of the nature of the elders' service. However, most of the scholars who hold to these arguments, especially number four above, do not deny the existence of female deacons, and many would see 5:3 + as a description of those servants.

A thorough discussion by Robert M. Lewis considered several possibilities: γυναικας as deacons' wives, as deaconesses, and as unmarried assistants to the deacons. After examining the first two possibilities, he sees both as suspect. He postulates that virgin assistants satisfy the criticisms against both of the former. The ministry of married women was centered on the home, while the unmarried were free to minister in various ways. "The issue is flexibility and availability to meet the service demands of an entire church. Both the married man and the unmarried woman can meet those requirements" (Lewis 167).

Lewis also states that if deacon's wives are assumed, then it must also be assumed that both a deacon and his wife are elected to fulfill these service obligations:

> Thus an office of "deaconess" is created, open only to those women whose husbands seek the office of deacon. Women who could not fulfill these functions.... negate their husband's chances of obtaining the deacon's office for themselves. (169)

J. G. Davies agrees with many scholars in doubting the Pauline authorship of the Pastorals. He sees no logical arrangement of materials within the book and suggests that 1Tm. 3:11 is possibly "an intrusive statement regarding women in general" ("Patristic" 2).

Chrysostom (A.D. 400) in his ancient commentary said, "Some have thought that this is said of women generally, but it is not so, for why should he introduce anything about women to interfere with his subject? He is speaking of those who hold the rank of Deaconesses" (Homily 11 on 1Tm. 3:8 +).

Theodoret (A.D. 450) agreed stating:

"The women likewise," that is to say, the [woman] deacons. . . . What he prescribed for men, [he prescribed] in similar terms equally for women. For just as he required deacons to be "serious," so he required women to be "serious." Just as he required deacons not to be "double tongued," so he required the women to be "no slanderers." Just as he required deacons to not be "addicted to much wine," so he required the women to be "temperate." (Interp. Epist. I ad Tim. 3:11, cited in Martimort 118)

Plevy was a seventeenth century church historian who prepared an *Ecclesiastical History* published in 1690. In his first edition, he wrote "deaconesses" for γυναικας in 1Tm. 3:11. However, in the English edition of 1726, "deaconesses" was changed to "their wives" because the Roman church had set about obliterating any trace of deaconesses (Echols Deaconesses 4).

1 Timothy 5:3 + - Widows

A further passage often connected with the female deacon discussion is 1Tm. 5:3 + where Paul gives instructions about church support of widows. Even though nothing is said in 1Tm. about widows being deacons, later church history reveals two classes of members who are often grouped with deaconesses: widows and virgins (Constitutions 2:25). The age of 60 for the enrollment of widows is later changed to fit the context of deaconesses (Tertullian On Veiling of Virgins 9; Council of Chalcedon 15).

Although the relationship of widows and virgins to the female diaconate will be discussed further in Chapter Seven, widows were the primary source of early deaconesses. Bingham oversimplifies the issue in saying, "None but such (elderly widows) were ordinarily taken into this office" (2:22:1). He goes on to list four ancient qualifications for deaconesses: 1) they were to be widows; 2) they should have borne children; 3) they should have been married but once; and, 4) they should have attained a considerable age - forty, fifty, or sixty.

Having said this, Bingham immediately gives an exception from an extremely early period (A.D. 107) where Ignatius greets "the virgins who are enrolled among the widows" (Smyrneans 13). The concept of a widowed virgin can only be understood in an ecclesiastical sense. Tertullian (A.D. 210) speaks with great disapproval of a young virgin who was made a deaconess (On Veiling of Virgins 9). Such references seem to indicate that the terms virgin, widow, and deaconess were synonymous or very closely related from a very early period. See also the discussion of "Young Men and Old Men" in the previous chapter.

Other scholars, such as Turner, deny any connection between deaconesses and widows in New Testament literature:

> The New Testament writings give us so far no hint at all of any order of women engaged in works of mercy: the widows correspond not to our sisters of charity but to the occupants of our almshouses. . . . Whenever widows are mentioned together with orphans, the emphasis is obviously being laid on the service which the church is to render to them, not on that which they are to render to the church."

He gives an example of a letter from Pope Cornelius to Fabius of Antioch which mentions the various orders of the clergy followed by mention of fifteen hundred and more "widows and afflicted" who were supported by the Roman church. He sees 1Tm. 5 as a list of those for whom the church provides financial support, whether passively as with widows or actively as with clergy (320 +).

In looking at the passage from Ignatius (Smyrneans 13), Turner sees the reference not to virgins who are ranked as deaconesses (widows), but of widows who through temperance are once again counted as virgins. He cites Tertullian who speaks "of widows who, not marrying again, are God's brides, God's maidens" (To His Wife 4).

Certainly, in the later centuries when the order of deaconess was well developed, the widows in need were a different group from the deaconesses who served. When and how the word "widow" (and the word "servant") took on a technical as well as a non-technical meaning has not been determined. It would appear that the widows of 1Tm. 5 were not church ministers in an official sense, but destitute widows who were supported by the church because of their exemplary Christian commitment.

New Testament Women

A company of women traveled with Jesus and were benefactors to his ministry. They are described as serving (διακονειν) him and were "many" in number. Among them were Mary Magdalene, Mary the mother of James and Joseph, Salome, and the mother of the sons of Zebedee (Mt. 27:55; Mk. 15:40). When the remnant met in the upper room after the Lord's ascension, they were there (Ac. 1:14). Echols wrote:

> Although it is certainly not suggested that these women were recognized as deaconesses in this early period, the functions they had performed during Jesus' personal ministry might very well have influenced the creation of a special sphere of activity for women disciples when similar needs were experienced by the community. (3)

Conzelmann sees the mention of the Galilean women in Lk. 8 and its parallels as theologically significant. He states:

> The Galilean women and Mary seem to stand in a similar relation to one another as the Twelve and the Lord's brethren. (48)

> Just as the male followers are turned into apostles, so the female followers are turned into deaconesses. (47)

Also connected to the interpretation of deaconesses as widows was the story of Tabitha (Ac. 9:36+). This Christian woman was "always doing good and helping the poor" and was a member of a band of Christian widows. Those grieving her death were widows, and when she was raised, she was presented to "the believers and widows." The text supports the recognition and organization of widows for benevolent service within the Christian community.

Both Paul and Apollos are called διακονος (1Co. 3:5) and συνεργος, "fellow worker," "helper." There is evidence to indicate that συνεργος and διακονος were interchangeable before διακονος became a technical term for an appointed ministry. Prisca and Aquila are called συνεργος, "fellow workers," with Paul in the Gospel, and may have been deacons, male and female, in the infancy of the diaconate, before διακονος became the formal designation (Ford 677+). The fact that Prisca's name normally appears first would suggest that she was known for her own ministry, not just as Aquila's wife. If the diaconate is more a function than an office, this thesis is even stronger.

1 Thessalonians 3:2 contains a strong textual variant to back up this suggestion. Metzger examines the five different variant descriptions of Timothy which have been transmitted:

(1) "God's fellow worker" (συνεργον του Θεου, D^P*, 33 ^d ^e, Pelagius, Ambrosiaster, pseudo-Hieronymus).

(2) "fellow worker" (συνεργον, B, Ephraem).

(3) "God's servant" (διακονον του Θεου, aleph, A, P^P, 424**, Goth, Boh, Arm, Syr^h, Eth, Basil, Theod. Mops.^lat.).

(4) "servant and God's fellow worker" (διακονον και συνεργον του Θεου, F^P, G^P).

(5) "God's servant and our fellow worker" (διακονον του Θεου και συνεργον ημων, D^p(c), K^P, L^P, Syr^P, most minuscules, Chrysostom, Theodoret). (240)

He explains that any of the first three could be the original. Bover, Nestle, UBS, and the New English chose the first; Weiss selected the second; and Tischendorf, Westcott-Hort, von Soden, and the R. S. V.

adopted the third. The first is the most difficult reading, therefore would explain the origin of the others. However, its manuscript evidence is less than impressive. Bruce and Frame prefer the third (Thessalonians 59; 126 +). Morris and Thomas recognize the transcriptional arguments for συνεργον, but prefer the third (100; Thessalonians 265). The variants are not easy to choose between, and demonstrate the interchangeability of συνεργος and διακονος in the earliest manuscript traditions.

Bertram also suggests that the words are synonyms and cites 1Co. 3:5 where Paul and Apollos are described as διακονοι of Christ followed by verse 9 where they are called συνεργοι. He says συνεργος in Paul corresponds to εργατας ("laborer") or δουλος in the synoptic kingdom parables (874). Epaphroditus is described as συνεργος (fellow-worker), συστρατιωτης (fellow-soldier), αποστολος (messenger), and λειτουργος (minister) in Phl. 2:25.

Conclusions

This writer sees as much evidence in the New Testament for the work of female deacons as he does for the male. 1Tm. 3 is most naturally understood if applied to female deacons, not wives or some informal un-named group. Phoebe is called a servant of the church, exactly what a deacon should be. The problems are created when the service function is solidified into an ecclesiastical office. The only reason to refuse the function to a female is her sex, not her activity.

Critics frequently object that the Scriptures do not say much about female deacons. Those critics should be reminded that the Scriptures do not say much about the male deacons either. It is scholastically dangerous to be dogmatic about either sex in the diaconal role in the first century.

The exact work of a female deacon is undefined in the New Testament.

Scholars on Deaconesses

Some readers might ask where certain commentators stand on the interpretation of Ro. 16:1 and 1Tm. 3:11. Following is a synopsis of their interpretations.

On Romans 16: Phoebe

In favor of the interpretation that Phoebe was an official "deacon" in Ro. 16 are: J. Barmby, A. Barnes, D. G. Barnhouse, J. Bingham, M. Black, E. C. Blackman, E. M. Blaiklock, P. C. Boylan, D. S. Briscoe,

C. Brown, F. F. Bruce, C. E. Cerling, J. Chrysostom, A. Clarke, W. J. Conybeare, C. E. B. Cranfield, C. H. Dodd, E. P. Echlin, J. M. Ford, C. Gore, F. E. Hamilton, L. R. Hennessey, M. Henry, K. Hess, R. J. Karris, K. E. Kirk, J. Knox, R. C. H. Lenski, J. B. Lightfoot, E. H. Maly, D. Moody, W. R. Newell, A. Nygren, J. C. O'Neill, R. C. Prohl, B. Reicke, H. Rolston, D. S. Schaff, K. H. Schelkle, J. R. Thomson, M. P. Truesdell, R. A. Ward, W. W. Wiersbe and K. S. Wuest.

Holding that Phoebe was an unofficial servant are: W. Barclay, H. J. Carpenter, J. Danielou, J. G. Davies, B. S. Easton, R. G. Gromacki, F. J. A. Hort, P. Hunermann, C. F. D. Moule, J. Murray, B. M. Newman and E. A. Nida, H. Rhys, C. C. Ryrie, W. H. G. Thomas, and D. C. Verner.

Those expressing uncertainty or not clarifying their interpretation of Ro. 16 include: C. K. Barrett, E. Best, H. W. Beyer, E. M. Blaiklock, W. Burrows, G. R. Cragg, H. E. Dana, C. R. Erdman, E. F. Harrison, J. S. Howson, A. M. Hunter, G. W. H. Lampe, A. T. Robertson, and W. Sanday and A. Headlam.

John Calvin saw Phoebe as an assistant and enrolled widow as described in 1Tm. 5.

M. Vincent held different opinions at various times.

W. Hendriksen said she occupied "a stable position, performed a definite and important function."

E. Kasemann saw her work as "an early stage of what became the ecclesiastical office." R. Gryson, A. Oepke, J. J. S. Perowne, and C. Robinson agree.

Uncertain, but leaning toward "deaconess" was H. C. G. Moule.

On 1 Timothy 3: Wives or Deaconesses

In favor of 1Tm. 3:11 as being qualifications for female "deacons" are: F. L. Arrington, W. Barclay, G. Barlow, J. Barmby, J. H. Bernard, C. Brown, R. E. Brown, F. F. Bruce, C. E. Cerling, J. Chrysostom, T. Croskery, J. Danielou, E. P. Echlin, R. Falconer, R. Finlayson, J. M. Ford, E. F. Harrison, A. C. Hervey, D. E. Hiebert, E. G. Hinson, F. J. A. Hort, J. S. Howson, A. J. Hultgren, R. J. Karris, J. N. D. Kelly, R. C. H. Lenski, J. B. Lightfoot, W. Lock, C. Robinson, H. Rolston, E. Schweizer, W. H. G. Thomas, M. P. Truesdell, C. H. Turner, and R. A. Ward.

Holding that 1Tm. 3:11 refers to the "wives of deacons" are: A.

Barnes, W. J. Conybeare, R. Earle, B. S. Easton, R. M. Gromacki, A. T. Hanson, M. Henry, J. L. Houlden, H. Kent, C. F. D. Moule, B. Reicke, C. C. Ryrie, J. Stam, C. Trentham, and W. W. Wiersbe.

Uncertain on the interpretation of 1Tm. 3 are J. G. Davies, G. W. Demarest, M. Dibelius and H. Conzelmann, D. Guthrie, and P. Hunermann. Uncertain, but leaning toward "deaconess" are C. K. Barrett, E. M. Blaiklock, E. G. Hinson, and A. T. Robertson. Uncertain, but leaning toward "wives" are M. S. Enslin and M. R. Vincent.

Holding that "women in general" was meant was A. Clarke.

Calvin stated that 1Tm. refers to "wives of deacons and bishops."

W. Hendriksen called them "deacon's assistants."

G. Fee called them "women who serve the church in some capacity."

Gryson refered to them as female ministers with the strong suggestion "that their service was analogous to that of deacons."

Holding that 1Tm. 5, not 1Tm. 3, refers to deaconesses are H. E. Dana, B. S. Easton, A. T. Hanson, and J. L. Houlden. This study has not dealt in detail with 1Tm. 5, and more of the above commentators may also see it as a reference to deaconesses.

Summary

Overall, in spite of their differences on the above, the following commentators recognized the existence in the first century church of female deacons: F. L. Arrington, W. Barclay, G. Barlow, J. Barmby, A. Barnes, D. G. Barnhouse, J. H. Bernard, E. Best, J. Bingham, M. Black, E. C. Blackman, E. M. Blaiklock, P. C. Boylan, D. S. Briscoe, C. Brown, R. E. Brown, F. F. Bruce, C. E. Cerling, J. Chrysostom, A. Clarke, W. J. Conybeare, C. E. B. Cranfield, T. Croskery, H. E. Dana, J. Danielou, C. H. Dodd, E. P. Echlin, R. Falconer, R. Finlayson, J. M. Ford, C. Gore, F. E. Hamilton, E. F. Harrison, L. R. Hennessey, M. Henry, A. C. Hervey, K. Hess, D. E. Hiebert, F. J. A. Hort, J. S. Howson, J. L. Houlden, A. J. Hultgren, R. J. Karris, J. N. D. Kelly, K. E. Kirk, J. Knox, R. C. H. Lenski, J. B. Lightfoot, W. Lock, E. H. Maly, D. Moody, W. R. Newell, A. Nygren, J. C. O'Neill, R. C. Prohl, B. Reicke, A. T. Robertson, C. Robinson, H. Rolston, D. S. Schaff, K. H. Schelkle, E. Schweizer, W. H. G. Thomas, J. R. Thomson, M. P. Truesdell, C. H. Turner, M. R. Vincent, R. A. Ward, W. W. Wiersbe, and K. S. Wuest.

The majority opinion is clearly that a group of women servants called deacons was recognized by the early church. Some commentators express questions whether Phoebe was too early in that development to be a deacon, however, most feel that 1Tm. 3:11 is a qualification statement for such a group.

CHAPTER 5

Qualities of a Deacon

Paul's first letter to Timothy lists the qualities that bishops and deacons (male and female) should possess. Although the duties are not given for either office, the qualifications are listed and are parallel in thought and structure. See Appendix C for comparison charts.

The qualifications given were not purely Christian; parallels existed in general Greek society (Barrett Pastoral 57, Dibelius and Conzelmann 51). Easton discussed such ethical lists at some length (197+). They were common in the writings of the Greek speaking Jews, most notably in Philo and in Wisdom. In their simplest form, they were learned by children. In the most advanced education, they were classified systematically. Some were arranged around common themes: "The Ruler," "The Philosopher," "The Good Woman," etc. Astrologers used lists to characterize those born under certain signs. They were also used on epitaphs. The lists appear to have been adapted, modified, and sometimes used without regard for the original purpose.

Stobaeus, a professional writer on ethics, lists the cardinal virtues, many of which are identical to those given in 1Tm. 3 and Tit. 1. Similar lists are found in Ptolemaeus, an astrologer, and Plutarch. In a multi-column form, Easton compares the qualities for the King, General, Elder (1Tm. 3), and Midwife (201). Onasander writes:

> I believe, then, that we must choose a general, not because of noble birth as priests are chosen, nor because of wealth as the superintendents of the gymnasia, but because he is temperate, self-restrained, vigilant, frugal, hardened to labor, alert, free from avarice, neither too young nor too old, indeed a father of children if possible, a ready speaker, and a man with a good reputation. (De imperatoris officio 1)

The passage continues with a commentary on the individual qualities (Dibelius and Conzelmann 158+).

Few of the virtues listed in 1Tm. are uniquely Christian. One assumes that a person entrusted with the ministry of the church is a person of deep belief in the Lord and love for people. They should be "full of the Spirit and wisdom" (Ac 6:3), but little is mentioned of such qualities in 1Tm. 3. Other concepts such as patience and confidentiality go unnoticed.

Alexander Campbell warned against strict interpretation of the qualifications:

> Consequently, the qualifications of its functionaries are relative, because no absolute standard could be ordained. A teacher, preacher, or bishop, for example, might be well qualified for one community and quite disqualified for another. Aptitude to teach, is a relative attainment or gift. The character and the attainments of a community must always decide what is suitable. There is no absolute maximum or minimum established, because it could not be done. . . . ("Church Organization, 3" 247)

> The New Testament alone does not furnish data enough from which to construct a complete system of church organization. ("Christian Organization, 8" 509)

Carroll Osburn said:

> This list was written to this man to be used with this church. It is not a complete list; it was never intended to be a complete list. It was never intended to be joined with anything else.

> The reason this list is in here is because in this congregation at this time you have a certain situation. . . . These are things at this point which if that congregation is going to make any progress they need to emphasize. Down on Crete there is a different situation. . . .

Any church leader must be of irreproachable character, free from scandal or selfish ambition. The major difference between elders and deacons is that elders oversee and are not novices while deacons serve. Although a specific age is not mentioned, "we scarcely meet with an instance of any one that was ordained before the age of twenty-five in all the history of the church" (Bingham 2:20:20). See Chapter Six for a more detailed discussion of the ages of deacons.

The passage will be broken down by element, and discussed for a clearer meaning:

> (3:8) Deacons, likewise, are to be men

> worthy of respect,

> sincere,

> not indulging in much wine, and

> not pursuing dishonest gain.

> (3:9) They must keep hold of the deep truths of the faith with a clear conscience.

> (3:10) They must first be tested; and then if there is nothing against them,

> let them serve as deacons

> (3:11) (Omitted, see below)

> (3:12) A deacon must be the husband of but one wife and

must manage his children and his household well.

(3:13) Those who have served well gain an excellent standing and great assurance in their faith in Christ Jesus.

Likewise

The use of "likewise," ωσαυτως, is a literary device. Three groups are discussed in this chapter. The bishop or overseer is described first. Then, verse 8 says "likewise the deacons." Verse 11 goes the next step, "likewise the women." Paul is saying that there are three groups: 1) bishops, 2) deacons, 3) women. The literary use denoting a list of similar items is important to the explanation of verse 11 to follow.

Chrysostom interpreted "likewise" differently:

That is, they should have the same qualities as bishops. And what are these qualities? To be blameless, sober, hospitable, patient, not brawlers, not covetous. And that this is what he means when he says "likewise" is evident from what he says in addition. (Homily 2 on 1Tm. 3:8)

Worthy of Respect

Σεμνος, is translated "grave" (K. J. V.), "serious" (R. S. V.), and "worthy of respect" (N. I. V.). Arndt and Gingrich list the meanings as "worthy of respect or honor, noble, dignified, serious, of deacons" (Arndt Gingrich 754). Gunther elaborates:

In Paul, it is used only once (Phl. 4:8) where directions are being given to Christians for the conduct of their everyday lives. Otherwise it occurs almost exclusively in the Pastoral Epistles. Σεμνοτης differs from ευσεβεια [godly, devout] in that it indicates, without direct reference to God, an ethical and aesthetic outlook resulting in decency and orderliness. Seriousness both of doctrine and of life is expected of the leaders of the church. (2:95)

Bales writes: "Those who come to him, or to whom he goes in the course of his duties, need to realize that they will be received with seriousness and dignity and not with contempt or scorn; nor will they be treated lightly and irreverently" (18).

Sincere

The words translated "sincere" (N. I. V.) are μη διλογος, and occur only one time in the New Testament. The King James and R. S. V. read "not double-tongued." The literal meaning is "not (μη) two (δι) words (λογος)." The deacon does not say one thing to one person, and another thing to someone else. Current slang would say that a deacon should not speak out of both sides of his mouth.

Fanning misinterpreted this as a requirement to be a good speaker, "He was not to be a stammerer, nor 'thick-tongued'" ("History 8" 360), and Durst followed Fannings logic (612). The possession of a good voice was considered a qualification by some patristic writers; however, this was more related to their liturgical duties after the diaconate developed beyond the second century. Chanting would have been an important part of the later development (Thurston "Deacon" 649).

Not Indulging in Much Wine

The K. J. V. states, "not given to much wine," while the R. S. V. reads, "not addicted to much wine." Elders are to be "temperate" (1Tm. 3:2) and "not given to wine" (Tit. 1:7). The need for sobriety is common to all Christians. Arndt and Gingrich interpret the Greek, "be addicted to much wine 1Ti. 3:8; enslaved to drink Tit. 2:3" (565). Brown states:

> The New Testament maintains a similar attitude to wine as the Old Testament. On the one hand, it is one of God's gifts of creation to be enjoyed. On the other hand, to refrain from drinking wine may be necessary for the sake of the gospel. . . . Moderation must not be confused with license. Bishops and deacons must not be drunkards. ("Vine" 922)

While the emphasis of the text is on self control, most spokesmen for Churches of Christ advocate total abstinence. Bales states, "On account of the influence and example one sets who drinks intoxicating liquor, a church would be foolish indeed to select a man as a deacon if he even drinks occasionally." He does agree that "there is no passage which literally says, concerning the deacons, 'no wine at all'" (30 +). His position is echoed in most of the authors of the Churches of Christ. Fulford writes, "This qualification, in addition to many other biblical principles, should preclude the social drinker from serving as a deacon in the church" (135).

Not Pursuing Dishonest Gain.

Both the deacon and the elder (Tit. 1:7, cf. 1Tm. 3:3) should avoid dishonest dealings. K. J. V. reads, "not greedy of filthy lucre," while the R. S. V. is "not greedy for gain." Considering the understanding that the deacons are treasurers of the church, the greed concern is not without warrant:

> The NT is critically opposed to the normal economic orientation of profit in so far as profit is looking for out of selfish motives. Tit. 1:11 is directed against teachers of false doctrine from Crete who were spreading abroad ideas with an eye to their own advantage. They teach "for base gain" (cf. also the warnings to the leaders and deacons of the congregation in 1Tm. 3:8; Tit. 1:17; 1Pt. 5:2) Anyone who is out for gain and whose view of life is dominated by the profit-motive falls into an arrogant self-centeredness, and thus into sin (Js. 4:13). (Siede 137)

Greedy men not only could misuse the funds of the church, but they also may be very slow to spend church money where it is desperately needed.

They Must Keep Hold of the Deep Truths of the Faith with a Clear Conscience

K. J. V. states, "holding the mystery of the faith in a pure conscience," with the R. S. V. in close agreement, "they must hold the mystery of the faith with a clear conscience:"

"The mystery of the faith" and "the mystery of our religion" both refer to the confessing of Christ and his redeeming work, i.e. mystery here is a paraphrase for the formulated confession of faith. (Finkenroth 505)

The Pastoral Epistles lay great emphasis on a good conscience. They speak of the "corrupt and unbelieving" whose "minds and consciences are corrupted" (Tit. 1:15), and "liars whose consciences are seared" (1Tm. 4:2). By contrast, Christians are to hold "faith and a good conscience" (1Tm. 1:19, cf. 1Pt. 3:16) and "to serve with a clear conscience" (2Tm. 1:3). . . . 1Tm. 1:5 names the consciences as the source of love in action. In short, the conscience can be regarded as the place where the "mystery of faith" is to be found (1Tm. 3:9). That is why "the appeal to God for a clear conscience," which is the essence of baptism (1Pt. 3:21), is so important. (Hahn "Conscience" 350+)

But the conscience is only part of our moral make-up. Its work is largely negative. As the pain we feel when we do something wrong, it acts like a red warning light. It serves as a sort of moral double-check on our actions. It operates largely on the basis of experience. It needs to be educated and carefully tended. (Brown "Conscience" 352)

Articles among Churches of Christ on this quality are very rare. R. C. Oliver penned such an article in 1971. Oliver explains that the mystery in Ep. 3 is "the fact that God has purposed from the beginning to save both Jews and Gentiles in one body, the church" (244). His conclusion is that:

. . . a deacon must be a man of faith who will administer both conscientiously and sympathetically to those in need and who will show no partiality in this administration. A true deacon is one who will deal equally with all men, without regard to their race or the color of their skin. (245)

Oliver's interpretation is too narrow. Some more traditional church members might add all sorts of secular doctrines to the "truths of the Faith." The truths are more clearly understood as the fundamentals of the Gospel: the incarnation, humanity and diety, death and resurrection of Jesus, and His plan for the salvation of creation. The deacon must be more than a kind serving man; he must be a man of deep faith.

The Husband of One Wife

Skipping to verse 12, the King James reads "the husbands of one wife," while the R. S. V. says "the husband of one wife." Literally it says, "the man of one woman." The words translated "husband" and "wife" are the basic words for man and woman and can be interpreted husband and wife in the context in which they appear. The word "wife" is the generic word used for "woman" in vs. 11 which will be discussed later.

The translation is easy, but the application is debated. The same requirement occurs in vs. 2 of the bishop, in Tit. 1:6 of the elder, and here of the deacon. On the feminine side, widows in 1Tm. 5:9 qualify for church support as "woman of one man." (In discussing this matter, some of the material to follow comes from writings on the qualities of elders, but the meaning is exactly the same for the deacon.) Several basic interpretations should be examined. The passage does not make the matter clear.

Must be Married

According to one view, only married men are eligible to serve as elders or deacons. The reasoning is simple - the home is a proving ground for one's leadership ability. If a man can't lead his wife and children, how can he expect to lead the church?

However, there is difficulty in reconciling this with 1Co. 7:1 +, 25 +. Paul in those passages shows the superiority of remaining single if God has given the temperament (gift) to be celibate. "An unmarried man is concerned about the Lord's affairs - how he can please the Lord. But a married man is concerned about the affairs of this world - how he can please his wife - and his interests are divided" (7:32b +).

Some scholars believe this passage refers to a specific local condition while others disagree. It is contradictory to say that the unmarried man has advantages in giving heed to the Lord's work and then prevent elders and deacons from having that advantage.

Possibly the earliest written argument in the Restoration Movement for unmarried elders comes from an anonymous author in Walter Scott's *The Evangelist* (1835). The writer, D. E., states:

> But I do not apprehend from what the Apostle says concerning the wife and family of a bishop that it is necessary for him to have either, in order to qualify him for the office. . . . This is undoubtedly said with a reference to the practice of polygamy which existed in those days, and it expressly forbids him from having two wives, but it does not necessarily imply that he should have any to qualify him for the office. ("Order No. 3" 243 +)

Alexander Campbell in the *Harbinger* of 1847 reviewed a new book (1845) by James Buchanan on church order. He quoted Buchanan as stating:

> A bishop or elder must, in case of the death of his wife, retire from office. . . . As

to having children - if it pleases God he should have none - the condemnation does not follow, it is having children not governed and ruled being in subjection. ("Church Order" 94)

Campbell did not agree with Buchanan and argued:

Now the husband of "one wife" stands in contrast with a polygamist, like Jacob, David, or Solomon; whereas the husband of "a wife" means no more than a person of family. In the primitive church many persons had, before conversion, a plurality of wives; and as the Apostles could not compel any one on his conversion to put away Martha and retain Mary, he inhibited such persons from exercising the bishop's office for two very obvious reasons - to discountenance polygamy and to prevent the bad example of disorderly families, inasmuch as the families of polygamists, from Abraham to Solomon, had become remarkable for disorderly and ungovernable children. But to divest a bishop of his office on the death of his wife, would be, in effect, to place the right of office in her keeping rather than in his. ("Church Order" 94)

Robert Milligan (1855) agreed:

These words [husband of one wife] would seem to imply that either celibacy or polygamy disqualifies a man for the office of a bishop. But there are some reasons which seem to imply that the latter only is intended.

First. Celibacy is not in itself an evil. In no part of the Bible is it so regarded. And at least two of the most eminent members of the Christian church were unmarried men. Hence it is not probable that Paul would condemn in others what he considered right and expedient in his own case. It is unreasonable to suppose that the chief of all the apostles would lay down, as a necessary qualification for the inferior offices, what is proved by his own example to be unnecessary for the superior; and which would have rendered both him and Barnabas ineligible to the eldership or deaconship in any Christian congregation.

Second. But polygamy is an evil. . . . Thomas Scott makes the following judicious remarks: . . . "Yet there was no direct command for a man who had previously taken more wives than one, to put the others away when he embraced the gospel; such a requisition might in some instances, have produced very bad consequences in domestic life and increased the opposition of the civil powers to the preaching of Christianity. But the rule that no man, however qualified in other respects, should be admitted into the pastoral office, who had more than one wife, or who had put away one to take another, tended to show the unlawfulness of polygamy and divorces on frivolous pretenses, and their inconsistency with the Christian dispensation. . . ." ("Elders" 688 +)

S. C., an unnamed writer in the *Harbinger* (1857), wrote in favor of married men:

The Apostle made no mistake, and while it is true that he excludes a polygamist, it is also true that he equally excludes a bachelor. How could a bachelor have faithful children?

The Greek church holds that neither a widower nor a married man to a second wife is eligible. (378)

David Lipscomb also wrote on the subject:

We do not think that language intended to require they should be married and have children; but as that was the common state of man, directions were given as to what kind of wives and children they should have. If it was prohibitory, Paul was unfit for a deacon; and he recommended that those who could restrain their passions should refrain from marriage that they might devote themselves exclusively to the service of God. (cited by McQuiddy "Query" 1921 550)

We believe an unmarried or childless man, if otherwise qualified, may be a bishop or a deacon. I think where the Scripture says "the husband of one wife," it means he must have but one wife and be true to her. Then he speaks of his having children. It means, since the rule was to have children, if he has them, he must rule them well. . . . This shows the end of the wife and children was disciplinary to teach and train the persons for the work of caring for the house of God. Now, if a man gets his training in some other way and shows his fitness of ruling, even though he has no family of his own, shall the church be deprived of his proved talent? (Lipscomb and Sewell 204)

In reacting to the writings of others such as Lipscomb, J. W. McGarvey said:

It would be unlawful to place a polygamist or bigamist in the office. But while the expression has this force, we think that candor requires the admission that it also has the effect of requiring a man to be a married man. . . .

Moreover, the context confirms the conclusion; for the apostle proceeds in both epistles to state how the overseer must govern his household, and especially his children; which statements imply that he is to be a man of family. (Eldership 56 +)

Kendrick agreed that marriage was essential (390). Hayden (1894) agreed with most of his predecessors that those unmarried and otherwise qualified could serve when circumstances demand their service (66). Morrison M. Davis cited Milligan in support of that position (Eldership 10).

A series of debating articles appeared in the *Gospel Advocate* between H. Leo Boles and J. C. McQuiddy. Boles held that it was necessary for a man to have a wife and children to qualify for the eldership, while McQuiddy felt that the clause was only prohibitive, expressing a limitation as to the number of wives a man could have to be qualified. McQuiddy stated that the elder need not have children if all else were equal and that the difficulty being addressed was polygamy. McQuiddy wrote:

The Bible nowhere says that an elder must be a married man. . . . Men who were divorced from wives or had more than one living wife were not qualified. (1920 999)

As polygamy was at one time practiced, the general opinion is that the Scriptures forbid an elder's having a plurality of wives, and that it is not an actual requisite that he be the husband of one wife, provided he is otherwise qualified for the position of an elder. . . . It is not actually necessary for a man to be the father of children in order to be an elder. (1917 795)

While it is decidedly better and more in harmony with the work of an elder for him to have a companion in the same faith, I know of no Scripture that teaches that on this account, provided there is nothing else against him, he should not do the work of an elder. (1920 222)

Boles, writing in response to McQuiddy, stated:

This shows that the elder is not only to be selected from the aged, but that he is to be the head of a family, "the husband of one wife," who has children which are old enough to be Christians and who have been trained by the father and have become Christians. The experience and responsibility of a Christian father have developed him so that he is prepared to take charge of the house of God. I do not say that his wife must be living at the time that he is selected, but the Scriptures do clearly teach that he must be a father and not a polygamist. (1920 1188)

(The series of articles by McQuiddy comes from the Gospel Advocate, 16 Aug. 1917; 4 Mar. 1920; 14 Oct. 1920; 4 Nov. 1920; 27 Jan. 1921; 9 June 1921, and 6 July 1922. Boles' responses are found in the 14 Oct. 1920 and 9 Dec. 1920 issues.)

C. R. Nichol and R. L. Whiteside (1923) quote J. W. McGarvey in support of their belief that marriage was required for the elder, and that the wife is alive at the time of the service. McGarvey says, "If I were an elder of the church, and my wife should die, I would go before the church the next Lord's day and resign" (3:92).

Deveny (1941) says that elders must be the head of a family with two or more children. "Adopting a child or children does not suffice. They must be his own flesh and blood." He reasons that men are born into God's family, therefore, the elder must be the biological parent. He overlooks the symbolism of the Christian's adoption by God. If the spouse later dies, that does not disqualify the man from serving (51+).

Winkler (1950) felt that marriage was not required of the elder or deacon and devoted a chapter to that discussion (94+). He said, "A bachelor can preach, marry people, preach funerals, baptize, wait on the Lord's table, and do everything that any servant of God should do - but you must not call him an elder (or deacon). How technical and legalistic" (107).

He sees a parallel to 1Co. 7:2, "Let each man have his own wife and let each woman have her own husband." He reasons that if both statements are seen as Christian requirements, no single could be a Christian at all. He holds that Paul was an elder and single (98+) and summarizes this qualification as, "blameless regarding the opposite sex" (328).

H. H. Gray, Jr., (1947) said deacons must be scripturally married, should have children, the children must be well-behaved, and if old enough, they should be Christians (40+). E. R. Harper (1950) was emphatic that only married men with faithful children could be elders. "This eliminates "old bachelors" from being elders. . ." (8). George Dehoff (1953) wrote that "an unmarried man can not be an elder or a deacon" (284). Fred Dennis (1954) required one and only one wife and further elaborated: "A brother who is unmarried or without a family cannot be a scriptural deacon in the church of God" (672). G. C. Brewer (1957) reacted against the view that an elder and deacon must be married with children: "It seems that that is an extreme view, but it would be best to have men who are heads of families. . ." (32). L. R. Wilson (1959) said they "must have one and only one wife" (52). Guy N. Woods (1977) felt that it was "obligatory upon the deacon to be both married and to have children" ("Criticism" 103).

Oliver Howard took a poll of over four hundred people at the Pepperdine Lectureship in 1988. Exactly one half held the marriage qualification as a matter of faith, while the other half viewed it as a matter of opinion. His unscientific quiz revealed a greater acceptance for female deacons than for unmarried deacons.

Across the ocean, Walter Crosthwaite of the British Restoration movement advocated single celibate elders and deacons. This was not the common view of his time, as many denied appointment to those who were not married and did not have a plurality of children (Worgan).

Some Baptist publications also emphasized that "the Scripture does not say at all that marriage is required for the office of deacon" (Naylor 121).

One must ask if the Scripture advocates one marital standard for leaders of the church and a less strenuous standard for the average member. Simpson states, "to postulate grades of official sanctity among members of the same spiritual body may be orthodox clericalism, but it is heterodox Christianity" (50). Tertullian in the third century writes the same: "Vain shall we be if we think that what is not lawful for priests is lawful for laics. Are not even laics priests" (On Exhortation to Chastity 7)? Both writers deny the possibility of a double standard.

Not a Polygamist

The argument against polygamy emphasizes the number "one." An elder is not to have multiple wives. Plummer denies that Paul is speaking of polygamy, yet he says, "It is quite true that polygamy in St. Paul's day still existed among the Jews." He quotes Justin Martyr's *Dialogue with Trypho*, "It is better for you to follow God than your senseless and blind teachers, who even to this day allow you each to have four or five wives" (119).

Calvin says:

> The only true exposition, therefore, is that of Chrysostom [Homily 10 on 1Tm. 3], that in a bishop he expressly condemns polygamy, which at that time the Jews almost reckoned to be lawful. This corruption was borrowed by them partly from a sinful imitation of the Fathers. (For they who read that Abraham, Jacob, David and others of the same class were married to more wives than one at the same time, thought that it was lawful for them also to do the same). . . . Polygamy was exceedingly prevalent among them: and therefore with great propriety does Paul enjoin that a bishop should be free from this stain. (1 Timothy 77)

Bingham sees this as the most probable interpretation of the prohibition. However, by polygamy, Bingham means not only "married to many wives at the same time" but also "married another after divorcing of the former" (4:5:4).

Looking at the broader view, the Scriptures taught in a variety of places that polygamy is not Christian behavior. It was against Roman law. It would seem inconsistent and redundant for the apostles to instruct the church not to have a polygamist in its leadership. The prohibition of polygamy was a common interpretation in the nineteenth century Restoration Movement, possibly in reaction to Mormonism and southern slave practices.

Only Married Once

The "once married" interpretation also places the emphasis on "one." J. N. D. Kelley writes, "to remain unmarried after the death of one's spouse or after divorce was considered meritorious, while to marry again was taken as a sign of self-indulgence." He refers to Paul's statement in 1Co. 7:40 to further support his suggestion and concludes by saying, "In the early Christian centuries, second marriages were not absolutely forbidden, but were regarded with distinct disapproval" (75+). Plummer adds detail:

> Hermas, Clement of Alexandria, of course Tertullian, and among later Fathers, Chrysostom [Homily 2 on Titus], Epiphanius, and Cyril, all write in disparagement of second marriages, not as sin, but as weakness. To marry again is to fall short of the high perfection set before us in the Gospel constitution. Athenagoras goes so far as to call a second marriage "respectable adultery," and to say that one who thus severs himself from his dead wife is an "adulterer in disguise." Respecting the clergy, Origen says plainly, "Neither a bishop, nor a presbyter, nor a deacon, nor a widow, can be twice married." The canons of councils are not less plain, either as to the discouragement of second marriages among the laity, or their incompatibility with what was then required of the clergy. The synods of Ancyra

> (Can. 19), of Neocaesarea (Can. 3 and 7), and of Laodicea (Can. 1) subjected lay persons who married more than once to a penalty.... The *Apostolic Constitutions* (6:17) and the so-called *Apostolic Canons* (17) absolutely forbid the promotion of one who was married twice, to be a bishop, presbyter, or deacon. (126+)

Bingham points out that Ambrose, Innocent of Rome, and the Council of Valentia state this opinion explicitly, excluding even those whose divorces or widowhood occurred before their conversion (4:5:2).

Such an interpretation also has problems. It eliminates any man who has married a second wife for any reason. That means that if a man's wife died, or if she was engaged in an adulterous relationship or abandoned her husband, he still must remain single. In Ro. 7:1+, Paul speaks of the freedom of Christians after the death of the Law. To make that point, he says that a woman is free to remarry after the death of her husband. His emphasis is freedom, not weakness. After the death of a mate, one is "no longer bound." It cannot be considered adultery against the dead spouse for the survivor to marry. She is free to marry, but only in the Lord (1Co. 7:39). In the case of young widows, he urges them to remarry (1Tm. 5:14). If a second marriage is considered a weakness, then what about Paul's indication that the first marriage could also be considered a weakness (1Co. 7:32)?

1 Timothy 5:9 brings up a parallel point. The qualification for a enrolled church widow is given as being a "one man woman," the exact opposite of the elder and deacon qualification. If this means that the only widows the church would support are the ones who have only had one husband in their life, then a difficulty follows with verse 14. Paul urges the younger widows to remarry instead of looking to the church for financial support. If they took Paul's advice and outlived their second husband, they would not be eligible to receive church support. It would seem more consistent with other teachings to interpret this passage "one-man kind of woman."

Once Married Since Baptized

Bingham cites a continuation of the thought above. The arguments are the same, except that the counting of wives does not begin until the man's baptism. If he was married to several women prior to his baptism, those divorces are forgiven by grace (4:5:2).

Never Divorced

Another interpretation prohibits men who have been divorced for any reason from being elders or deacons. Some churches have taken this beyond the diaconate to a variety of other ministries including teaching, preaching, and leading in public worship.

Plummer says this interpretation "has a fair amount of probablility:"

> They might be admitted to baptism; but they must not be admitted to an official position in the Church. A regulation of this kind might be all the more necessary, because in a wealthy capital like Ephesus it would probably be among the upper and more influential classes that divorces would be most frequent, and from precisely these classes, when any of them had become Christians, officials would be likely to be chosen. (121)

Although Chrysostom (Homily 10 on 1Tm. 3:2; Homily 2 on Tit. 1:6) and Theodoret (Commentary on 1Tm. 3:2) viewed this as the correct interpretation, many exceptions to this rule can be found in the appointees of the early church, including those of Theodoret who ordained a twice married bishop and defended the practice on the grounds that it was common practice (Bingham 4:5:4). Divorce was rampant in the first century. As with the twentieth century, any church that was evangelistic naturally brought into its fellowship a number of divorced and remarried people. Nowhere did Scripture bind restrictions on these converts or label them as second class Christians.

No regulations are given for the wife's former marital situation. Was she to be the "wife of one husband?" Nothing in this passage indicates that the wife of the elder or deacon can not have married and divorced a number of times as long as she was the only wife of the elder or deacon.

One Woman Kind of Man

The most desirable interpretation is that the bishop or deacon is faithful to his wife. But if this is the case, why does Paul insert the word "one" in the text? Possibly the translation could read "a one woman type of man" or "one woman at a time man" (Glasscock 250). The verb is in the present tense; "he is (currently) the man of one woman."

This understanding emphasizes the character of the man, not his marital status. It places the emphasis on his behavior currently as a result of Christ and not on the past when he was unredeemed. He is not a playboy; he is loyal and sexually pure. If he is married, he is faithful to his spouse in all things. The deacon, like the elder, will be in situations where they will serve the poor of this world; and many of those poor are abandoned women. Anyone who is easily sexually tempted will find this service very difficult and may yield to sexual temptation, bringing harm to the church (Glasscock 250+).

The safe position to take is to bar all men from the eldership and diaconate who are single or who have been divorced or widowed at any time. The question, which cannot be dogmatically answered, is whether or not that is in keeping with the overall teaching of Christ. Are there within the body of Christ two classes of people: those who are saved but cannot officially lead or serve, and those who by circumstance of birth, culture, past life, and conviction are Christians on a higher level? Should a man be barred from service because he sinned before he was saved? If so, none can serve. John T. Hines addresses some of these questions in the 1932 *Advocate*:

> It should not be forgotten, however, that we may become slavishly literal in our interpretations. . . . But the accident of an otherwise well qualified man to be elder, not having children, never having had any or all being dead, not being fit for the place, may well be studied before we become too radical about it. Or requiring an elder to resign because his wife has died, an absolute necessity if we are too strict in conditions, might also become a subject for study. Maybe Paul was showing more what should be true in normal situations than saying that every item mentioned must be one hundred percent full. (395)

Service is required of all Christians. Leadership is not something that can be commanded by a title but something that is earned by service. There is no way a church by decree can prevent members from following the leadership of one who has proven himself. The church can deny him a title, but not leadership, and such a denial achieves nothing. It seems that Paul is not saying that any man who has been divorced or married more than once in his entire life, pre- or post-baptism, is barred from leadership and service. Rather he is speaking of the character of the individual - a man who is faithful to his woman.

Must Manage His Children and His Household Well

"Ruling their children and their own houses well" is the K. J. V. reading, while R. S. V. states, "let them manage their children and their households well." Προιστημι (rule) is closely related entomologically to πρεσβυτερος (elder) and πρεσβευω (ambassador) (Coenen 192). In classical Greek it means, "to set before or over someone or something, to come forward, be set over, rule:"

> It is used to refer, especially in the participial form to the functions of leadership in an army, a state, or a party. A position of this sort involves the task of guarding and responsibility for the protection of those over whom one is placed. Thus the verb can express the meanings of support, care for, and even concern oneself with. (Coenen 193)

In biblical Greek, it carries the more spiritual sense of leadership through caring. Elders and deacons are to rule (προιστημι) their households well (1Tm. 3:4, 5, 12). Ruling elders (1Tm. 5:17) are worthy of double honor:

> Προιστημι is found only in the writings of Paul and the Pastorals [in the N. T.].

1Th. 5:12 has the participle in the plural for those who labor in the church and who are "over you in the Lord." They help others to live rightly and therefore deserve special esteem and love. The reference here seems to be to a group exercising leadership in the church. The present writer believes that there were as yet no institutionalized or precisely differentiated offices in the church known to Paul. . . . Behind 1Tm. 3:4, 5, 12, where the participle is used with "his own house," there is the picture of the patriarchal head of the household or father of the family. If he is capable of fulfilling this role well, he fulfills a vital qualification for being leader in the church.

He was influenced by the pattern of the charismatic community: "Whoever is filled with zeal, whoever does not shrink hard work, proves himself thereby to be one who can lead the way for others." This is confirmed by the list of gifts in Ro. 12:8, where the προισταμενος is characterized by zeal. The προισταμενος is here listed alongside he who teaches, he who exhorts, and he who does acts of mercy. All of these words are participles which suggest an activity rather than an office. . . . (Coenen 197+)

Reicke states:

1Tm. 3:12 describes good deacons as those who care well for their own houses (families and servants). The author certainly has in view the authority of the head of the household, but his attention is primarily directed, not to the exercise of power, but to the discretion and care to be shown therein. ("προιστημι" 702)

Additional comments on προιστημι and προστατις appear in Chapter Four with the discussion of Phoebe.

As for children, evidence indicated that the term may be used generically, and a plurality of children is not part of the requirement (1Tm. 5:4; Ep. 6:1+; Gn. 11:30; 21:7). J. C. McQuiddy said, "I do not understand that a man who is childless, through no fault of his own, is on that account barred from being an elder in the church" (1916). The same would be true of deacons. Reicke mentioned that "household" would be broader than children. The phrase also included slaves, otherwise the addition of "and household" to "children" would be superfluous:

Thus here the author betrays his assumption that prospective church officers will be householders with sufficient means to own household slaves. This fact in itself locates these householders in the higher social strata of the Asian Cities. It is most important to recognize that relatively high social standing does not appear here as a requirement which the author is intent on imposing on would-be office holders, but as a casual assumption that he makes about them. (Verner 133)

As a humorous aside, Campbell in the *Millennial Harbinger* (1858) reported on the faithfulness of the children of ministers and deacons:

In 241 families of ministers and deacons, there were 1164 children over fifteen years of age. Of these children, 814 - more than three fourths - were hopefully pious; 732 had united with the church; fifty-seven had entered the ministry, or were engaged in their preparatory studies; and only fourteen were dissipated, about one-half of whom became so while residing with their parents. In twenty-seven of those families, there were 123 children, of whom all but seven were hopefully pious; seven of them were deacons, and fifteen ministers. In fifty-six of those families there were 249 children over fifteen years of age, and all were hopefully pious. ("Children" 336)

The reference to home management can be seen as a reference to the leader's administrative capacity and caring nature, something that would be useful in their church ministry.

They Must First be Tested; And Then if There is Nothing Against Them,

The K. J. V. reads, "and let these also first be proved... being found blameless," while the R. S. V. reads, "then if they prove themselves blameless." The emphasis parallels that of the elder (1Tm. 3:6) and expresses concern for experience. It also highlights the official nature of the deacon's service. A deacon should be one who has proven his service. His life is open to examination and has passed the test. Haarbeck describes the word meanings as, "test, accept as proved, approve, pronounce good, establish by trial, recognize, interpret, test for the office of deacon" (Haarbeck 808). "Testing" is used of assaying ore to prove the genuineness and quality of precious metal (Gromacki 92). It is best understood here in the sense of an examination of character and conduct, not as a probationary period (Kelly 84).

Thomas Campbell was asked to explain this verse. His reply was:

And how could this be ascertained but by personal and social investigation? - that is, by conversing freely with the person by himself upon the specified subjects both of knowledge and practice; and also with his acquaintance, both in the church and out of it; . . . (220)

Wahrisch states concerning the state of being blameless:

The meaning of ανεγκλητος in the Pastorals (Tit. 1:6 +; 1Tm. 3:10) is akin to the usage in Hellenistic colloquial speech. . . . The other adjectives used in this context indicate that the meaning is beyond reproach, in the ordinary sense of common respectability. Thus in addition to qualifications of a spiritual nature, ordinary standards of decency are made into preconditions of office in the church, for the sake of the church's good name in the world. (924)

Results: Excellent Standing and Great Assurance.

Here is a paradox. The lowly servant gains a high standing through service. This is what Jesus said, "Whoever would be great among you must be your servant" (Mk. 10:43). The complete K. J. V. statement is, "purchase to themselves a good degree, and great boldness in the faith which is in Christ Jesus." The R. S. V. reads, "gain a good standing for themselves and also great confidence in the faith which is in Christ Jesus." For the deacon "in relation to God. . . here joyousness, confidence is the result or the accompaniment of faith" (Arndt and Gingrich 636). The following quotations add to our understanding:

Since the church on earth is always subject to temptation and is therefore in danger of losing its unique confidence (παρρησια), it is necessary for the church to show itself unshaken in its trust in God and its expectation of the future, i.e. in its assurance of salvation and that it should be ready to withstand every attack (Hb. 3:6, 14). (Schonweiss 660)

We should approach the future not in fear of judgment but in full confidence, openness to God and in hope of the fullness of the glory of God (cf. 2Co. 3:11 +). . . . He who perseveres in faith, holds to Christ in love (cf. 1Jn 4:17; cf. also the emphasis laid on 'parresia' gained through faithful service, 1Tm. 3:13). (Hahn "Openness" 736)

Lipscomb adds:

The Scriptures do not contemplate a man going among the sick and afflicted administering to their necessities without teaching them the word of God, admonishing them as to their duties and so gaining strength as a Christian, and giving him courage and boldness in teaching the Word of God. (I Timothy 151)

Lock sees the above as a reference to the growing of a deacon into an elder. The deacon who serves well will be promoted, eventually, to a bishop of the church (41). Most scholars from a hierarchal clergy/ laity background agree that this passage does offer the prospect of promotion to a higher order. Many Churches of Christ also view the diaconate as a training ground for the eldership.

Special Qualities for Women

In the discussion of deaconesses, vs. 11 is mentioned. The New International translation reads:

(3:11) In the same way, their wives are to be women

worthy of respect,

not malicious talkers but

temperate and

trustworthy in everything.

For the purposes of this discussion, it will be assumed that these women are female deacons.

Worthy of Respect

"Worthy of respect" is the same Greek used of the men in vs. 8. See that discussion for details.

Not Malicious Talkers

The K. J. V. and R. S. V. state "not slanderers." The Greek, μη διαβολος, comes from the root "to throw over or across" and grew to mean "to divide, set at variance, accuse, bring charges, slander, misrepresent, deceive." Through this development the word comes to mean "the devil" (Bietenhard 468). The concept is similar to the bishop's "not quarrelsome" (1Tm. 3:3) and deacon's "not double tongued" (1Tm. 3:8).

Some Restoration writers, such as Dennis, show their bias against women in statements such as, "Perhaps women are a little more given to slander than men" (672).

Temperate

"Temperate" is the translation in the N. I. V. and R. S. V., with the K. J. V. saying "sober." The word occurs only three times in the New Testament: of bishops in 1Tm. 3:2 and Tit. 2:2 and the current passage. It parallels the instruction of vs. 8, "not indulging in much wine." "The main point in these contexts is the self-control necessary for effective ministry" (Budd 515).

Trustworthy in Everything.

The R. S. V. and K. J. V. say "faithful in all things." For Paul in the Pastorals, faith becomes a type of doctrinal summary. He can say in the opening verses of 1Tm. as he opposes false teachers, "the goal of this command is love which comes from a pure heart and a good conscience and a sincere faith" (1Tm. 1:5). Some brethren, following the false teachers, are said to have "shipwrecked their faith" (1Tm. 1:19). Paul describes himself as a "teacher of the true faith to the Gentiles" (1Tm. 2:7). A logical interpretation of 3:11 is that the women maintain doctrinal purity in everything. "Soundness in faith sets a new standard that distinguishes the Christian life from all false teaching" (Michel "Faith" 604).

Summary

One must question whether these are all of the qualifications, or if other qualities are taken for granted. 1 Corinthians 12:28 lists among the gifts of the spirit the gift of "serving," as if serving is from God and beyond human capacity. Some see that gift as a reference to being a deacon. If Ac. 6 is to be taken as a model for what later developed as the diaconate, one would naturally add, "full of the Spirit and of wisdom" (Ac 6:3).

One requirement is made of the deacon which is not demanded of the bishop - "not double tongued." The qualifications desired of a bishop which are not mentioned for a deacon are: "hospitable," "an apt teacher," "able to encourage," "not quarrelsome," "well spoken of by outsiders," "not wild," "not rebellious," "not arrogant," "a lover of good," "righteous," and "devout."

The qualities given in this passage are not meant to be a formal and complete checklist. Those who are formally recognized as special servants of the church should be of the highest character. Proof of that character results from the use of spiritual common sense, not just a check of membership and attendance records.

PART TWO

HISTORICAL DEVELOPMENT

CHAPTER 6

Deacons in the Post-New Testament Church

Much more is known of the activities of deacons in the second through fourth centuries than in the first. Appendix B is a chronological list of some of the early church writings related to deacons.

It is important to note as one begins this chapter and Chapter Seven that no single picture of the deacon, male or female, is found. The structure of the church varies from one geographic location to another, from one period of time to another. It is a mistake to compile a strict description of the deacon frozen in time and geography and call that description normative.

Second Century

At the end of the first century, as seen in the *Didache* and *I Clement*, "bishops and deacons" is a formula for the leaders of local congregations in the Roman world.

Clement (c. A.D. 100) states that a church is not mature until bishops and deacons are appointed. He then quotes Is. 60:17, "I will make peace your governor and righteousness your ruler," though modifying the *LXX* rendering to become, "I will establish their bishops in righteousness and their deacons in faith" (I Clement 42). Clement asserts that apostolic authority and succession is to be transmitted in an orderly fashion by the direction of the apostles through the appointment of bishops and deacons with the consent of the church. Easton sees in Clement the term "presbyters" applying to both elders and deacons. The elders are the presbyters who were especially concerned with overseeing the community while the deacons are the presbyters concerned with serving. Easton describes these as the "governments" and "helps" of 1Co. 12:28 (Hippolytus Apostolic Tradition 79). Early Greek Christians seek to identify the titles which they take over from contemporary societies with positions mentioned in the Old Testament (Porter 104). Clement and Irenaeus (Against Heresies 4.26.5) find that support for elders and deacons in Is. 60. Irenaeus does not cite Clement, however, but the Hebrew and Septuagint forms of the Isaiah text.

In the Syrian *Didache* (c. A.D. 100), bishops and deacons are described as appointed officials and are compared to "prophets and teachers" (15). Note that the mention assumes that the work of bishops and deacons parallels that of prophets and teachers, and, possibly, that the names "bishop" and "deacon" were not as known or accepted in the Syrian church as the other titles were. It is speculation as to how far one should carry the comparison in defining the work of elders and deacons. If parallel, the passage gives a teaching responsibility to deacons. Ferguson believes that the context suggests primarily leading in worship, which would include teaching (Letter). There may be some difficulty with the Jewish Syrian churches accepting elders and deacons. In Acts, Syrian Antioch has prophets and teachers, but there is no mention of elders and deacons (Ac. 13).

Ignatius (c. A.D. 107), the martyr-bishop of Antioch, is the first to describe a hierarchical pyramid for the churches of Syria and Asia minor which includes the elevation of one presbyter to the position of bishop within the congregation. The formula for Ignatius is "bishop (singular), presbyters, and deacons." The presbyters take on sacerdotal dignity - the priesthood (Philadelphians 4). The structure has definite levels of authority as two quotations from *Magnesians* demonstrate:

> I exhort you to study to do all things with a divine harmony, while your bishop presides in the place of God, and your presbyters in the place of the assembly of the apostles, along with your deacons, who are most dear to me, and are entrusted with the ministry of Jesus Christ. (6)

> As therefore the Lord does nothing without the Father, for says He, "I can of mine own self do nothing," so do ye, neither presbyter, nor deacon, nor layman, do anything without the bishop. Nor let anything appear commendable to you which is destitute of his approval. (7)

The deacon is an important member of this authority structure. The church is urged to "respect the deacons as the commandment of God" (Smyrneans 8).

Ignatius is the writer who first draws a distinction between the leaders of the church and the average member, or the "layman" (Magnesians 7). He also says that without all three clergy positions in place, "it is not called a church" (Trallians 2). Careful emphasis is made between the "right reverend (most worthy)" bishop, the "reverend (worthy)" elders, and the "fellow servants," that is, the deacons (Magnesians 2). The reference to "fellow servants" demonstrates the affinity that Ignatius feels for the serving ministry.

Some scholars feel that the mono-episcopal Ignatian bishop was not a monarch ruling over the church, but that he was the president of the local Christian community elected by his fellow presbyters. He is "chairman of the elders," so to speak, and the presbyterial council has the overall local ruling authority (Barnett 48).

Frend sees Ignatius, and less Polycarp, as very concerned about Christian orthodoxy in belief, organization, liturgy and conduct. In the first phase of Christianity down to A.D. 100, "we may recognize differing patterns of ministry reflecting the influence of James's church at Jerusalem and the Hellenistic churches respectively." In the absence of the apostles, with a the diminishing number of Christians who had personal contact with the twelve, and recognizing the cessation of prophets, Ignatius is concerned to solidify the corpus of belief. There is no room in his orthodoxy for variations in congregational organization (Frend 139).

Ignatius' brief job description for deacons is seen in *Trallians*: "deacons, who are ministers of the mysteries of Christ Jesus; for they are not ministers of meat and drink, but servants of the Church of God. They are bound, therefore, to avoid all grounds of accusation, as they would a burning fire" (2).

The "mysteries" are often connected with the liturgical function of the Lord's Supper or Eucharist. The picture that is painted may be of the combined αγαπε feast and Eucharist. The feast and Lord's supper seem to remain together in some eastern churches until near the end of the second century.

The question that is raised by this citation centers around the deacons not being "ministers of meat and drink." This may indicate that the servant and benevolent aspects are giving way to the sacerdotal. It seems to indicate that the spiritual handling of the mysteries is being elevated above common service. While at first the deacons may have business responsibilities, they soon begin to assume liturgical and pastoral activities.

The Shepherd of Hermas (c. A.D. 120) lists deacons along with apostles, bishops, and teachers as the building blocks of the church, deacons ranking lowest. Their job includes care for the widows and orphans, a concept that is repeated in later writers, and bad deacons are rebuked for misappropriating benevolent funds (3:9:26). He also links deacons with teachers, as they are frequently mentioned with catechetical teaching.

Polycarp (c. A.D. 155) details the qualifications of the deacons when he writes to the Philippians: "They are not to be slanderers, double tongued, nor lovers of money, but self-controlled in all things, compassionate, attentive, walking according to the truth of the Lord, who became the servant of all" (5). He also credits the deacons with authority by saying, "Wherefore it is necessary that. . . you be subject to the elders and deacons as to God and Christ. . ." (Philippians 5). These instructions are written to the same location Paul addressed Phl. 1:1 a century earlier.

Justin Martyr (A.D. 155) states that the deacons took the Lord's Supper to those who were sick and not present in the assembly, emphasizing the place of the communion in the early church (First Apology 67). Those absent are primarily the sick, so this reference illustrates a combined duty to care for the sick and to serve communion (Symonds 410).

In the worship, deacons distributed the bread and wine. This was a development from the table service of food to the service of the Eucharist (First Apology 67). Deacons arranged the altar, cared for the ornaments and utensils, presented the offerings of the people, read the gospel, and otherwise took the lead in worship. Only the clergy could lead in the worship. Inferior clergy, such as the sub-deacons, exorcists, etc., were prohibited from coming into the high altar area (Bingham 2.20.4).

Clement of Alexandria (A.D. 180-200) confirms the three-fold "grades in the church of bishops, presbyters, deacons" as "imitations of the angelic glory." The work of elders is the "most excellent," while that of deacons is "ministerial" (Stromata 6:13.106). He views deacons as married and holds that the qualification "husband of one wife" is a universal virtue (Stromata 3:12:90). The celibate deacon appears later.

Irenaeus (c. A.D. 185) speaks of deacons, but only as he sees Nicholas and Stephen, two of the Seven from Ac. 6, as the first deacons (Against Heresies 1:26:3; 3:12:10). He is the first writer to call the Seven "deacons."

Third Century

Tertullian (A.D. 208-217) stated that deacons could baptize with the specific authority of the bishop. If no chief priest (bishop), presbyter, or deacon was on the spot, then other disciples could be called to the work (On Baptism 17). The highest ranking cleric in a community was always looked to for authority in any sacramental work. He further argued that all Christians, including deacons, should be men of one marriage, "Hence we are bound to contend that the command to abstain from second marriage relates first to the laic; so long as no other can be a presbyter than a laic" (Exhortation to Chastity 7). Tertullian ranked deacons with bishops and presbyters as "honorable titles of guides and leaders to the laity," and he saw deacons as overseers and pastors of the flock of Christ (Bingham 2.20.1).

Hippolytus (A.D. 215) wrote a manual which included the ordination process for deacons. Reflecting the practice of the church in Rome, he stated that deacons were elected by the people and were "not ordained to the priesthood but to serve the bishop and to carry out the bishop's commands." The deacons did not take part in the council of the clergy. The bishop's control strengthened, while the deacon's freedom lessened. The deacon no longer served the church; he served the bishop (Apostolic Traditions 9:1, 2).

The deacons' connection with the Eucharist is emphasized. They bring the Eucharist to the bishop for consecration (AT 4), a work that is mentioned in their prayer of ordination (AT 9). Hippolytus speaks of deacons being "diligent in giving the blessed bread to the sick" (AT 26). They also have a teaching responsibility in the assembly (AT 33).

Hippolytus gave a detailed account of baptism which included the role of deacons, and, by inference, female deacons in baptism. Baptism was administered by a bishop or, possibly, a presbyter, assisted by deacons. Only when no bishop was available could a deacon baptize (AT 26). Flowing water from a stream was preferred. Before the baptism the candidate fasted, was exorcised, took a bath, and meditated all night. Baptism took place at the first cock crow. Children were baptized first, then men, and finally women. No jewelry or clothing could be worn. Deacons stood on either side of the bishop holding the oils that were used. The bishop anointed each candidate with the oil of exorcism after the renunciations, probably over the entire body of the naked individual. This was not considered improper, as the non-Jew in the Graeco-Roman world was accustomed to the nakedness of his own sex in the public baths. A deacon, also naked, accompanied the candidate into the water for the baptism. After being baptized three times, the bishop anointed each convert with the oil of thanksgiving. Then the convert was clothed in new white garments and brought into the church for the laying on of hands, prayer, and further anointing (AT 21).

Hippolytus also reports that the church in Rome owned a catacomb which was placed under the control of a deacon at the time of Pope Zephyrinus (A.D. 199-217) (Refutation of all Heresies 9:12:14). This is the first evidence for a church holding property as a corporate body (Frend 284).

The clergy of the third century were married, although Hippolytus complained of those who had been married two or three times (Refutation of all Heresies 9:7). The first command relating to celibacy was recorded in the Council of Elvira (A.D. 305), (Canon 33) which required married clerics to no longer have any conjugal intercourse with their wives. Canon 27 allowed the clergy to have living in their house only their sisters or their own daughters who were virgins and had taken a vow of virginity (Hefele 1.148). In the fourth and fifth centuries, marriage was not forbidden, but sexual relations often were. The tendency continued to shift toward celibacy, a practice which was firmly established by the sixth century.

The pseudo-Clementine writing, the *Epistle of Clement to James* (A.D. 220), described the deacons as:

> ... eyes to the bishop, carefully inquiring into the doings of each member of the church ascertaining who is about to sin, in order that, being arrested with admonition by the president, he may haply not accomplish the sin. Let them check the disorderly, that they may not desist from assembling to hear the discourses, so that they may be able to counteract by the word of truth those anxieties that fall upon the heart from every side. (12)

In the same period, Origen (A.D. 200) saw the deacon as having a ministry of the word (Jos. 2:1). Much of the discussion over his preaching duties centered around the ministries of Stephen and Philip, who were known best for their preaching, and traditionally were called the first deacons.

The earliest systematic description of deacons appears in the *Didascalia Apostolorum* (A.D. 220-240). The authority of the deacon, and his apparent superiority to the presbyters, is shown:

> Let the bishop... be honored by you as God, the deacon is with you as a type of Christ, so let him be loved by you. Let the deaconess be honored by you as a type of the Holy Spirit. Let the presbyters be looked on by you as a type of the apostles. (2:26)

The deacon and deaconess are compared to deity, while the presbyters are seen as mortal. The citation demonstrates the closeness of the deacons to the bishop. Other passages show the deacons to be the mediators between the congregation and the bishop:

> But let them [the people] have free access to the deacons, and let them not be troubling the head (bishop) at all times, but making known what they require through the ministers, that is through the deacons. For neither can any man approach the Lord God Almighty except through Christ. All things therefore that they desire to do, let them make known to the bishop through the deacons,

and then do them. (2:28)

And let the deacon make known all things to the bishop, even as Christ to His Father. But what things he can, let the deacon order, and all the rest let the bishop judge. Yet let the deacon be the hearing of the bishop, and his mouth and his heart and his soul; for when you are both of one mind, through your agreement there will be peace also in the Church. (2:44)

It is required of you deacons therefore that you visit all who are in need, and inform the bishop of those who are in distress: and you shall be his soul and his mind; and in all things you shall be taking trouble to be obedient to him. (3:13)

The deacons have become servants of the bishop with a special closeness that would become the root of conflict between deacons and presbyters.

Widows are to report to and obey the bishop and deacons. No mention is made in the passage concerning presbyters. The widows at this time are probably an organized body of special servants, but they were not to do anything "without the command of the bishops and deacons" (3:8).

Selection of the deacons (male and female) is left to the bishop. He is to choose and appoint them as he pleases. Men are to serve men; women serve women. Female deacons are especially important for the baptism of females: "It is not fitting that a woman should be seen by men. . . . For there are houses whither thou canst not send a deacon to a woman. . ." (3:12).

The number of deacons to be selected is to be determined by the needs of the church. Enough are needed to "relieve every one; so that to aged women that are infirm, and to brothers and sisters that are in sickness, to every one of them they shall provide the ministration that is right for him" (3:13).

In describing the church's financial support of its servants, the deacon receives double the amount given to widows. In talking of presbyters, *Didascalia* states, "but if anyone wish to honor the presbyters also, let him give them a double portion as to the deacons" (2:28). Support of presbyters is less significant than the support of deacons.

The ministry of the deacon in the public worship is seen in 2:57. He is to stand by the Eucharist and generally maintain order in the service. This includes making sure that every person sits in his proper place in the assembly and that "no one whispers, or falls asleep, or laughs, or makes signs."

Cyprian (A.D. 249), bishop of Carthage, makes the point that deacons are to serve and obey their bishops. In his letter concerning a rebellious deacon, he says that the Lord appointed the apostles (bishops), but the apostles (bishops) appoint the deacons ("To Rogatianus" 64:3). Rebellions against the bishop are the things that "are the beginnings of heretics and the origins and endeavors of evil-minded schismatics" (Epistle 64:3). He also shows that the deacons were involved in distributing the communion cup, although this evidently was not a common practice and was resisted by some (Treatise 3, On the Lapsed 25).

If a work was necessary, if an authorized cleric was not present, and if the deacon had obtained permission, he could do just about any sacramental work. This included baptism, taking confession, and granting absolution. The determining factors were the necessity and permission for sacramental activity (Bingham 2.20.12). Cyprian reported concerning the last rites:

> If, says he, they are seized by any dangerous distemper, they need not expect my return, but may have recourse to any presbyter that is present; or if a presbyter cannot be found, they may make their confession before a deacon; that so they may receive imposition of hands and go to the Lord in peace. (Epistle 13)

Cyprian saw deacons as celibate and wrote of the difficulties they experienced with sexual appetites. He commanded the excommunication of deacons and virgins who were sleeping together without intercourse as a way of fulfilling their sexual needs without violating their celibate vows (Epistle 41:1).

Eusebius (A.D. 324) in his *Ecclesiastical History* saw Stephen and the Seven as deacons appointed for public service (2:1). He spoke of the participation by deacons in the Council of Novatus (c. A.D. 250) and quoted a communication between Cornelius, bishop of Rome, and Fabius, bishop of Alexandria, concerning seven deacons and seven sub-deacons in Rome under Cornelius (c. A.D. 250) (6:43).

A papyrus written in the fourth century, probably in Egypt, revealed the only example of a formal Greek contract between a deacon and his bishop. The deacon was appointed by his bishop and returned to lay status if he acted without the bishop's consent. Excommunication awaited him if he contravened the contract. The deacon in this contract was illiterate, using a secretary to write the document. It has been suggested that illiteracy was not a major liability, as the deacon was not a lector - a reader - but a practical servant (Horsley 80 121+).

About the same time, June 6, 324, to be exact, Isodoros, son of Ptolemaios from the village of Karanis in Eqypt, filed a damage suit and petition of assault to his local government because he was attacked by some livestock owners. Their livestock had trampled his field. When he went to complain, the owners beat him. He would probably have been killed if Antonios, a deacon, and Isak, a monastic (monk) had not come by at the right time.

This petition is significant because it is the earliest reference in secular correspondence to a church deacon and is the earliest mention of monks in the church. It probably shows that the titles and life styles of deacons and monks were widely known and accepted by Egyptian secular society at this early date. It also confirms the previously conjectured theory that the monastic orders were formed by A.D. 300 (Judge 124 +). At least seventeen documents from the fourth century are published which identify monastics - monks and nuns (Horsley 82 128).

Since its decisions were multi-regional, the First Council of Nicaea (A.D. 325) marked a landmark in the definition of the diaconate. Canon 3 revealed that deacons were probably celibate. They were forbidden to have a female living with them except a mother, sister, aunt or "such persons who are beyond suspicion." The presbyters were bound to put deacons in their place. Canon 18 reminded deacons that they were "the inferiors to the presbyters." They were to take the Eucharist after the presbyters and were not to sit among the presbyters. Their handling of the Eucharistic emblems was critically scrutinized, and they were told not to offer it without the bishop being present.

The 4th century *Apostolic Constitutions* (c. A.D. 380) has many parallels to *Didascalia*. Although its origin is uncertain, most scholars feel that *Constitutions* is a compilation or adaptation of earlier materials. Many scholars see the first six chapters as based on *Didascalia* and chapter seven based on the *Didache* (Riddle 388). A comparison is made between church and Jewish leaderships: bishops = High priest; presbyters = priests; deacons = Levites (2:25). Another comparison is made between Moses as the bishop and Aaron as a deacon (2:30). Modern Roman Catholic thought strongly supports the Levitical parallels (Biskupek 1 +).

Sometime in the second half of the third century, the diaconate began to change. Instead of being a significant independent ministry, the church came to see the diaconate as a transitional step to the priesthood. The order was clearly established by this time and significantly different from its New Testament origins (Hennessey 83).

Yet another parallel in the *Constitutions* is the bishop's likeness to Almighty God while the deacon resembles Jesus Christ (2:28). As the Christian approaches God through Jesus, so the laity can approach the bishop only through the deacon.

Constitutions 2:28 also refers to the bishop as governor and the deacon as minister. As Jesus is the prophet and messenger of God, so the deacons are the prophets and messengers of the bishop (2:30). They are "ready to carry messages, to travel about, to minister, and to serve" (3:19). By this period the ministry is strongly liturgical.

Deacons emerge as servants of the bishop. They are to minister to the bishop as "Christ does His Father" (2:26). Presbyters are not mentioned in this concept. Only the bishop can ordain deacons (3:11), and deacons can not ordain any other cleric (3:20). Specific prayers are given for the ordination of deacons and deaconesses (8:17+). In those prayers the deacon is compared to Stephen while the deaconess is honored with Miriam, Deborah, Anna, Huldah, and Mary.

The deacon is not a servant of the church, but an assistant to the bishop. He is to be the "ear, and eye, and mouth, and heart, and soul" of the bishop, "as Jethro did appoint for Moses" a counsel of helpers (2:44). Deacons are delegated authority to solve the lesser problems of the churches.

By this time he was not allowed to baptize or offer the Eucharist, but he did distribute the Eucharist, not on his own authority, but as a minister of the priests, once the bishop had blessed it. The bishop delivered the bread to the communicant saying, "Body of Christ," and the deacon delivered the cup saying, "The Blood of Christ, the Cup of life" (8:13). This activity later became debated, especially if presbyters were present, because its seemed to give precedence to the deacon over the presbyter. The deacon, therefore, could only serve the host, not bless or consecrate it.

The authority of deacons and lesser orders is detailed (8:28). The deacon is in charge of the sub-deacon, readers, singers, and deaconesses. In the worship, only the bishop, presbyter, and deacon can read the Gospel, although readers could read other parts of the Scripture (Bingham 2.20.6). The deacon is clearly not of the priestly clergy, yet he is above the lower orders and the laity.

Other duties of the deacon are also detailed in the *Constitutions*:

And if anyone be found sitting out of his place, let the deacon who is within reprove him and make him to rise up and sit in a place that is meet for him. (2:57)

> Let the deacon oversee the people, that nobody may whisper, nor slumber, nor
> laugh, nor nod; for all ought in the church to stand wisely, and soberly, and
> attentively, having their attention fixed upon the word of the Lord. . . . As to the
> deacons, after the prayer is over, let some of them attend upon the oblation of
> the Eucharist, ministering to the Lord's body with fear. (2:57)

The deacon was the sacred crier of the congregation. When the
bishop had completed his sermon, the deacon announced, "Let the
hearers and the unbelievers depart" (8:5). He called the catechumens
to prayer and generally dictated the activity of the congregation in worship. All of this was determined by the bishop for whom the deacon
spoke.

When a Christian moved to another town, he took with him letters
of recommendation. It was the responsibility of the deacons to receive
those letters and verify the faithfulness of the member. The same text
refered to deacons securing help for the poor, a right which appeared
to have been validated by the letter of recommendation (2:58):

> If then our Lord did thus, will you, O deacons, hesitate to do the like for them
> that are sick and infirm, you who are workmen of the truth, and bear the likeness
> of Christ?. . . It is required of you deacons therefore that you visit all who are in
> need, and inform the bishop of those who are in distress; and you shall be his soul
> and his mind. . . ." (3:13)

The deacons were charged with seeing that everyone received a
proper burial. This sometimes applied to the non-Christian dead (Constitutions 3:7). Christians were opposed to cremation. Bodies were to be
rescued from the birds who might take the body from the earth. Man
was made from dust, and to dust man should return.

Constitutions also give details of the baptismal service, although
not as detailed as Hippolytus. Here the distinctive roles of men and
women are emphasized:

> For we stand in need of a woman, a deaconess, for many necessities; and first is
> the baptism of women, the deacon shall anoint only their forehead with the holy
> oil, and after him the deaconess shall anoint them; for there is no necessity that
> the women should be seen by the men. (3:15)

> After that, either thou, O bishop, or a presbyter that is under thee, shall in the
> solemn form name over them the Father, and Son, and Holy Spirit, and shall dip
> them in the water; and let a deacon receive the man, and a deaconess the woman,
> that so the conferring of this inviolable seal may take place with a becoming
> decency. (3:16)

The number of deacons within a church was to be determined by
the size of the church (3:19). Deacons could be married, but they could
not marry an actress, widow, slave, or public woman (8:18). The community financially supported them (8:4).

Ross summarized the deacon's work from the third and fourth centuries as:

> a) Liturgical: keeping order during divine service, leading the prayers of the people, reading the Gospel, receiving the offerings and presenting them to the presbyter, serving the Eucharistic elements (or at least the cup) to the communicants, and dismissing the people at the end of the service. With the bishop's permission, deacons could administer baptism and absolve penitents.
>
> b) Educational: if no presbyter were available, deacons could read the homilies of the fathers, and some were licensed by the bishop to preach; deacons were also employed in teaching catechumens.
>
> c) Charitable: the deacons reported necessitous cases to the bishop and acted as his almoners in the distribution of charity; they also visited the sick and clothed and buried the dead.
>
> d) Administration: the deacons not only secured orderly behavior in church, but were expected to keep an eye on the congregation at all times and report misdemeanors to the bishop; the deacons were responsible for the altar and its utensils, and doubtless also for church property in general; they sometimes (as also did presbyters) attended General councils as proxies or attendants to bishops, and also sometimes served on provincial and consistorial synods.

In this period, the deacons were primarily full time paid officials, while presbyters were mostly part-timers employed in secular work (Ross "Reconsideration" 153).

The minimum age for deacons was around twenty-five. Siricius, Bishop of Rome, set the age at thirty (A.D. 385) but later lowered it to twenty-five, following Nu. 8:24 (Ep. I ad Himer 14 cited in Bligh 422). The Council of Hippo (A.D. 393) said that twenty-five was the earliest age (Second Series, Canon 1, Hefele 2.397). The Maronite required that a deacon be over twenty-one. The East Syrian or Nestorian "Book of Canon Law" said that readers must not be ordained until past boyhood, sub-deacons when nearly grown, deacons a little later, and presbyters about eighteen, although it added that the ancient age for presbyters was thirty. Modern Anglicans set the minimum age at twenty-three (Cross "Deacon" 380).

The period from Ignatius until the Council of Nicaea was considered the golden age of the diaconate. The diaconate developed from a lay ministry to a professional one and from the ministry of a family man to that of the celibate. The deacons became special ministers to the bishop, frequently exercising more authority than the presbyterate. Herein was its downfall. As the presbyters banded together in strength, their ministry grew and the functions of the deacons came to be assumed by presbyters. Later, other religious orders of men and women were conceived to provide for the diaconal ministry.

Deacons in the Orthodox East after A.D. 337

From the time of the death of Constantine (A.D. 337) the eastern and western churches grew more independent of each other, and the diaconate developed differing responsibilities. Although the western church fought the power and expansion of the diaconate, deacons flourished in the East (Gillet 415).

John Chrysostom of Antioch (A.D. 345-407) spoke of the deacons in many of his homilies. He was a deacon himself from A.D. 380-386 before being ordained a priest. The deacon was the one who called the people to worship and directed them in prayer for the clergy, catechumens, and other specific concerns. He generally was responsible for orderliness in the worship, including silence at the appropriate time and sitting in the proper location. He received the offering with an exclamation of "Holy things for the Holy" and warned the recipients of the Eucharist not to partake unless penitent (Halton 54+).

At Antioch, Alexandria, Jerusalem, and Constantinople, the atriums of the basilicas were the gathering places for beggars. Over three thousand poor were supported in Antioch from church funds. St. John the Almoner (c. A.D. 400), patriarch of Alexandria, fed as many as 7500 people daily. Deacons became responsible for hospitals and other social centers to distribute assistance. These charitable institutions became known as deaconries (Gillet 416).

The church of Edessa in A.D. 451 had thirty-nine deacons. Justinian (A.D. 535) prohibited Constantinople from having more than sixty priests, one hundred deacons, ninety subdeacons, one hundred ten lectors, forty deaconesses, twenty-five cantors, and one hundred doorkeepers (Novellae 3.1 cited in Martimort 109). By A.D. 692, the number of deacons had risen to one hundred fifty. These deacons served three functions: (1) an elaborate system of charitable distribution; (2) an administrative body for the local church; (3) and a strong liturgical body (Gillet 415).

Quite early the eastern areas became welfare states, and this created a conflict between the church and state. Justinian in Constantinople began the process, and the Byzantine Empire was an example of fully developed care. With the state taking over the social welfare, there was little need for the deacons. The church was described as:

   ... more anxious to accumulate wealth than to give it away, more preoccupied

> with adorning temples than with feeding the hungry, and so little inclined to wish, with St. John Chrysostom, that the generous distribution of alms might empty its treasury. (Gillet 417)

While the deacon's charitable duties contracted, the administrative duties expanded. By the time of Constantine, a chief deacon became pre-eminent in many churches, the bishop's deacon. As a young and enterprising individual, he was the bishop's confidential collaborator. He was charged with special missions for the bishop, often exceeding the presbyters in authority. By nature deacons were young and active while presbyters were older and retiring. The archdeacon was first recognized at the Council of Ephesus (A.D. 431), and the position grew in authority until by the eighth century he became a rival and opponent to the bishop (Gillet 417).

The liturgical function of the deacon remained primary. While the priest was to "enlighten" and the bishop was to "bring to perfection," the deacon was to "purify." The deacon was to separate the sacred from the profane and to insure that the holy objects were treated with respect. He was also to prepare candidates for initiation. This work was significant in baptism, confirmation, marriage, unction of the sick, and ordination. In many things, the deacon could take the place of an absent priest with the consent of the bishop. At various periods in history, he could hear confessions and pronounce absolution. Deacons were always associated with the Eucharist; however, the part they played changed through the centuries (Gillet 418).

Deacons in the Latin West after A.D. 337

In the West, the diaconate had become a stepping stone to higher orders by the time of Constantine. It was significant to the *cursus honorum* (graded ranks of clergy). An extreme example was Ambrose of Milan, who was not even baptized when he was elected bishop. "Thus, when he was baptized, he is said to have fulfilled all the ecclesiastical offices, so that he was consecrated bishop on the eighth day with the greatest favor and joy on the part of all" (Paulinus 3.9).

Not all deacons did advance. Sixth century epitaphs from Gaul show deacons who died at age fifty-eight, sixty, seventy, or even eighty. Pope Zosimus determined that a cleric could become a deacon at age twenty-five, a priest at age thirty (Ep. IX, 1, 2, cited in Bligh 422). It became normal for a cleric to serve as deacon for five years before being advanced to the priesthood, regardless of age. Most deacons were in their twenties and did not serve over five years in this position (Bligh 422).

Requiring a cleric to serve five years, and restricting the number of deacons to seven proved difficult. It limited the number of men who could rise to the priesthood to seven in any five year period for any one diocese, and that was not enough for the rapidly expanding church. Efforts to expand the number were at first resisted. In some cases auxiliary deacons, or deacons for stational churches, or deacons for the care of tombs of the martyrs were appointed. By A.D. 520 Rome had one hundred deacons (Bligh 423).

As has already been indicated, the deacons had power struggles with the presbyters. Their closeness to the bishop, youthful energy, and elite number caused them to overstep their bounds many times. The decisions of the various councils indicated attempts to put them in their place. Some people questioned whether deacons should serve the bishop instead of the priests, or, even broader, the church (Bligh 424). Ambrosiaster wrote a treatise, "On the Boastfulness of the Roman Deacons" (c. A.D. 370), because the deacons were taking precedence over the presbyters. Jerome objected that presbyters were selected only on the recommendation of the deacons and that they sat among the presbyters when the bishop was absent (Letter 146.2).

The duties of the western deacon varied from diocese to diocese. Most bishops patterned their charge to the deacons after the work of the Levites and of the Seven in Acts 6. They had control of collections and distribution of the alms to the poor, and they cared for church property and treasures. Rarely were they allowed to baptize (Bligh 425). They generally read the Gospel in the worship (Bingham 2.20.6).

Jerome tells of the deacons announcing the names of contributors to the congregation as gifts were made. He tells of "extortioners and oppressors who made their oblations out of their ill-gotten goods, that they might glory in their wickedness" as the deacons announced their generosity to all (Comm. on Eze. 18 reported in Bingham 2.20.5).

Great care was expressed by church fathers to separate the reading the Gospel and calling the congregation to worship from preaching, which was strictly forbidden to the deacon. At times the deacon was authorized to read a homily from the church fathers in the absence of the bishop, but he was never to preach an original message. These readings required the bishop being absent and the permission of the bishop for the readings to take place (Bingham 2.20.11). The preaching ministry of the deacon probably developed more fully when the diaconate became an interim and training office for the priesthood (Barnett 80).

Gregory the Great curtailed much of the liturgical function with the transfer of music duties to the cantors in A.D. 595 (Cross "Deacon" 380). Regular cantors took over the chanting of the Psalms. On major feast days, deacons assisted the bishop. Isidore reported that deacons were to enhance the solemnity of the occasion by providing a sort of screen between the celebrant and the people, "lest they see what they ought not to see" (De Ecclesiasticis Officiis 2:8).

Archdeacons

In the East and West, one deacon in each church grew to be the bishop's deacon. He presided at Mass, and presbyters, like Jerome and Chrysostom, demanded to know why deacons had so much power, especially the archdeacon in Rome (Bishops' Liturgy 20). By A.D. 400, archdeacons appeared in every Latin diocese, although the Council of Merida (A.D. 666) showed that it was not universal in Spain (Canon 10, Hefele 4.483). At first, the archdeacon was equal with his fellow deacons and probably was the deacon with greatest seniority. Possibly due to the strenuous duties, he changed from being the senior deacon to being elected by fellow deacons. Politics finally took over and the bishop appointed the archdeacon directly (Bingham 2.21.1).

The archdeacon was the immediate minister and attendant of the bishop, at the bishop's side and assisted in any duty. Gradually he was given more administrative duties until he was the supervisor of the other deacons. In Rome the archdeacon was frequently in charge of the diocese when the bishop was absent. Archdeacons attended councils as representatives of their bishops, supervised and instructed junior clergy, and had overall supervision of collections, care for the poor, and direction of schools for boys. Isidore showed the ultimate development of power: "The archpriest must know that he is under the archdeacon and must obey his orders just as he obeys the bishops" (De Sac. Ordinationibus 3:219 cited in Bligh 427). His power was often resented as tyrannical (Bligh 427+).

By the fourth century, archdeacons considered it a demotion to be made a priest. Jerome reported: "An archdeacon thought himself injured if he was ordained a presbyter" (Comm. on Eze. 100.48 cited in Bingham 2.21.3). Several archdeacons were chosen as the bishop's successor even though they had not served as presbyters (Bingham 2.21.3).

As a result, the work of the archdeacon was eventually given to priests so that lower orders had no control over higher orders. The deacons were finally restricted to the liturgical duties with the presbyterate handling the administrative work of the church:

Once an associate of the bishop, now an assistant to the priest; once a minister of charity, now a mere "waiter at tables;" once a minister of worship, now a ceremonial appendage. . . and all because the deacon was not a presider of the Eucharist. (Bishops' Liturgy 20)

Conclusion

At the close of the New Testament, a variety of styles of congregational organization were observed. However, by A.D. 150 - 170 orthodoxy demanded uniformity, and most communities were governed by a single bishop who was assisted by a corps of presbyters and served by a body of deacons. As with all movements, time gave way to tradition, and the basic organization was unified. It is during this time that definition was given to deacons. Service gave way to authority and liturgy, and those roles carried with them a lot of political baggage. It was the political authority of the presbyters that eventually overcame the diaconate. Unfortunately, the original concept of service ceased to be a major consideration after the first few centuries.

Many fundamentalists are unconcerned about what happened after the close of the New Testament. All the later developments seen in this chapter cloud the issue for them. If one does not consider the post apostolic writings, it is very hard to paint a picture of the work of deacons based on the limited texts of New Testament. The New Testament simply speaks of service without detailing that service or expressing concern for clerical authority.

CHAPTER 7

Female Deacons in the Post-New Testament Church

In studying the New Testament, evidence for the existence of female deacons is somewhat circumstantial. Scripture tells us little about the work, but when sandwiched between the writings that predate and postdate the New Testament, female deacons are understood as significant to early Christian ministry. A clearer understanding of the work of female and male deacons comes from examining extra-biblical materials.

Deaconesses in the Apostolic Fathers

In the first centuries of the church, widows and virgins were two significant organized female ministry groups. They performed different roles in different periods, but the widows were often synonymous with deaconesses in later times. The term "widow" was used generically when Ignatius (A.D. 107) spoke of "the virgins who are called widows" (Smyrneans 13:1). He obviously spoke of young unmarried women who did the same work as enrolled widows and were called by the same title (Easton Pastoral 185). Gryson described these women:

> Christian virgins who resolved to remain chaste "for the honor of the Lord's flesh" were called "widows;" since both groups of women had a profession of continence as their chief characteristic, their ideals and life-styles seemed similar. In the case of these virgins, continence most probably went hand in hand with asceticism, prayer, and acts of charity; when no close relatives were available, they also, like widows, were assisted by the community. (13)

The earliest mention of Christian deaconesses outside of the New Testament was found in the letter of Pliny, Roman Governor of Bithynia, to the Emperor Trajan (A.D. 112). Pliny was trying to find something illegal in the activities of Christians. To do so, he tortured "two maidservants who were called deaconesses" (Latin *ministrae*, translated by most as "deaconesses") in an attempt to secure information from them (Pliny Letters 10.96.8). *Ministrae* was the same term used to translate Ro. 16:1 in the Latin. The use here paralleled what was said of Phoebe and the women of 1Tm. 3. Whether they were part of a recognized order or office is unclear.

The Shepherd of Hermas (c. A.D. 120) testified to women's work as he wrote to a female servant or deaconess named Grapte. Her work was to admonish the widows and orphans (1:2:4). Others interpreted the official group that Grapte represented as the "order of Widows" (Danielou 14).

Clement of Alexandria (A.D. 180-200) speaks of female ministry when listing four offices, or, as he puts it, "chosen persons:" presbyters, bishops, deacons, and widows (Instructor 3:12:97). He recognizes the Apostolic origin of female deacons by saying:

> The women whom. . . the apostles. . . took around with them were not wives but, as befitted the apostles' dedication to an undistracted preaching ministry, sisters, fellow ministers to the women who kept house. So the Lord's teaching made its way into the women's quarters too, and in a manner above reproach; for we know what the honorable Paul in one of his letters to Timothy prescribed regarding female deacons. (Stromata 3:6:53)

Tertullian (A.D. 208-217) wrote with reprobation about a twenty year old virgin who was ordained to the "order of widows" which some interpret as deaconess (On the Veiling of Virgins 9:2-3; Thurston "Deaconesses" 4:651). He spoke of two classes of women in the service of the church: virgins and widows (Schaff "Deaconess" 3:374). The bishop was responsible for admitting the proper women. Just like the male clergy (bishops, presbyters, and deacons), widows had to be "once married" (Exhortation on Chastity 13:4).

Great stress was placed on a widow having been a mother. Tertullian saw the responsibility of educating children and experiencing the tenderness and compassion of parenting as extremely valuable to a servant of the church (Veiling of Virgins 9). The Theodosian Code (A.D. 390) also made the same emphasis. The work of these widows was counseling and encouraging, but nothing was said of the benevolent activities prevalent in later centuries. Tertullian did not permit a woman to teach, exorcise, baptize, or have anything to do with the sacramental functions that were reserved for men (On Baptism 17; Against Heretics 41:5). The home was her primary sphere.

In the above writers, διακονισσα does not appear; all of the passages refer to women's ministry in other words (Greek and Latin) or with the masculine διακονος. It is only in the fourth century, beginning with *Apostolic Constitutions*, that the word "deaconess" is coined for the female ministry. Gryson states, "Those scholars, therefore, who interpret 'widow' in Tertullian as a synonym for διακονισσα. . . do so arbitrarily" (22). It is true to say that deaconesses did not appear before the third century because the word had not been formed. However, female deacons and other official female service groups are attested from the infancy of the church.

Didascalia Apostolorum (A.D. 200-240) summarized the work of female deacons (Easton Pastoral 186). She is referred to specifically as a γυνη διακονος (woman deacon) or η διακονος (feminine deacon). Her work was to assist at the baptism of women, especially in the act of anointing, "to go into the houses of the heathen where there are believing women... to visit those who are sick, and to minister to them in that of which they have need, and to bathe those who have begun to recover from sickness" (Shepherd "Deacon" 786). She did not administer baptism (3:9) She was granted in some churches the right to distribute communion to women and children and was regarded as the community's guardian of women and children (Hunermann 327+).

In reporting the importance of the deaconess, *Didascalia* states: "Let the bishop. . . be honored by you as God, the deacon is with you as a type of Christ, so let him be loved by you. Let the deaconess be honored by you as a type of the Holy Spirit. Let the presbyters be looked on by you as a type of the apostles" (2:26). It is significant in this report that the deaconess is likened to one of the Trinity, while the presbyters (elders) only rank with mortal apostles.

In the detailed account of baptism, *Didascalia* demonstrates the propriety of having deaconesses. A deaconess can go into a home where a deacon cannot. She can study with the candidate. She is essential in baptism because baptism is by immersion and in the nude. She also performs the anointing with oil of the nude body of the candidate. "It is not fitting that a woman be seen by men" (3:12).

A woman was instructed to teach women, but the instructing of men was forbidden (3:6). Her ministry, although parallel in some respects to the male deacon, was much more limited.

It is also evident from *Didascalia* that at this time deaconesses and widows were two separate but recognized groups. The deaconess was a type of the Holy Spirit, while the widow was lower in rank - a type of the altar (2:26). The bishop choose the deaconesses, but nothing indicates that he was restricted to selecting her from the widows. If the duties of the deaconesses were as strenuous as has be suggested, they were probably young women. The widows received instructions to be in prayer and to fast with and pray for the sick.

Hippolytus (c. A.D. 215) did not mention female deacons, but did discuss at length the work of widows who were appointed (not or-dained) by the bishop. Two types of widows existed: those who were indigent widows, and those who were set apart as a special group for prayer. Neither could take part in the liturgy of the church (Apostolic Tradi-tion 11). Virgins also had a part in this ministry of prayer: "Widows and virgins shall fast often and pray on behalf of the church" (A. T. 23).

Hippolytus gave us a detailed account of baptism which included the role of deacons. Although female deacons were not mentioned specifically in Hippolytus, his description did add detail to the account of *Didascalia*.

Origen (c. A.D. 240), author of a commentary on Romans, saw Phoebe as a "deaconess of the church" and an office holder. He used Ro. 16 as a proof text for the existence of the female diaconate in Paul's time (Romans 10:12, 17, cited in Martimort 82). Since female ministry was not universally accepted, Origin may have been defending the practice:

> If by this time women deacons were frequently found in the churches of Egypt, this remark would have been pointless, for there would have been no need of a text to teach with the authority of the Apostle that women were instituted deacons in the church. (32)

Another publication, *Ecclesiastical Canons of the Holy Apostles* (c. A.D. 300), is only known to us through various translations. In the Sahidic and Bohairic text, the Apostle Andrew suggests that women be made deacons. After considerable discussion, James concludes by saying, "Where shall we be able to set apart women for a ministry, ex-cept this ministry of this kind only, that they should help the needy" (28:15:27+)? The Ethiopic adds, "it is not fitting for women to raise voice while they stand in the church... but only this ministry that they should help the needy" (21:25+). The point is that women could not teach or celebrate the Eucharist, but they could be deacons in the context of service, charity, and good works (Gryson 84+, Martimort 86+).

The First Council of Nicaea (A.D. 325) defines deaconesses as "such as have assumed the habit, but who, since they have no imposi-tion of hands, are now to be numbered only among the laity." It is clear that their significance has been reduced to a lower order. The coun-cil gives instructions for their examination and appointment (19).

A great deal of information comes from the *Apostolic Constitutions* in the late fourth century. In the first six books of *Constitutions*, the masculine διακονος is used for the deaconess, while the balance of the work coins a new title, διακονισσα. The first portion may be based on *Didascalia* which uses the masculine term and is of earlier origin

(Turner 329).

Deaconesses were clearly a step lower than deacons in the hierarchy of the church. Below the deacons were "readers, singers, porters, deaconesses, widows, virgins, and orphans" (2:25). It should be noted that deacons, widows, and virgins were separate groups at this point. Deaconesses were in subjection to deacons and were "ministers to the deacons" (8:28). Widows were subject to deaconesses (3:7) and were to address their needs to deaconesses, deaconesses to deacons, and deacons to the bishop (2:26; 3:7).

As in *Didascalia*, the deacon serves the bishop "as Christ does His Father," and the deaconess is "honored by you in the place of the Holy Ghost." She is not to say anything without the deacon, as the Spirit says nothing "of Himself but gives glory to Christ" (2:26). In her service to the bishop she is "ready to carry messages, to travel about, to minister, and to serve" (3:19).

Women provided ministry to other women and to orphans:

The very same thing let the deaconess do to those women, whether poor or rich, that come unto them" (2:58).

Ordain also a deaconess who is faithful and holy, for the ministrations towards women. For sometimes he [the bishop] cannot send a deacon, who is a man, to the women, on account of unbelievers. Thou shalt therefore send a woman, a deaconess, on account of the imaginations of the bad. For we stand in need of a woman, a deaconess, for many necessities; and first is the baptism of women, the deacon shall anoint only their forehead with the holy oil, and after him the deaconess shall anoint them; for there is no necessity that the women should be seen by the men; but only in the laying on of hands the bishop shall anoint her head. (3:15)

In the worship services, men and women were seated separately. The church building was compared to a ship, with the deacons and deaconesses being mariners or shipmen. The bishop's throne was placed in the middle of the assembly with the presbyters seated on each side of him and the deacons standing near at hand. Deaconesses were to stand at the entries of the women and oversee them as the deacons did the men. They were to insure that the women did not whisper, sleep, laugh, nod, or otherwise withdraw their attention from the service (2:57).

Among the qualifications, virginity is stressed: "Let the deaconess be a pure virgin; or, at the least, a widow who has been once married, faithful, and well esteemed" (6:17). This demonstrates the closeness between the concepts of virgin, widow, and deaconess (see Chapter Four). The three female groups are distinct, but the deaconesses are chosen from the other two. All have some role to play in the church. *Didascalia* and *Constitutions* divide the service of prayer and active work mentioned in 1Tm. 5 between the widows and the deaconesses, with the deaconess above all other women in rank. In addition to the enrolled widows, the church community also has the usual widows.

The presbyters could not ordain deacons or deaconesses; this was the exclusive right of the bishop. However, the exclusive nature of this selection and ordination demonstrated the elevated position of the deacon and deaconess over the presbyter (3:11). The *Constitutions* gave a prayer and procedure for the appointing of deaconesses (8:19-20). In that ordination her ministry was compared with that of Miriam, Deborah, Anna, Huldah, Mary, and the women at the gate of the Temple.

As with *Didascalia*, the women were not to baptize anyone, and they were prohibited from teaching men. The argument was that men have a natural superiority to women, and therefore, to allow a woman to teach or baptize publicly would have violated natural order and divine law (3.9). Dissimilarities existed between her work and the work of the deacon:

> A deacon does not bless, does not give the blessing, but receives it from the bishop and presbyter: he does not baptize, he does not offer; but when a bishop or presbyter has offered, he distributes to the people, not as a priest, but as one that ministers to the priests. But it is not lawful for any one of the other clergy to do the work of a deacon. A deaconess does not bless, nor perform anything belonging to the office of presbyters or deacons, but only is to keep the doors, and to minister to the presbyters in the baptizing of women, on account of decency. A deacon separates a sub-deacon, a reader, a singer, and a deaconess, if there be any occasion, in the absence of a presbyter. It is not lawful for a sub-deacon to separate either one of the clergy or laity; nor for a reader, nor for a singer, nor for a deaconess, for they are the ministers to the deacons. (8:28)

The Fourth Council of Carthage (A.D. 398) reported: "Widows or virgins consecrated to God, who are to be employed at the baptism of women, must be competent to instruct rude and ignorant women how to answer at their baptism and how to live afterwards" (Canon 12, Hefele 2.412).

An inscription from Stobi, Yugoslavia, dated in the fourth century, reports of a female deacon (masculine διακονος with feminine adjectives), Agrippiane, who paved an exedra with a mosaic in fulfillment of a vow (Horsley 109 194+).

On the Mount of Olives, a fourth century tombstone reads, "Here lies the slave and bride of Christ, Sophia, deacon, the second Phoibe, who fell asleep on the twenty first of the month of March. ..." It is presumed that Sophia is compared to Phoebe because she is a benefactor to her church and city (Horsley 122 239+).

Horsley's articles give other information on ancient documents which discuss female deacons. These include διακονισσα Athanasia of Delphi in the early fifth century. A family tombstone at Melos from the fourth century reveals a host of church titles within one family: πρεσβυτεροι Asklepis (female ?), Elpizon, and Asklepiodotus and διακονος Agaliasis (masculine title, female person) (Horsley 122 240+).

1 Timothy 5:9 stated that a widow was not to be enrolled until she reached the age of sixty. Tertullian confirmed this same age limit when speaking of the notorious irregularity of a virgin who had been admitted into the order of widowhood at the age of twenty (Veiling of Virgins 9). The *Didascalia* listed a deaconess's age as fifty (3:1). The *Theodosian Code* (A.D. 390), which demonstrated the confusion between deaconesses and widows, required the Pauline age of sixty years for widows to be applied to deaconesses (cited in Martimort 107). The Council of Chalcedon (A.D. 451) changed it to forty after the woman had appropriate probation (15). Olympias (c. 420), the deaconess of Constantinople, became a widow at eighteen and was accepted as a deaconess at a very early age because of her exemplary life (Schaff "Deaconess" 375). The Council of Trullo (A.D. 692) fixed the deaconess's age at forty. Justinian required fifty at one point (Novellae 6:6) and forty at another (Novellae 123:13, cited in Martimort 110).

All of this concern for age took a back seat later as the vow of perpetual virginity came into the qualifications. The *Apostolic Constitutions* reported two life situations for deaconesses: widowhood and chaste virginity (6:17). Once a woman became a deaconess, if she decided to marry, she was declared anathema (Chalcedon 15).

The *Theodotian Code* stated that if the deaconess had children under age, she must appoint a guardian for them and entrust the management of her property to others. She could, however, continue to receive an income. She also could not bequeath her property to the church or to a cleric (Robinson 76).

The prohibition against a twice married widow (1Tm. 5) was interpreted generally as a prohibition against a woman who had been married successively to two husbands, although lawfully and scripturally acceptable marriages. This was the interpretation of Tertullian, Epiphanius, the *Apostolic Constitutions*, and Justinian. Theodoret saw it as a prohibition against a woman who had remarried after divorcing her first husband, a scandalous act. "Husband of one wife" in Chapter Five discussed this in greater detail.

Although beginning as a table function, the male diaconate developed into a liturgical function in the post-Biblical writers. The female diaconate, on the other hand, remained in service to women and children. As the years passed by, male dominance of church offices remained the norm.

The interpretation of Canon 11 of the Synod of Laodicea (A.D. 343-381) has led some to see this as the beginning of the end of deaconesses. The Canon reads, "The appointment of the so-called female elders or presidents shall not take place in the church." Balsamon interprets the canon to refer to certain venerable women who oversaw other older women, but due to arrogance or selfishness, brought scandal on themselves (Nicene and Post-Nicene Fathers 14:130). Hefele cites Neander and Fuchs as interpreting the Canon as a prohibition of the appointment of deaconesses in general, since they preside over the rest of the female populace (2.305).

The Western Church

The office of deaconess was noticeably absent in the Latin church. Evidently no such feminine ministry was considered necessary, and female clergy aroused suspicion. The *Apostolic Tradition* of Hippolytus was the manual of discipline, and that writing did not mention deaconesses, only widows and virgins.

Ambrosiaster, a Latin commentator, considered the women of 1Tm. 3:11 to be women in general. He saw the bishop and deacon establishing a model, and he wrote, "Therefore, since the church must be pure, he [Paul] wants even women, who seem inferior, to be without reproach." Ambrosiaster described as "foolish audacity that deaconesses should be ordained." His commentary on Romans interpreted Phoebe as a servant in the broad sense (Gryson 156+).

Pelagius also wrote Latin commentaries on 1Tm. 3, and stated his opinion that such were the women of the 1Tm. 3. The way he words his statement showed that he did not know of deaconesses in the western church, only in the eastern church. He also viewed the women of 1Tm. 5 as deaconesses.

The Council of Nimes (A.D. 394) forbade women to be admitted to the Levitical ministry, but it was unclear exactly what was being addressed at this point. Possibly the Priscillians had permitted women to become priests and may have had deaconesses (Rand 372). The Coun-

cil of Orange (A.D. 441) stated, "Deaconesses shall no longer be ordained, and (in divine service) they shall receive the benediction only
in common with the laity (not among those holding clerical offices)"
(Canon 26, Hefele 3.163). Likewise, the synod at Epaon (A.D. 517) continued
the condemnation (Title 21, Hefele 4.111). However, deaconesses seemed to
have been in Gaul as late as the sixth century, as attested by the Second
Council of Orleans (A.D. 533) which stated that "no woman may any
longer receive diaconal benediction due to the frailty of her sex" (Canon
17, Hefele 4.187). Venatius Fortunatus (A.D. 650) and the Council of
Worms (A.D. 868) showed that deaconesses were active in some
western churches (Martimort 118). By the twelfth century, the order was
generally extinct (Bingham 2.22.14).

The Eastern Church

Theodore of Mopsuestia (c. 395), in his commentary on 1Tm. 3:11,
translated γυνη as women who performed the duties of deacons, not
the wives of deacons. He emphasized that the age of sixty is for
widows, not deaconesses. Since no age requirements were given for
bishops or deacons, there should be no specific age requirement for
the female deacon (Martimort 118 +).

John Chrysostom (A.D. 400) talked of deaconesses in the context
of Ro. 16 and 1Tm. 3. In his commentaries he called Phoebe a deaconess and referred to the women of 1Tm. 3 as having the "dignity of the
diaconate." In the later case, he elaborated that they were deaconesses
and not female Christians in general.

As did Chrysostom and Theodore, Theodoret of Cyrrhus (A.D.
425) had no doubt that the women of 1Tm. 3 were deaconesses. He
stated in his commentary on 1Tm.:

> "The women likewise," i.e. the (women) deacons, "must be serious, no slanderers,
> but temperate, faithful in all things." What he prescribes for the men, he
> prescribes also and in about the same terms for the woman. Since he says that
> the deacon must be "serious," he also says that the woman must be "serious." Just
> as he forbids the men to be "double-tongued," so too he forbids the women to be
> "slanderers." And, as he forbids the men to be addicted to much wine, so also he
> commands the women to be "temperate." (cited in Martimort 118)

He saw the ordination of Phoebe as a deaconess in Cenchreae as
evidence for the rapid development and importance of that
congregation.

The current word "nun" comes from the Latin *nonna* which means
"nun, child's nurse, or old lady." Ultimately it is baby talk referring to
a grandmother. The relation of the word to the status of the widow is

easily understood. The Greek μοναχαι carries the monastic idea ("live alone, separate ones self") in the early development of the order of nuns. A papyrus from Oxyrhynchos, Egypt, dated June or July A.D. 400, is a lease agreement for a residence between two μοναχαι and Aurelius Jose. Several things are significant in this lease: it is one of the earliest mentions of female monastics; they did not use an intermediary or church official to make the lease arrangements; and it is curious that monastics would live in the Oxyrhynchos instead of a seculuded location (Horsley 82 126+).

The *Testament of Our Lord* (circa A.D. 450) comes from Syria and is not available in its original Greek language. The roles of widows and deaconesses in the church hierarchy are reversed in its text from what is seen in *Constitutions*. The deaconess is below the widow who serves as her supervisor. The deaconesses have a humble position which includes little, since the widows provide most of the service, including assistance with baptisms. They do take communion to the pregnant women who could not attend Easter services (2:20), but this sacramental role is remarkable (Martimort 50).

The emperor Justinian (A.D. 535) wrote to Epiphanius, Archbishop of Constantinople, in *Novellae* 3. Epiphanius had expanded the clergy to such a great degree that the budget of the church was overburdened. Therefore, the number was restricted: sixty priests, one hundred deacons, forty deaconesses, ninety subdeacons, 110 readers, and twenty-five singers (3:1:1, cited in Martimort 109). All were full time employees of the church. When he talked of the ranks of clergy, he spoke of "male and female deacons" and gave them authority over the subdeacons, readers, and singers.

Deaconesses had to be once married widows or virgins with a minimum age of fifty, later reduced to forty. Celibacy was required. Deaconesses who "defiled their ordination," like unfaithful vestal virgins, were liable to capital punishment and had their possessions distributed to the church (6). The condemnation changed with time. *Novella* 123 put the majority of the blame on the man who seduced her and required capital punishment for him while only banishing the deaconess to a monastery (43). She was not allowed to have a male in her house unless he was her son or father; she could not live with a brother, cousin, or other male. The only work Justinian detailed for the deaconess was assisting in the baptism of females (Martimort 109).

Epiphanius wrote that the ministry of deaconesses was centered around the female sick and baptismal candidates as detailed earlier.

He forbade women to speak in the church or have authority over men. He did consider them to be clergy, but he ranked them lower than the subdeacon and higher than the exorcists, interpreters, grave diggers, and janitors. They were selected from the virgins or once married widows, or from those women who had promised to remain continent in marriage. Widows were never mentioned as an order (Panarion 3.2. cited in Martimort 112 +).

Epiphanius reports:

> There is in the Church, however, the order of deaconesses, but it does not exist for the purpose of exercising priestly functions or for the purpose of confiding certain tasks to women. It exists for the purpose of preserving decency for the female sex, whether in connection with baptism or in connection with the examination of women undergoing sufferings or pain, or whenever the bodies of women are required to be uncovered, so that they need not be exposed to the gaze of the men officiating, but instead be viewed only by the deaconess, who receives from the priest the order to take care of the woman at the time of her nudity. (Panarion 3.2.79, cited in Davies "Deaconess" 87)

He echoes the words of *Didascalia* and *Apostolic Constitutions* in denying women any role except service. The male diaconate has taken on a liturgical function that is denied to women.

A sixth century tombstone from Archelais, Cappadocia, reads:

> Here lies Maria the deacon, of pious and blessed memory, who in accordance with the statement | of the apostles reared children, practised hospitality, washed the feet of the saints, distributed her bread to the afflicted. Remember her | Lord, when you come in your kingdom.

Although she was called a deacon (masculine), her attributes were virtually a quote of 1Tm. 5:10. She was probably a widow at the time of her appointment to the diaconate (Horsley 109 193 +).

Balsamon (A.D. 1070), commenting on Justinian's report, stated that the deaconesses were really nuns and bore little resemblance to the original sense (Thurston "Deaconesses" 652). The terms "deaconess" and "archdeaconess" were used as designations of the officers in convents at Constantinople (Schaff "Deaconess" 375).

Hunermann remarks:

> The female diaconate in the Eastern churches gained the greatest ground during those long periods of peace when the Christian communities imparted momentum to an intensive, ever-growing missionary action and took in multitudes. It was the time before the official recognition of the church, the time of quite energetic expansion... The moment the churches proceeded to lose their missionary character, this office began to die out. (330)

The western church develops the work of deaconesses. Some scholars feel that it originated in the East and never developed in the

West. Others suggest that the eastern church had a greater need for structure. Perhaps the western church was more suspicious regarding female ministry. It is hard to say with certainty (Rand 373).

As adult baptism by immersion became rare and infant baptism became common, the office of deaconess declined in significance. When deaconesses took on a greater liturgical function, abuses occurred. In the Montanist and Nestorian communities deaconesses administered Holy Communion and read the Scriptures in public. Prohl credited the "gradual strangling" of deaconesses to the "false doctrines of the class priesthood and the sacrifice of the mass" (76). Men and women began sitting together in the assembly, removing the need for females to maintain order over the women (Robinson 95). The cultural conventions of the times also took their toll (Hunermann 330). Generally, the order of nun evolved and the growth of monastic houses for nuns offered them refuge. This distinct religious and clerical calling for women ended deaconesses (Schaff "Deaconess" 375).

In the middle ages, the term deaconess did surface again, but it was used exclusively of the deacon's wife just as πρεσβυτερα was used of the wife of the presbyter and επισχοπα of the wife of the bishop (Bingham 2.22.15).

Conclusions

The major cause of a revival of interest in deaconesses comes from the question of ordination of women to ministries in the church. For most religious groups, the terms "ordination" and "clergy" are primary to this study. All agree that the church had female servants. The question is whether they were laity or clergy. Only if they are clergy would most groups recognize these servants as deacons. Many denominational studies must be seen as an effort to prove or disprove that the ordination of women to the diaconate justifies female clergy today. Unfortunately, the emphasis is on office and not on function.

Turner, in summarizing the roles of widows, deaconesses, and virgins, has remarked:

> Now the course of our investigation has. . . shown us that in early or ante-Nicene times there is really no confusion whatever between widow, deaconess, and virgin. They were throughout distinct persons, with distinct qualifications and distinct duties: distinct, too, in the times and sometimes also in the places, at which they acquire prominence, and distinct in the degree and the sense in which they can be spoken of as constituting an order in the Church. The widow is both primitive and universal; and she is from the first enrolled in a class: but the class is not, and substantially it never became in early times, a ministering class; what it gave to the church was not ministry, but intercessory prayer. The woman deacon is

primitive, though from the complete absence of any traces of her in the West we can hardly say universal: but what the steps were which connected the primitive women-servants of the Church with the wealthy and influential deaconesses of the Greek Church of the fourth century, our scanty evidence does not enable us to say. We do not know whether evolution or revival would be the truer word to characterize the course of the history. Individual self-dedication to the virgin life goes back to the earliest times and was doubtless found in all quarters of the church: but it was of its very essence to be private, and Tertullian urges that virgins ought to be, Cyprian deplores that in fact they are not, distinguishable in outward appearance from other women. Doubtless the impulse to the virgin life received a great impetus with the rise of monasticism: and just as the solitary life for men was quickly followed by the coenobitic, so too about the middle of the fourth century we rather suddenly begin to hear of the body or order of virgins.... and it is true that a time did come when the outlines that had once been sharply defined came to be blurred and indistinct. (349+)

That blur comes in a complete merger of situations in the fifth century (351).

Gryson states:

One thing is undeniable: there were in the early church women who occupied an official position, who were invested with a ministry, and who, at least at certain times and places, appeared as part of the clergy. These women were called "deaconesses" and at times "widows." (xi)

Martimort adds:

The Christians of antiquity did not have a single, fixed idea of what deaconesses were supposed to be. In the enumeration of the various groups distinct from the Christian people as a whole, they listed them in different places: sometimes they were listed after deacons; sometimes they were listed after all other ministers; sometimes they appeared in the middle of a listing of consecrated states of life. (241)

For the fact is that the ancient institution of deaconesses, even in its own time, was encumbered with not a few ambiguities.... In my opinion, if the restoration of the institution of deaconesses were indeed to be sought after so many centuries, such a restoration itself could only be frought with ambiguity. (250)

Gryson and Martimort are writing from a Roman Catholic hierarchal background and are defining "deacon" with concern for sacerdotal ecclesiastical leadership.

Female servants of the church did exist in the early church. It is valid to ask if that service was carefully structured into an ecclesiastical office. However, it is equally valid to ask the same question about the male deacons. It appears to this writer that the internal structure of the church was in a state of evolution. The style and recognition of leadership varies with the cultural environment of the congregation. No single fixed universal organization is apparent.

One additional point needs to be made. Current debate over

female deacons centers around the equality of male and female in sharing ordained clerical roles. Historically, deacons and deaconesses have never served equally. The females minister to other females and children, not to males. Propriety is always a consideration. In the hierarchical structure, the females are always considered under their male counterparts. Any attempt to justify female preaching ministers does not find support in historical studies of the diaconate.

Chapter 8

Deacons Redefined: The Reformation

In contrast to the liturgical function of the medieval deacon, the Reformation leaders redefined the diaconate in an attempt to restore the New Testament church. The direction that restoration took was determined in part by the sizable social needs of the period. Deacons had been cloistered for too long, it was now time to redefine their work in terms to meet the needs of the poor.

European Influence

From the time of the Waldensians and Moravians of pre-Reformation Protestantism, deacons were valuable ministers. The Waldensians had preaching presbyters (called *barbe*) and deacons (often called *minores*) who were assistants to the *barbe*. The deacons accompanied and served the presbyters on their frequent preaching tours. Among the Moravians or Hussites of the fifteenth and sixteenth centuries, the deacon was an assistant to the priest, living with him, helping him teach, accompanying him on trips, preaching, assisting with communion, and baptizing as necessary. The care of the poor was not his charge (Ross "Deacons" 429).

The Protestant Reformation included the concept of deacons in the reform of the Papal system. Luther, in 1520, stated:

> The diaconate is the ministry, not of reading the Gospel or the Epistle, as is the present practice, but of distributing the church's aid to the poor, in order that the priests might be relieved of the burden of temporal concerns. (Wentz and Lehmann 36:116)

After the preacher, Luther saw no higher office in the church than the man who handled the funds justly and honestly, helping those poor who could not earn their own livelihood (Ross "Deacons" 430). He viewed the deacon as part of the laity rather than an order of the priesthood (Deweese Emerging 19).

It was primarily to administer the funds of the church that he called for a diaconate elected from the congregation. The funds were kept in a chest at the church building, and in most cases three or more keys were required to open it, giving some safeguards against misuse of funds. Annual audits were required (Atkinson 87).

The deacons kept records on all people served and closely scrutinized the resources of the poor. Certain towns issued an identity badge to the consistently poor, but others rejected this as unloving. The deacons also served the hospitals, and efforts were made to bring the hospitals under the control of the deacons (Atkinson 88).

Calvin joined Luther in tracing the deacons to Acts 6:

> Scripture specifically designates as deacons those whom the church has appointed to distribute alms and take care of the poor, and serve as stewards of the common chest for the poor.... Here, then, is the kind of deacons the apostolic church had, and which we, after their example, should have. (Institutes 2:1061+)

The church constitution which Francis Lambert drafted for Philip of Hesse (1526) claimed three orders of ministry: pastors, elders (for discipline) and deacons (for the poor). Luther found the concepts too democratic, but Calvin adopted them in his discussion of Ro. 12:6+ and 1Co. 12:28. The earliest edition of his *Institutes* recognized two offices: presbyter and deacon, but the final edition advocated four: pastors, teachers, elders, and deacons (Reid 104).

Calvin's strong social concern was reflected in his two function approach to the diaconate: the *procureurs* who gathered alms and the *hospitallier* who distributed those alms in caring for the poor and sick. This may have been the custom in the society of Geneva in Calvin's day rather than an innovation based on his scriptural understanding (Reid 106). Calvin laid down the method of selection and fixed the number at four procurators and one hospitaler per church with mandatory periodic reviews by the pastor and elders (Kingdon 60). Each was a laymen or part-time volunteer who rarely took on teaching functions. Calvin was quick to attack the Roman church for corrupting the diaconate.

An individual could hold the position of elder and deacon at the same time in Calvin's Geneva. This frequently occurred, especially after Calvin and other pastors began to intervene in the process. After 1562 three out of four *procureurs* were also elders. This small, elite, completely devoted group of laymen gave the pastor extreme power since they held most of the lay offices of the church (Kingdon 63).

Deacons were an important part of Anabaptist - Mennonite life in the 1500's. Jan Pauw, a deacon, was martyred in Amsterdam in 1535. Deacons in Moravia and Transylvania administered church discipline in 1537. The 1580 Confession of Faith of the Dutch Anabaptists demonstrated the importance of deacons to church life.

The *Concept of Cologne* (1591) stated, "Deacons shall be chosen. . . to whom is to be assigned the care of the poor." They were "to distribute to the poor the gifts received for this purpose, so that the giver shall remain unknown, as Christ teaches" (Neff and Bender 21). The *West Prussian Confession* (1895) added:

> We hold fast to the Apostolic arrangement according to which, along side of elders and preachers, deacons or alms-keepers are maintained in the church, who support the poor through the alms which are given by generous hearts, supply the wants of needy members, practice mercy with gladness, and otherwise lend a helping hand in the church in order that it may be well administered. (Neff and Bender 22)

The British Isles

John Knox (Scottish Presbyterian) instituted deacons at the very outset in the first Book of Discipline (1561):

> Their office is to gather the alms diligently and faithfully to distribute it, with the consent of the ministers and elders; also to provide for the sick and impotent persons, having ever a diligent care, that the charity of godly men be not wasted upon loiterers and idle vagabonds. (Ross "Deacons" 432)

Presbyterian leaders Robert and James Haldane and John Glas established independent "Churches of Christ" in the British Isles prior to the restoration movement in America. The Haldanes and Glasites observed the Lord's Supper weekly, practiced believer immersion, the holy kiss, foot washing, and sought to restore New Testament church order. They also practiced a plurality of elders and deacons (Brown Churches 43; Garrett 51). The Campbells were often accused of being Haldanes or Glasites (Garrett 53).

In the seventeenth and eighteenth centuries, the role of the deacon faded in the Church of Scotland mainly because social and welfare concerns were assumed by the government. It was not until J. G. Lorimer's book, *The Deaconship: A Treatise on the Office of Deacon, with suggestions for its Revival in the Church of Scotland* (1843), and the separation of the Free Church from the Church of Scotland, that a revival of the diaconate took place (Ross "Deacons" 433).

Late in the 1500's the Church of England discussed the role of elders and deacons. Months were spent debating the work and powers of the presbytery, but only one day was devoted to the diaconate. The *Directory of Government* said simply that deacons were not to preach or administer the sacraments, "but to take special care in distributing to the necessities of the poor" and that the office was perpetual. At this period the state social welfare system was developing, and the state church had difficulty working out the relationship of deacons to benevolent needs (Yule 126).

A key figure in the re-establishment of the elder and deacon form of church order in Britain was John Smyth. Smyth led a separatist congregation which had fled from England to Amsterdam. When Smyth concluded that infant baptism was wrong, he convinced his congregation and baptized himself and his church. Thereafter, believers' baptism was a mark of his "Baptist" church (Maring and Hudson 12).

In 1608 Smyth delivered an address on "The Differences of the Churches of the Separation," describing the British Separatist movement. He raised objections to the staff of officers maintained by the Catholic church, a staff which the Geneva Bible recommended in its notes. In his last confession, Smyth stated that the only offices should be in the local church and that those should be elders and deacons:

> We believe that Christ hath set in His outward church two sorts of ministers: viz. some who are called pastors, teachers, or elders, who administer the word and sacraments, and others who are called Deacons, men and women: whose ministry is to serve tables and wash the saints' feet. (Beasley-Murray 72)

Smyth saw elders, overseers, bishops, pastors, teachers, governors, and leaders as the same office with the "chief work of feeding and applying the covenant" to the church (Whitley 307).

The deaconry, as he put it, cared for the body and bodily necessities of the saints. They were servants of the eldership and church as the Levites were given to serve the priests and people in the tabernacle, and were concerned with the treasury of the church: who is to contribute, when to collect, and how to use the funds. The weekly participating in the Lord's Supper, weekly treasury collection and church maintenance of widows were all a part of his revival (Whitley 316 +).

The American Frontier

The Particular Baptists of Philadelphia can be studied through the work of Morgan Edwards (1768), *The Customs of Primitive Churches*. Edwards believed that the biblical pattern provided for "teachers; elders; deacons; deaconesses; and clerks." The Separate Baptists of Virginia and the Carolinas also had deacons and deaconesses. Barton Stone's movement drew heavily from the Separate Baptists, with 13,000 of them becoming Stone's "Christians" by 1811. Campbell had success with Separate Baptists also, reporting the recruiting of eleven churches and 500 members by 1832 (Allen and Hughes 64 +).

The prayer book which John Wesley sent to America provided for an order of deacons, as well as elders and superintendents. At the Christmas Conference of 1784, the church decided that deacons should be a part of the ministry in America. The Methodist Protestant church in 1828-30 did away with the deacon, having only the order of elders and the bishop (Harmon 1:639).

A contributing factor to the growth of the Restoration Movement was the "disestablishment" of American Religion. In 1775, nine of the colonies had "established" churches. Citizens were required to attend and maintain these churches, and dissenting sects such a Methodists and Baptists faced some restrictions. In Connecticut, dissenters were forced to pay taxes to support the Congregational church until 1777. It was around the turn of the century that various states "disestablished" the churches. Thereafter no denomination had automatic precedence over another, and no one was obligated to participate. This resulted in a new voluntary spirit. Churches had to recruit in order to survive resulting in aggressive proselytizing. In 1800, only seven percent of the American population belonged to religious societies. By 1850, that percentage had doubled. Diaconal and lay ministries were significant to that growth (Douglas 22 +).

Contemporary Thought

It is a serious mistake for any student of the diaconate to avoid examining the struggles of various denominations with the subject. All claim scriptural authority for their position. In the past twenty years a revival of interest in the diaconate has occurred and many excellent scholarly works have been produced that examine the historical background in greater detail than this volume and which struggle honestly with the implications of Scripture and tradition on the role of deacons in their own groups. Excellent works include Barnett (Episcopalian), Nowell (Roman Catholic), Gribble and Swartz (Anabaptist) and the World Council Study. These four are valuable resources.

The work of deacons in most churches is ever evolving. The newly created (1987) Evangelical Lutheran Church of America has formed a committee to consider the role of deacons and deaconesses. The Catholics began appointing permanent deacons in 1971 and continue to evaluate their role and debate the addition of deaconesses. As this book goes to press, the Pope has charged the Bishops to further consider the ordination of women. Episcopalians parallel the Catholics in their study. Some Southern Baptist churches have begun appointing deaconesses, and this activity has contributed to the liberal/moderate/conservative battle for control of the Southern Baptist

Convention. Reading the documents of these groups often creates a sense of *deja vu* to readers from Churches of Christ. In most denominations, a description of the diaconate that was written twenty years ago is obsolete today.

Another group currently studying polity is the Commission on Faith and Order of the National Council of Churches. Dr. Lynn Mitchell is the only member of Churches of Christ who is serving on this study group. It should produce a volume much like the World Council Study.

The World Council of Churches, meeting in Lima, Peru, issued in 1982 their monumental statement, *Baptism, Eucharist and Ministry*. Represented in this statement were virtually all of the major church traditions: Eastern Orthodox, Oriental Orthodox, Roman Catholic, Old Catholic, Lutheran, Anglican, Reformed, Methodist, United, Disciples, Baptist, Adventist and Pentecostal. Their statement summarized the role of deacons today:

> The New Testament does not describe a single pattern of ministry which might serve as a blueprint or continuing norm for all future ministry in the Church. In the New Testament there appears rather a variety of forms which existed at different places and times. (Ministry 19)

> The presbyters become the leaders of the local Eucharistic community, and as assistants of the bishop, deacons receive responsibilities in the larger area. (Ministry 21)

> Although there is no single New Testament pattern, although the Spirit has many times led the Church to adapt its ministries to contextual needs, and although other forms of the ordained ministry have been blessed with the gifts of the Holy Spirit, nevertheless the threefold ministry of bishop, presbyter, and deacon may serve today as an expression of the unity we seek and also as a means for achieving it. (Ministry 22)

> The threefold pattern stands evidently in need of reform. . . . In others, the function of deacons has been reduced to an assistant role in the celebration of the liturgy: they have ceased to fulfill any function with regard to the diaconal witness of the Church. (Ministry 24)

> Deacons represent to the Church its calling as servant in the world. By struggling in Christ's name with the myriad needs of societies and persons, deacons exemplify the interdependence of worship and service in the Church's life.

> They exercise responsibility in the worship of the congregation: for example by reading the Scriptures, preaching and leading the people in prayer. They help in the teaching of the congregation. They exercise a ministry of love within the community. They fulfill certain administrative tasks and may be elected to responsibilities for governance. (Ministry 31)

In a marginal commentary on "Ministry 31," the writers pose these comments:

In many churches there is today considerable uncertainty about the need, the rationale, the status and the functions of deacons. In what sense can the diaconate be considered part of the ordained ministry? What is it that distinguishes it from other ministries in the Church (catechists, musicians, etc.)? Why should deacons be ordained while these others ministries do not receive ordination? If they are ordained, do they receive ordination in the full sense of the word or is their ordination only the first step towards ordination as presbyters? Today, there is a strong tendency in many churches to restore the diaconate as an ordained ministry with its own dignity and meant to be exercised for life. As the churches move closer together there may be united in this office ministries now existing in a variety of forms and under a variety of names. Differences in ordering the diaconal ministry should not be regarded as a hindrance for the mutual recognition of the ordained ministries.

Suggested Reading

Anabaptist

Gibble, June A., and Fred W. Swartz, ed. *Called to Caregiving*. Elgin, IL: Brethren, 1987.

Huffman, Cathy Simmons. "Deacon." *The Brethren Encyclopedia*, Vol. 1. Philadelphia: Brethren Encyclopedia, 1983. 368.

Neff, Christian Weierhof, and H. S. Bender. "Deacon." *The Mennonite Encyclopedia*, Vol. 2. Scottdale, PA: Mennonite, 1956. 21.

Baptist

Beasley-Murray, George R. "The Diaconate in Baptist Churches," *The Ministry of Deacons*. Geneva: World Council of Churches, 1965. 72+.

Deweese, Charles W. *The Emerging Role of Deacons*. Nashville: Broadman, 1979.

Forshee, Howard B. *The Ministry of the Deacon*. Nashville: Convention, 1968.

Graves, Allen W. *A Church at Work: A Handbook of Church Polity*. Nashville: Convention, 1972.

Howell, R. B. C. *The Deaconship*. Valley Forge, PA: Judson, 1847.

Maring, Norman H. and Winthrop S. Hudson. *A Baptist Manual of Polity and Practice*. Valley Forge: Judson, 1963.

McMinn, J. B. "Deacon." *Encyclopedia of Southern Baptists*, Vol. 1. Nashville: Broadman, 1958. 352.

Naylor, Robert E. *The Baptist Deacon*. Nashville: Broadman, 1955.

Smith, Michael A. "Baptist Deacons in the Nineteenth Century." *The Quarterly Review* Oct. - Dec., 1982: 67+.

Church of England

Barnett, James M. *The Diaconate: A Full and Equal Order.* Minneapolis: Winston, 1981.

Every, George. "The Diaconate in the Anglican Communion," *The Ministry of Deacons.* Geneva: World Council of Churches, 1965, 45 + .

"The Lambreth Conference of 1958." *The Encyclical Letter from the Bishops Together with the Resolutions and Reports.* Greenwich, CT: Seabury, 1958.

Lutheran

Bouman, Stephen Paul. "The Diaconate: A Gift We Offer the New," *Lutheran Perspective* 26 Oct. 1987: 14 + .

Krimm, Herbert. "The Diaconate in the Lutheran Church." *The Ministry of Deacons.* Geneva: World Council of Churches, 1965. 54 + .

Winter, Sister Mildred. "Deacon." *The Encyclopedia of the Lutheran Church*, Vol. 1. Minneapolis: Augsburg, 1965. 659.

Methodist

The Book of Discipline of the United Methodist Church - 1984. Nashville: United Methodist, 1984.

Harmon, Nolan B. "Deacon." *The Encyclopedia of World Methodism,* Vol. 1. Nashville: United Methodist, 1974. 639.

Wakefield, Gordon S. "Diakonia in the Methodist Church Today." *Service in Christ: Essays Presented to Karl Barth on his 80th Birthday.* Ed. J. I. McCord and J. H. L. Parker. London: Epworth Press, 1966. 182 + .

Presbyterian

The Constitution of the Presbyterian Church (U. S. A.): Part II, Book of Order. New York: General Assembly, 1987.

Henderson, Robert. "Notes on the Diaconate in American Presbyterianism." *The Ministry of Deacons.* Geneva: World Council of Churches, 1965. 63 + .

Roman Catholic

Bishops' Committee on the Liturgy. *The Deacon, Minister of Word and Sacrament.* Washington, D.C.: U. S. Catholic Conference, 1979.

Bishops' Committee on the Permanent Diaconate. *Permanent Deacons in the United States: Guidelines on their Formation and Ministry.* Washington, D.C.: U. S. Catholic Conference, 1971.

Bishops' Committee on the Permanent Diaconate. *A National Study of the Permanent Diaconate in the United States.* Washington, D.C.: U. S. Catholic Conference, 1981.

Biskupek, Aloysius. *Deaconship.* St. Louis: Herder, 1944.

Dowd, Dick. "Too Many Deacons? Or Not Enough?" *Deacon Digest* May 1986: 8.

Nowell, Robert. *The Ministry of Service: Deacons in the Contemporary Church.* New York: Herder and Herder, 1968.

O'Rourke, J. J. "Deacon." *New Catholic Encyclopedia*, Vol. 4. New York: McGraw-Hill, 1967. 667.

Rashke, Richard L. *The Deacon in Search of Identity*. New York: Paulist, 1975.

Riley, T. J. "Deacon." *New Catholic Encyclopedia,* Vol. 4. New York: McGraw-Hill, 1967. 668.

CHAPTER 9

Deaconesses Rediscovered: Kaiserswerth and Beyond

The female deacon had disappeared in the Roman church by the time of the Reformation. Only the nunneries remained to reflect an organized role for women in the church. The reformers looked to the women of the New Testment for models of female activity. The deaconess was rediscovered to care for the benevolent needs of women and children, to enter the developing sphere of medical care, and to offer a protestant alternative to the Roman nun.

John Calvin (c. 1540) in his commentaries held that female deacons or deaconesses were a part of the early church. His commentary on Ro. 16:1 called Phoebe a deacon in the official sense. In 1Tm. 5 he saw a double role for the church and its widows who were deacons. The church provided for the welfare of the poor widow who in turn spent her ministry helping other poor in the community (Reid 107).

Mentions of deaconesses occurred among protestant reformers such as the Church of Wesel (1575) and the Synod of Middelburgh (1581). The Puritan Ministers in 1575 wrote a clause that reads, "touching deacons of both sorts, namely men and women." Both were elected by the congregation and ordained with prayers. Gov. Bradford spoke of "one deaconess who visited the sick, relieved the poor, and sat in a convenient place in the congregation with a little birchen rod in her hand and kept little children in great awe from disturbing the congregation" (Schaff "Deaconess" 376). By the beginning of the eighteenth century, the Mennonites of Holland also appointed deaconesses who were part-time volunteers to serve the sick and poor (Winter "Deaconesses" 660).

Robert Haldane, who heavily influenced the Campbells in Scotland and Ireland, stated concerning Phoebe, "As deacons were appointed to attend to the poor, so deaconesses were specially set apart in the churches in order to attend to the wants of their own sex" (633).

At least three movements led to a deaconess revival. The early non-conformists of Europe and the British Separatists began independent movements in the seventeenth century, but it was the influence of the Kaiserswerths that made the greatest impact on the nineteenth century movement.

The Baptists

John Smyth wrote of "deacons, men and women: whose ministry is to serve tables and wash the saints' feet" (Beasley-Murray 72). Thomas Helwys who formed the first Baptist church in England (1611) held that deacons could be men or women (Deweese Deacon 25). The 1611 *Confession of Faith* from Amsterdam stated that deaconesses, along with other church officers, were to be elected and approved by their church with fasting, prayer, and the laying on of hands (Deweese "Deaconesses" 53). Minutes of the Broadmead church in Bristol, England, showed that that church selected deaconesses in 1662, 1673, and 1679. These women were widows over the age of sixty who vowed not to marry. They were to visit, provide for and encourage the sick and report to the elders and deacons any special needs they discovered (Deweese Deacon 30).

Kaiserswerth Deaconesses

The Kaiserswerth institutions of Germany were credited with the primary revival of deaconesses in the Christian church. In 1836, Pastor Theodor Fliedner founded an institution of deaconesses at Kaiserswerth on the Rhine, near Dusseldorf. He was animated in part by the Mennonite deaconesses and by practical considerations to meet the need of his day for the proper care of the sick and the training of neglected children. He was struck by the contrast between the fine architecture of hospital buildings and the poor care within. Impressed by the needs for trained women, he prepared a constitution for "The Order of Deaconesses for the Rhenish Provinces" in 1836. Gertrud Reichard was the first to enter the institute and two years later was sent to the city hospital of Elberfeld. The concept spread rapidly. Kaiserswerth deaconesses were soon serving in Hospitals in England (1846), America (1849), Jerusalem (1851), Constantinople (1852), Smyrna (1853), and Alexandria (1857) (Winter "Deaconess" 660+).

Three kinds of deaconesses were developed: 1) those to care for the sick and poor; 2) those to be teachers; 3) and those to aid ministers in their local work. They obligated themselves for five years of service, received maintenance, an allowance, and lifelong care. They wore the simple dress of the married woman (Winter "Deaconess" 661). By

1905, 14,501 Kaiserswerth deaconesses served in seventy-five institutions around the world (Schaff "Deaconess" 377).

The Church of England in the early nineteenth century was primarily composed of the upper class. There was little contact with or concern for the poor. In the 1830's external reform by the state and research into the nature and authority of the church began the process to alleviate the misery and poverty that abounded.

The first Church of England deaconess, Miss Elizabeth Ferard, was dedicated in 1861. However, the movement goes back to Florence Nightingale and Elizabeth Fry. Miss Nightingale studied at Kaiserswerth before taking charge of a sanitarium in London, and Mrs. Fry set up a nurses' training school in London in 1840 after a visit to Kaiserswerth. The first protestant sisterhood was established in 1847 near London and was copied in the same year by the Sisterhood of Mercy in Devonport. This led to much discussion at Canterbury from 1858 to 1871 on woman's work in the Church of England, including a call to revive the order of deaconesses (Schaff "Deaconess" 378).

In 1858, Elizabeth Catherine Ferard went to stay in the Deaconess Institution at Kaiserswerth. She trained for medical service and offered herself to revive the deaconess order in England in 1861. In 1871, rules were laid down by the Archbishop of Canterbury for diocesan deaconesses homes (Schaff "Deaconess" 378). Those rules stated:

> The object of the Institution is the renewal of the primitive Order of Deaconesses in the Church of England, for the purpose of engaging in works of Christian usefulness... the care of the sick and poor, education of the young, etc... shall be formed as far as circumstances permit upon the model of the Institution at Kaiserswerth. (Joanna 220)

All women were called by the title "Sister," a term that remains the address for modern British registered nurses. Gifted deaconesses from Kaiserswerth were sent to England to train English Sisters. However, there remained many difficulties, partly because the class system left much misunderstanding about educated women working among the poor. Many deaconesses also did not receive sanction from the church (Joanna 222).

The Church of Scotland quickly followed the Methodist and Anglican churches in appointing deaconesses. They began discussing deaconesses in 1886 and in 1887 commended the establishment of deaconesses' training schools patterned after the Kaiserswerth deaconesses. Edinburgh House was begun that year with the first deaconess installed in 1888 (Cross "Deaconess" 381).

American Developments

The early Baptists in America were served by deaconesses, although the office probably was accepted by the minority. Morgan Edwards was an influential writer who published *The Customs of Primitive Churches* in 1774. He gave the most detailed account of Baptist deaconesses in America, including deaconesses in thirteen churches in Virginia, North Carolina, and South Carolina. He favored deaconesses based on Ro. 16 and 1Tm. 3 to nurse the sick, tend to the poor, and do "those things wherefore men are less fit" (43, quoted in Deweese Deacon 38). Edwards found deaconesses in Separate Baptist, Particular (Calvinistic) Baptists and Tunker (German) Baptist churches in the early Eighteenth Century. The Separate Baptists had the largest number of deaconesses, due in part to the influence of American liberty on the equality of men and women and to the heritage of the separate mother church in Sandy Creek, North Carolina, which had deaconesses and spawned at least forty-two other Baptist congregations (Deweese Deacon 38+). Both Campbell and Stone had considerable success preaching to Separate Baptists.

The number of Baptist deaconesses declined in the nineteenth century in part because the diaconate took on more of an administrative, business, and management role to the neglect of the caring and supportive ministries. The concern for submission prevented women from taking this role (Deweese "Deaconesses" 55).

In the 1840's, Pastor William Passavant of the Evangelical Alliance of the Lutheran Church began deaconess work in the United States. He utilized the pattern of the Kaiserswerths and established forty-five hospitals, schools, and orphanages for the Lutherans. He stated his principles as:

1. The association of Christian females is purely voluntary. The members unite without persuasion, remain without vows, and retire without restraint.

2. It is not an order, but the restoration of an office, that of "Servant" or Deaconess in the primitive church.

3. Its members heartily confess the faith, engage in the worship and observe the discipline of the Evangelical Lutheran Church.

4. Its object is habitually to engage in works of mercy among the sick and poor, the ignorant and fatherless, and other suffering members of our Lord's body. In the better attainment of this object, the association is incorporated and fully empowered to establish and conduct the necessary charitable institutions.

5. Not earthly reward and honor but the desire for an opportunity to manifest

their gratitude to Jesus Christ in the way revealed in His work, has influenced the members to associate themselves as servants of Christ and His church. (Keller 269)

This influence spread to other protestant groups and influenced the current status of deaconesses.

The Protestant Episcopal Church followed the Lutherans in deaconess work in the United States. A sisterhood was organized in New York city in 1843 which developed into St. Luke's Hospital. Although sisterhoods were not officially approved, the office of deaconess was. A training school for deaconesses was opened in New York in 1890 with a two year course of training for students eighteen years and older (Schaff "Deaconess" 379).

The General Conference of the Methodist Church discussed whether or not women could serve as delegates in 1888. Their answer was a negative, much to the disgust of five regular delegates and eighteen reserves on the floor, all female. However, one week later the church recognized the deaconess as an official of the church. One irate delegate said, "The women delegates asked for a crumb of the bread of life and were given the stony consolation of Deaconesses" (Dougherty 90+)! As with other religious groups, historians have labeled the Methodist deaconess movement as a response to Industrialism, the beginnings of the "Social Gospel." The concerns were for the social needs of mankind. As the *Deaconess Advocate* put it in 1906:

> If the pastor needs a stenographer let him hire one. If the church needs some one to collect funds for the preacher's salary let stewards be appointed. A deaconess trained in soul-winning is too valuable to be used for such routine. (Dougherty 92)

As much as leaders denied that they were creating a Protestant nunnery, the movement relied heavily on Catholic sisterhoods for functional models. The deaconess' duties were:

> ... to preach the Gospel, to lead the worship of a congregation, to teach both young and old; you may be required to feed the flock of Christ, to nurse the sick, to care for the poor, to rescue the fallen, to succor the hopeless, to offer friendship, even at cost to many who but for you may never know a Christian friend. But, in all this, you must be true evangelists of Our Lord Jesus Christ, translating your Gospel into the language of personal service. (Wakefield 185)

In those early days, the deaconesses were forbidden to take a vow, although they had rules that simulated them. They adopted a religious costume, lived communally, survived on an allowance, not a salary, and remained single. Conforming to the rules was required, but there was little stigma in leaving the movement for other walks. By 1900, over one hundred deaconesses' homes and training schools were found in the U. S. (Schaff "Deaconess" 379).

In the beginning, Methodist deaconesses worked primarily in social areas: nursing, teaching, and social work. In the early twentieth century, those ministries became professionalized, thus secularizing some of the deaconess' work. Those best skilled no longer volunteered their talents for an allowance; they earned a salary. A decline was evident. The real peak of activity was the period of 1888-1910 (Dougherty 97+).

Contemporary Views

Frederick S. Weiser wrote of the diversity he experienced at the North American Deaconess Conference (1970):

> The wide variety of forms assumed by those who claim an apostolic office, a form of ministry present in earliest Christianity, revealed at once that historical forces had played a decisive role in shaping the diaconate as the several churches know it today. There were the Lutherans - some attired in a special garb, addressed as "sister" and generally committed to celibacy. There were the Episcopalians - all attired in a special garb with a veil, addressed as "Deaconess" and specifically committed to a life of celibacy in the one order of ministry their church opens to women. There were the Methodists, Presbyterians, the rest of Lutherans and the others - dressed as any American women might be, addressed as "Miss" or "Mrs." depending upon the state of life in which they found themselves. And throughout there were nurses, parish workers, social workers and a wide variety of unique positions, each representing in one way or another Christ among the world "as one who serves." (17+)

Such was the diversity of workers that Christendom labeled "deaconesses."

One major question among denominations is the use of the term "ordination." For some, deacons are ordained, for others they are not. This ordination question is a major concern. The *Baptism, Eucharist and Ministry* statement of the World Council of Churches (1982) points out this discussion:

> The church must discover the ministry which can be provided by women as well as that which can be provided by men. A deeper understanding of the comprehensiveness of ministry which reflects the interdependence of men and women needs to be more widely manifested in the life of the church.

> Though they agree on this need, the churches draw different conclusion as to the admission of women to the ordained ministry. An increasing number of churches have decided that there is no biblical or theological reason against ordaining women, and many of them have subsequently proceeded to do so. Yet many churches hold that the tradition of the Church in this regard must not be changed. (Ministry 18)

> Those churches which practice the ordination of women do so because of their understanding of the Gospel and of the ministry. It rests for them on the deeply held theological conviction that the ordained ministry of the Church lacks fullness when it is limited to one sex. This theological conviction has been reinforced by

their experience during the years in which they have included women in their ordained ministries. They have found that women's gifts are as wide and varied as men's and that their ministry is as fully blessed by the Holy Spirit as the ministry of men. None has found reason to reconsider its decision.

Those churches which do not practice the ordination of women consider that the force of nineteen centuries of tradition against the ordination of women must not be set aside. They believe that such a tradition cannot be dismissed as a lack of respect for the participation in the Church. They believe that there are theological issues concerning the nature of humanity and concerning Christology which lie at the heart of their convictions and understanding of the role of women in the Church.

The discussion of these practical and theological questions within the various churches and Christian traditions should be complimented by joint study and reflection within the ecumenical fellowship of all churches. (Ministry, "Commentary" 18)

With the increasing acceptance of women in ordained roles, the work of deaconesses virtually disappeared in most denominations. In the nineteenth century when women were expressing their equality, the diaconate was as high as women could rise in most church structures. With the openness of the current period, most women seeking professional ministry were not content to stop with the lower orders. This is written with the understanding that the deaconesses in most traditions from the rediscovery to the present were full time, often celibate, servants supported by their denominations. They were the Protestant nuns.

Suggested Reading

In addition to the readings suggested at the end of the preceding chapter, some of which include female deacons, the following shed light on deaconesses in various denominational traditions.

Anabaptist

Huffman, Cathy Simmons. "Deaconess." *The Brethren Encyclopedia,* Vol. 1. Philadelphia: Brethren Encyclopedia, 1983. 369.

Neff, Christian Weierhof. "Deaconess." *The Mennonite Encyclopedia,* Vol. 2. Scottdale, PA.: Mennonite, 1956. 22.

Smith, Lena Mae. "Deaconess." *The Mennonite Encyclopedia,* Vol. 2. Scottdale, PA.: Mennonite, 1956. 22.

Baptist

Agar, Frederick A. *The Deacon at Work.* Valley Forge, PA: Judson, 1923.

Burroughs, P. E. *Honoring the Deaconship*. Nashville: Sunday School Board of the Southern Baptist Convention, 1929.

Deweese, Charles W. "Deaconesses in Baptist History: A Preliminary Study." *Baptist History and Heritage* Jan. 1977: 52.

Church of England

Joanna, Sister. "The Deaconess Community of St. Andrew." *Journal of Ecclesiastical History* 1961: 215+.

Lutheran

Winter, Sister Mildred. "Deaconess." *The Encyclopedia of the Lutheran Church*, Vol. 1. Minneapolis: Augsburg, 1965. 659+.

Methodist

Dougherty, Mary Agnes. "The Methodist Deaconess: A Case of Religious Feminism." *Methodist History* Jan. 1983: 90+.

Presbyterian

Bridel, Claude. "Note on the Diaconal Ministry in the Reformed Churches." *The Ministry of Deacons*. Geneva: World Council of Churches, 1965. 58+.

Roman Catholic

Norpel, Mary Louise. *The Relevance of the Lutheran Deaconess Tradition in America for Post-conciliar Religious Life Among Roman Catholic Women*. Ph.D. Diss. Catholic Univ. of America, 1971.

PART THREE

THE RESTORATION MOVEMENT

CHAPTER 10

Deacons in the Restoration Movement

The early leadership of the Stone-Campbell movement came from a Presbyterian background, but the membership largely had roots in the Baptist tradition. The Campbells were originally Old Light, Anti-Burgher, Seceder Presbyterians. Their background in Scotish Presbyterianism included the diaconate understanding of John Knox. The Baptists, developing from the thought of Smyth, also considered deacons to be essential to church development. From the Puritans onward the diaconate was a part of frontier America.

The exact role of male deacons in the Restoration Movement underwent an evolution. Their activities moved from being financial custodians, to varied servants, to ministry system leaders. Throughout that development, others questioned whether the diaconate was ever intended to be an office in the church. This chapter seeks to piece together the changes through the writings of restoration leaders.

The Papers

Alexander Campbell began the *Christian Baptist* in 1823 and followed it seven years later with the *Millennial Harbinger*. The name change took place partly to prevent the restoration movement churches from being called "Christian Baptist" churches. Publication continued into the 1860's.

The *Gospel Advocate* (Nashville) was begun in 1859 and is the oldest of the papers still in existence. Talbert Fanning began the *Advocate*, and other nineteenth century editors included David Lipscomb and E. G. Sewell. The *Advocate* was known as the most conservative of the restoration periodicals and was critically blamed along with editor Lipscomb for making too many things a test of fellowship, resulting in division between the Churches of Christ and the Christian Church (Brown Church 97).

The *Christian Standard* (Cincinnati) was begun in 1866 under Isaac Errett because:

> . . . the Restoration was threatened with the danger of being dwarfed into something narrower and smaller every way, than was contemplated by its originators or consistent with the spirit and purpose of the movement. It was thought that there was a tendency to erect matters of human opinion and expedience into tests of fellowship and thus re-entangle the brethren in the meshes of human authority and domination from which they had so happily escaped. (Brown Church 95).

The *Standard* led the movement along an ecumenical course and campaigned for greater acceptance of women in church activities. Errett was influential in the creation of the Christian Women's Board of Missions (Bailey "Status" 11).

Some members felt that the *Standard* was moving too much toward liberalism, so the *Apostolic Times* (Lexington, KY) was formed in 1868 with editors Moses Lard, J. W. McGarvey, and others. The name was later changed to the *Christian Companion* (Brown Church 96).

The *Christian Evangelist* (St. Louis), begun in 1864, was the other primary early publication. Editors James Garrison and B. W. Johnson took a conciliatory stance and were described as "progressively conservative." They were criticized for glossing over seemingly irreconcilable differences (Brown Church 96).

The Nineteenth Century

When Thomas Campbell (1763-1854) was refused admission into the Pittsburg Synod of the Presbyterian church because of his connection with the Christian Association of Washington, he transformed that association into a church meeting at Brush Run. That church was organized on Saturday, May 4, 1811, with a handful of members, one elder (Thomas Campbell), four deacons, and Alexander Campbell ordained to preach the gospel (Brown Church 52).

Alexander Campbell gave some of his ideas concerning church polity in *The Christian Baptist*. He taught (1826), "When congregations were fully set in order there was always a plurality of elders or a presbytery instituted in each congregation" ("Ancient Order XIV" 260). In the early days, however, having only one elder was not uncommon.

He described the deacon as "the steward, the treasurer, the almoner of the church:"

> For as the deacon's office had respect to the temporalities of the church, and as these are in general some way connected with pecuniary matters, the office of treasurer and almoner is identified with, or is the same as that of deacon. . . . Out

of the same fund three sets of tables were furnished. These were the Lord's table, the bishop's table, and the poor's table.... Conversant with the sick and the poor, intimate with the rich and more affluent brethren, familiar with all, and devoted to the Lord in all their services, they became eminent for their piety and charity, and out of high reputation amongst their brethren. (1826) ("Ancient Order No. XIX" 77)

They must be regarded as were the deacons in the synagogues - the public servants of the church in all things pertaining to its internal and external relations - in all matters of temporal concern.

There ought to be a plurality of deacons in every church. As keepers of the treasury of the church, it is most satisfactory to him that officiates to have a companion or companions in office; and on many occasions the duties are too oppressive for a single individual. ("Order" (1835) 507)

Campbell was very critical of the reckless use of religious titles. After looking at the variety of names used in denominations, he listed those which he felt were scriptural:

The following are the nearest approach I can make: ... Deacons, to those males who are the public servants of the whole congregation. Deaconesses, to those female public servants, who officiate amongst the females. (1829) ("Ancient Order XXXII" 17)

Campbell saw elders and deacons as the biblical pattern for every church:

In every city, town, and country where the Apostles gathered a community by their own personal labors, or by their assistants, in setting them in order, for their edification, and for their usefulness and influence in this world, they uniformly appointed elders, or overseers, to labor in the word and teaching, and to preside over the whole affairs of the community. To these, also, we added deacons, or public ministers of the congregation, who, under the direction of the overseers, were to manage all the affairs of these individual families of God. This the very names Bishop and Deacon, and all qualifications enjoined, fairly and fully import. (1839) (System 147)

When the nature of a community... is better understood... it will be unnecessary to elaborate arguments to show that there never can be in any society but two distinct offices in reference to its usefulness and happiness - the office of presiding, i.e. instructing and directing; and the office of ministering, i.e. of executing all the wishes of the community. No two words better express these two offices than the words selected in the New Institution: bishops and deacons, or overseers and ministers. (1835) ("Order" 243)

Bishops and deacons were "permanent and stationary officers of one single congregation" (1835) ("Order" 244).

Campbell did express some caution in his understanding of polity. He stated that elders and deacons:

... are the mere germs of a ministerial organization, since it does not appear how many presbyters and deacons were ordained in each church; whether the deacons were amenable to the presbyters, to the body of believers, or to the Apostles alone; and whether the Apostles in the chief ordinary government of the church had successors or not.

There can be no question that these things were perfectly understood at the time, both in principle and practice; but the notices concerning them being purely incidental, we are left to the further induction of such incidental notices as subsequently occur, until the system stands forth complete. (1843) ("Nature XII" 13)

The organization of the church continued to be a topic of considerable interest. In addition to Campbell's *The Christian System* and special number on organization in the *Harbinger* (1835), he also had a series of five articles in the *Harbinger* of 1849 and five more in 1853. Both series spoke of officers in the church, but the emphasis was clearly on the evangelist and elder. Both offices were dealt with in detail, while deacons were glossed over. In 1849, he introduced the subject stating that:

... there are but four classes: - Apostles, Prophets, Evangelists and Pastors - even teachers. A Pastor and a Teacher are equivalents - for the Teachers fed the church - and were overseers or shepherds of the flock. Apostles and Prophets were ministers extraordinary. Evangelists and Pastors were ministers ordinary. (460)

After stating that apostles and prophets were no longer needed, he introduced deacons without citing a biblical precedent. "Evangelists, Bishops and Deacons are as essential now as in the days of Paul and Peter. Their work will be commensurate with time, or until the Lord comes" (461). This was the only mention of deacons in the 1849 series. The other officers are discussed in detail.

The 1853 series is much longer that the 1849 series, and Campbell's local officers are clearly and repeatedly mentioned as "bishops, deacons, and evangelists." His use of "deacons" is clearly generic for male and female. Yet in this series, the deacons receive scarce mention when compared with the treatment given to elders and evangelists:

Deacons were the hands and the feet of the Christian Church.... As hands, they were its almoners; as feet, they were its messengers and public servants. (183)

The deacon's office is a more important office than many imagine It was not merely to serve tables, though that called it forth. They were not mere almoners of the Christian bounty, or the mere presidents of tables. They were "ministers" of the church, domestic and foreign.... (184)

Timothy and Erastus acted as deacons for Paul. ... The Primitive church had also deacons. Such was Phebe, of Cenchreae.... Deacons... performed foreign service for the church and the Apostles. Such was Onesimus and such was Tychicus. (185)

I say it [the church] is an organized body. Its organs are pastors or teachers, deacons and deaconesses; and for foreign missions and influence, evangelists or missionaries. . . .

We shall, therefore, take as a minimum church some ten or twelve members, by way of example. Of course it does not need a plurality of elders nor deacons. But it will require one elder and one deacon, or both offices absorbed by one person. . . .

But a church of one or two hundred members might require a plurality of elders - a presbytery or eldership, of more than a simple plurality, and a corresponding number of deacons and deaconesses. (247)

In the 1836 *Harbinger*, Robert Richardson wrote that the offices of bishop and deacon were "very essential to the perfection of a church." However, he cautioned against appointed men too soon. He advocated a probationary period, "being on trial," which could require many months. Only after they were fully proved could they be ordained by fasting, prayer, and the laying on of hands, all of which he considered essential for the appointment. He reacted against the common view of the day that the deacons' only work was to serve the Lord's Supper. Their peculiar duty was "to receive the contributions for the poor, and make the proper application of them to the wants of the society in which the congregation is located" (517+).

A contemporary of Campbell was Walter Scott, who edited *The Evangelist*. In 1834 he wrote:

A deacon never, and a bishop seldom, perhaps never, receives any pecuniary compensation for his labors, unless he teach and proclaim the Gospel as well as preside; and he is changed at the pleasure of the brethren if the interests of the society are not advanced by his administration. ("Address" 18)

When asked about the necessity of a church having elders and deacons, he strongly urged the appointment of only fully qualified men. He felt that a church could function well without elders until men were recognized with the qualifications. He also advocated the appointment of deacons in the absence of men qualified to be elders ("Query" 268).

Everett Ferguson and others have published some of the minutes of the Chestnut Grove Church of Christ in Kelton, PA. This church was started after three Christians moved from Baltimore to New London, PA. On December 30, 1838, the church was organized with eleven members. Daniel Sommer later preached at this church (1875-1880). It only had one elder in 1845, a practice common in the early restoration. Records showed the selection of two deacons in 1845, two deacons in 1846, the reinstatement of one of those in 1848, two deacons to serve with three deaconesses in 1860, and two deacons in

1864 and 1865. Deacons were re-examined and reappointed periodically. John Kitsleman was deacon in 1845 and 1846 and was reinstated in 1848 as "deacon of the church treasurer [sic] and at the same time elected as sexton of the said church." In 1860, William Atwood served as deacon and as secretary and treasurer (Ferguson, Olbricht and Roberts 225+).

After looking at Phl. 1:1 and 1Tm. 3, Robert Milligan maintained, "These passages, therefore, prove, beyond all reasonable doubt, that the Deacons of the primitive Church were a distinct order of Christian Ministers." Concerning the duties, Milligan examined Ac. 6 and concluded:

> To wait on the secular concerns of the Church was, therefore, the limit of their official duties. . . . It conferred no authority whatever, either to teach or to preach, in either the public or the private assembly.

> The obvious conclusion, then, from these premises is: that the first office created under the apostles was the deaconship; that those first appointed to perform the duties of the office were deacons; that their office comprehended all the secular interests of the congregation and nothing more; and that from this time, the term *diakonos* had an official or specific signification as well as a generic one, just like the words elder, bishop, evangelist, president, governor, and almost every other official name.

> Enough to justify the conclusion that all the deacons, elders, and evangelists, of the primitive church, were ordained by the imposition of hands, with prayer and fasting; and consequently, that no one can be legally set apart to the duties of any office in the Christian church, without these solemnities.

> We, therefore, conclude, that as the administration of the deaconship has not been made the subject of special legislation or approved precedent, the duly elected and ordained deacons of every congregation should organize, and discharge the duties of their office according to the generic laws and the ruling motives of the gospel. This rule, of course, leaves much room for the exercise of sound judgment and the Christian virtues. (1855) ("Of Deacons" 624+)

Milligan attached a special place to preaching and indicates that the only authority that a deacon had to preach or teach was that of any other Christian, "and not as an officer of the church." He also introduced the reader to the order listed in *Constitutions* stating, "And to supply the deficiency in the Diaconate, they appointed Sub-Deacons, Acolytes, etc." (1868) (Redemption 338+; Constitutions 8:28).

Milligan concluded that the work never required preaching or teaching. The office was concerned with only the secular interests of the church: "There is not a single intimation that preaching or teaching is any part of his office. . . . Were it so, women would never have been made deaconesses" ("Of Deacons" 626).

Tolbert Fanning, as editor of the *Gospel Advocate* (1859), observed a shortage of deacons: "Nevertheless there were deacons in earnest in ancient times, and we see no reason for concluding there will not be deacons again. . . . A deacon, anciently, was one who gave himself to the ministering to the poor saints" ("Deacons" 83+). He advocated that the deacon be supported out of the church treasury: "They and their families should have a comfortable living on earth, and great honor in heaven" ("Deacons" 85).

He later (1866) remarked concerning the concept of office:

We have been satisfied that the Brethren generally employ the words "office" and "officer" in a very equivocal and unscriptural sense, to say the least. Furthermore, we are satisfied, that by affixing to the words "office" and "officers" unscriptural ideas, immense mischief has accrued.

Each church is scripturally organized the moment it is planted. . . . We are not prepared to affirm that some of the members in the church are officers, and others are not, as our brethren teach.

We have failed to learn that the elders, deacons, bishops, deaconesses, evangelists or others were not constituted officers in the Apostolic churches by virtue of an election or ordination, or both together. ("Official Service" 724+)

Elders, or seniors, are made by years of labor, deacons and deaconesses by servitude, preachers by labor, and bishops by overlooking the flock; Carpenters are made by using the saw and hatchet; Blacksmiths by the use of the hammer, and gentlemen, by lives of devotion to rules of right, and we had just as soon attempt to make a scholar by prayer and imposition of hands, as a church officer. (1867) ("Officers of the Church" 681+)

Regarding the labor of both deacons and deaconesses, it is clear that it is their business to relieve the needy, especially the sick, the widowed, and orphans. (cited in Stroop, Church Organization 215)

Fanning later established another periodical, *The Religious Historian.* He had a lengthy discussion of church polity in that publication in 1873. Fanning expounded his understanding that leaders grow up naturally. They matured and became leaders, servants, or preachers, and were followed because the congregation recognized their gifts and expertise, not because of any ceremony in the church to bestow authority upon them. Fanning found no set office of elder. All serving members were deacons with the diaconate encompassing every aspect of Christian service and leadership including overseeing and elderly advice:

In Christ's body, there is no earthly head - no higher and lower orders of councils, no clergy and laity, but the members are all kings and priests to God, the sons and daughters of the same Father. ("History No. 4" 237)

We are fully aware that members of the church of Christ, in ancient times, were known as apostles, prophets, pastors, leaders, shepherds, bishops, evangelists, elders, deacons, and ministers. . . but we stoutly maintain that, such names "incidental," are characteristic of labor, and never were conferred by sacred authority, as official designations. We are satisfied moreover, that, all elections and ceremonies employed to "make" officers in the church, are self-assumed, devoid of scriptural authority. ("History No. 6" 297)

In the congregations of the saints anciently, all the members were commanded to be "subject one to another," and no one was to be respected as teacher or ruler beyond the measure of his intelligence and his moral influence as exhibited in successfully instructing others and his good works as shepherd or pastor of the flock. ("Ministers" 3:57)

The attempt to change the meaning of the word "elder," "older," or one "more wise" and "experienced" than another, into a suddenly created officer, is a complete subversion of the meaning of plain Greek and English words. ("History No. 7" 343)

No one can possibly read the passage [1Tm. 3] as intended by the inspired writer, till he can banish from his mind all idea of honor, or authority in the shape of office; and till convinced that the Apostle was speaking of the work, and not of the authority, to perform service. ("History No. 8" 359)

In short, all Christian service, whether by men or women, whether it is feeding the hungry, clothing the naked, preaching the Gospel, baptizing the believers, arranging the members in their places, stopping the mouths of false teachers, or building up the saints in the faith, was performed by them as ministers, deacons and servants of the Lord.

Our conclusion then is, that the deacons were, by no means, menials, performing the common-place work of the church, such as waiting at tables, preparing meals, passing about bread, etc.

Neither have we any authority to conclude that it is their special duty to take charge of "the finances of the church." There is, indeed, neither a command nor example for such a conclusion. The elders, or seniors, were not only the custodians of the funds to the starving Judeans, but the contributions were sent to the elders.

Instead of the deacons being merely committee-men, hand laborers, and inferiors, we can discover no work too high or too spiritual for them; and no position too elevated for them to occupy. Whether men or women, such as minister in things holy, supply the needy, establish the saints, and comfort the suffering are God's ministers.

The name arises from the service performed as the name "Baptist" comes from the work of baptizing. Simon was called "the Tanner" from his work. Philip was called "the Evangelist" because of his labor, and Phoebe was called Deacon in consequence of her labor in the cause of Christ. ("History No. 8" 361+)

James Challen wrote an outline of the "Deacon's Office" in the *Harbinger* of 1866:

A servant (or deacon) in a family is called upon to do whatever his relation to the family implies. It is not necessary that any specific duty shall be defined.

1. He should give special regard to all the secular affairs of the congregation.

2. He should attend to the gathering of all the money necessary for the support of the cause and the wants of the poor.

3. He should watch over the education of the poor; and be an efficient help in the Sunday School [originally literacy training].

4. The deacons of the church and the Elders should have their stated meetings for conference and mutual help.

5. They should serve at the Table of the Lord.

6. They should be earnestly engaged in the cause of Christ, as they stand in the light of representative men of the congregation.

7. They should see that all debts due by the congregation should be faithfully paid, and that all repairs to the meetinghouse should be made; that fuel should be provided, the house kept in good order, and every comfort compatible with the necessities of the case be given to the worshipers.

8. They should call to their aid at stated times others in the church, male and female, as occasion requires, that nothing be wanting.

9. They should be elected for life or during good behavior. The yearly election of elders and deacons is an abomination. It is simply ridiculous and insupportable. Permanency is attached to these offices.

W. K. Pendleton, son-in-law of Alexander Campbell, writing in the *Harbinger* in 1848, defended the title "deacon" as applying to an "office" within the church. The only work the deacons were sanctioned to do was the "taking care of the destitute, by collecting and appropriating the bounty of the church for their comfort and support." He concluded, "it is generally regarded, among our brethren, as an essential element in the restoration of primitive order, to ordain, in every church, both deacons and deaconesses" ("Discipline" 290+).

Later (1866) he reacted against a British tract on church order. The tract supported the view that "there is not a single act of episcopal or diaconal authority on record in the New Testament." Pendleton disagreed, seeing elders and deacons as having peculiar powers and privileges of office.

Pendleton in 1870 carried on a published discussion with John C. Miller concerning the diaconate. Pendleton was asked, "Has the Christian Church a divine right to have Deacons in the Church?" He understood that the church structure was based on the synagogue where three men collected alms. After briefly examining 1Tm. 3 and Phl. 1, he turned to Ac. 6 to finally support his belief:

This is an important passage; for although the Seven are not called deacons, yet the office they were to perform was *diakonia* (deaconship); as they acted, in its discharge, by a solemn official appointment, there can be no doubt of the propriety of denominating them official Deacons. ("Deacons" 52)

We may sum up what we understand . . . :

1st. Every church must have its deacons - a plurality in all cases - and after the analogy of the Jewish synagogue, we think, never less than three. . . .

2nd. The duties of the deacons are to collect the bounty of the church, appropriate it to the necessities of the destitute brethren, and execute whatever function may be proper and necessary to the discharge of these. This will involve a general care for the sick. . . . But besides this. . . they are to serve the church in its public worship, ministering upon the Lord's table, attending to the current expenses, and other secular interests essential to the good order and comfort of the body.

3rd. Besides deacons, every church should have deaconesses, whose duty it is to perform such offices as cannot be so well performed by deacons, and especially such to females, as could not with delicacy and propriety be laid upon the deacons. ("Deacons" 53 +)

John C. Miller responded with an article in 1870. He began by asking if the transfer of the diaconate from the synagogue to the church was made by inspired men or simply the adaptation of men to their society. Since the scriptures did not require the office, he rejected it as of human origin. He then affirmed his belief that διακονος should be uniformly translated "minister" in every instance and that the context be allowed to determine the meaning for the reader:

Diakonos as a Greek word cannot possibly contain all the meanings that deacon does, as an English word; and I do not believe it contains any of the official meanings now attached to the latter. In the *Christian Quarterly* for April, page 2565, I find the following translation and remarks in an article from the pen of our esteemed brother Dr. S. E. Shepherd: "Paul and Timothy, servants of Jesus Christ, to all the saints in Christ Jesus who are at Philippi, with the overseers and ministers. Phil. 1:1. There is no more reason why the word (διακονος) should be translated deacons here than there is for translating it by the same word in all the places in which it is found in all the Epistles. It is first assumed that there was an order of men in the primitive church called deacon, and then this assumption is made a reason for this rendering of the word. That there was a class of men called minister is admitted. But there was no class answerable to the order of deacons. The same is true of 1Tm. 3:8, 12." ("Office" 137)

He continues, using Pendleton's logic, to show that there is more evidence to support calling Timothy a deacon than there is for calling the Seven deacons. He also points out that "the text does not inform us that they raised, disbursed or had anything whatever to do with money" (139). "The account of ordaining elders is very full - why should not that of ordaining deacons be equally so" (141)? He does admit that 1Tm. 3 is difficult to understand in light of his reasoning.

Pendleton's reply in the same issue (1870) states that much of the argument in support of deacons is based in conjecture. A lot of what is said about elders is also based on sketchy information. After discussing 1Tm. 3 and the support of the Apostolic Fathers, he continues:

> I do not desire to make this case any stronger than it is and would not be understood as holding the position that the Scriptures are very definite as to all the duties and privileges of the deacon. I think that very large freedom was given to all Christians to do for the infant and struggling kingdom, as opportunity offered, whatever their gifts enabled them to do; and that, whilst the primary and peculiar official duty of the deacon was to collect and disburse the alms of the church, their office almost necessarily called out their gifts of prayer, of exhortation, of comfort, and of teaching. . . . ("Reply" 145 +)

Miller and Pendleton have one more round of discussions in the May issue. Miller argues for the translation of διακονος, not the transliteration of it into "deacon:"

> I contend for the same principle in the translation of *diakonos*; reject modern church titled of diverse meanings, translate by its simple English representative, and let the context show when such word becomes an official term. I have not aimed to assert that *diakonos* never indicates an official position in the church; think it so used frequently. Bishop should give place to overseer for the same reason that presbyter and deacon should give place to elder and minister. ("Deacons Again" 252)

He continues to try to prove that the διακονος were actually preachers of the Gospel or evangelists, as illustrated by Stephen, Philip, and Timothy (253+).

Reacting against Fanning was John W. McGarvey. His *The Eldership* (1870) attacked Fanning's position directly:

> Individuals have been found who. . . admit that there should be an eldership in the churches of all ages; who also ascribe to the eldership of modern churches the functions which belonged to those in the primitive age; but who deny that the term eldership designated an office, or that elders are properly styled offices. They deny, indeed, the existence of office in the church and would use the term work where the term office is commonly employed. We regard the distinction as one between words rather than ideas; for one of a body of men, who has any work specially assigned to him by the body, is an office of that body, in the full import of the term. (9+)

E. G. Sewell, editor of the *Gospel Advocate* and co-author of *Queries and Answers* with Lipscomb, wrote:

> The word deacon is by no means an official title. . . . But there is work or service to be performed in the church of a general character, work which one or two members may do for the whole congregation, such as carrying around the bread and wine, looking after the finances of the church, looking after the poor, and such like. . . . Such men are not officers, but workers, servants for the congregation. . . . They [the Seven] were appointed to do a certain work and when the necessity for that work ceased, they went to something else. . . . Every congregation that has any men of suitable character should appoint some of them

to do whatever general work may be needed for their success and prosperity. And that such appointment or ordination may be made by fasting and prayer, is we think, plainly authorized. But the laying on of hands, as we understand it, belonged to the age of miracles and was used to impart miraculous power in some way. This cannot be done now. . . . (1882) ("Ordination" 403)

Officers in the church are men that have been installed into authoritative positions, by virtue of which they have authority to do things they would have no right or authority to do outside of such positions. . . . In this sense the word office is not found in connection with any worker in the church in the entire Greek Testament, and ought not to occur in any translation of it. (1891) ("Appointment" 182)

We have shown in preceding articles that by a literal translation of the scriptures, the word deacon would disappear from the oracles of God. And we have also shown that there is no such thing as a class or order of men in the church called deacons. But on the other hand we have shown that there are numerous instances of men being chosen to serve the church in different capacities. . . . In all such cases, the men chosen were simply workers, not officers in the church. (1892) ("Seven" 388)

In the early days of the church, when some sort of work or service was to be done that the whole church as such could not do, men already qualified and trustworthy were appointed, chosen to do that work, and when thus chosen, they were the ministers or servants of the church till that work was done, no matter what it was, as the Seven, Paul and his companions to minister to the saints, and such like. . . . Such servants are never in the Greek represented as a separate order or class of men, official, or anything of that sort. A pure and literal translation of the word of God would relieve the church of a world of trouble, and lead the Lord's people in the right way. (1892) ("Diakoneoo" 377)

Ministering to widows belonged to the *diakonia*, and this work in the church is set apart for the deacon. Serving tables was a general name for their work. Last, the ministry of the word is the *diakonia*. (1893) ("Apostolic" 121)

The Savior never intended that anything like official authority should ever reign among the members of his body. Hence elders and deacons, whatever may be meant by these words, can do nothing by what is called official authority into which they are to be installed by something called ordination. (1897) ("Organization" 356)

But in the Greek, regarding elders, bishops, there is no word for office. This has been put in by the translators without a particle of authority for it that I know of. Elders and deacons are necessary workers in the church, but not officers in any sense, but as workers. . . . (1921) (Lipscomb and Sewell 196)

He wrote as if passing the Lord's Supper was the only ministry that his readers understood for the deacons. He also placed great stress on the deacon desiring to better himself so that he could become an elder ("Apostolic Church" 121). Sewell taught strongly against electing elders and deacons by popular vote, though he does not give a good substitute for the practice ("Appointment" 182).

David Lipscomb was asked in the 1883 edition of the *Gospel Advocate*, "What authority have we for considering the deacon's work to be attending to the temporal affairs of the church?" This was in response to the questions raised by Fanning's *Religious Historian*. After looking at the meaning of the word "servant," he moved to the selection of the Seven in Jerusalem:

> If these be the typical deacons of the church, the work of looking after the poor of the church and of seeing that their wants are supplied, is clearly their duty. . . . The character of service is drawn from the supposition that the Seven were the class of servants referred to as deacons. This idea is somewhat strengthened, by the example of the early churches, as it comes to us through church history. Still the ground is not as clearly defined as we would suppose from the certainty with which it is usually regarded. (1883) ("Queries" 499)

Lipscomb openly faced the lack of strong biblical information by summarizing:

> I have never been able to speak with confidence in reference to the position and work of these servants, as I would like. The work of the deacons is gathered from the work these seven were appointed to do. Their work was temporary, . . . the work of looking after the poor of the church and of seeing that their wants are supplied. ("Queries" (1883) 499)

> They seem to have been helpers to the elders, or bishops. It has been generally assumed there business was to collect, keep, and distribute the funds of the congregation. . . . The elders were recognized as the proper persons to control the means sent. So if the deacons dispensed it, they did it under the direction of the elders. ("Duties" 36)

This lack of information did not stop him from making other comments.

When asked by a reader if it was scriptural for a deacon to preach, Lipscomb responded that, "It is not only scriptural, but the duty of all Christians to preach. I doubt whether there is a class of preachers distinct from other Christians" ("Queries" (1898) 555). When asked about the method of ordaining or appointing deacons, he remarked that scripture does not give details to be followed. "How are appointments made, save to agree and announce the agreement to the world?" He saw disputes over such matters as "a querulous fault finding disposition over nonessentials. . ." ("Appointment" 424).

To the question, "Is a deacon a deacon for life," he responded:

> The doctrine of "once a deacon, always a deacon," partakes of Romanism, rather than Christianity, and people who hold to this position usually magnify their official relationships and regard the church as under their authority and guidance. . . . Although a thoroughly good man, he might be inefficient as a deacon, so that the brethren would conclude that it would be better for him not to serve in this relationship. . . . Thus it is clearly seen that the deacon is one who serves, and when he ceases to serve, he is no longer a deacon. (1905) ("Life" 468)

John S. Durst, in the *Gospel Advocate* of 1883, agreed with Fanning's position:

> The generally received idea is that they [deacons] are to clean up the houses, ring the bells, prepare the supper, wait on the brethren in passing to them the emblems of the death and sufferings of our Savior, bury the deceased, keep the lights in order, etc. When we appeal to God's word for authority, however, we find them to be a different class of workers. They were the parties who set in order the things that were wanting, or the regulators in the congregations of the first Christians. . . . It seems that none were higher in congregational labor than the deacon. They were to establish the members of the congregations, to do the work of evangelists, set in order the things that were wanting, to regulate the elders and teachers, and to stop the mouths of pretenders. Their labor was comprehensive, and included, perhaps, every department of work.
>
> The deacons, we think, were persons of more wisdom and experience than any other class of workers. They regulated all the internal affairs of the churches, and labored in the highest ranks of the saints.
>
> Does not the word deacon denote simply a servant or minister, without reference to the manner of appointment or the character of work to be performed? . . . It has occurred to me that we must get out of our minds the idea of honor, or authority in the shape of office. The apostle, to my mind, was speaking of the work, and not the authority to work.
>
> With Bro. Fanning we will say that "we have not yet seen a command to make deacons, or to elect them or ordain them to office. They, like preachers, bishops, and elders, grow up in their positions as ministers of Jesus Christ." (612)

L. C. Wells addressed an *Advocate* questioner (1884) who asked if elders and deacons went out of existence in the same manner as the apostles and prophets. He pointed out that in most churches, deacons do little more than serve the Lord's Supper. He used this article to attack Lipscomb for some of his uncertainties, and said that since the scriptures advocated deacons, and those same scriptures were designed to furnish the church for every good work, Lipscomb should have been more definite on the work of deacons (178).

In 1888, J. M. Mathes edited a collection of twenty-three sermons from noted preachers entitled, *The Western Preacher*. A. I. Hobbs wrote "Ecclesiastic Polity." Hobbs stated that the church had two classes of offices, the ordinary (elders, deacons, and evangelists) and the extraordinary (apostles, prophets, and workers of miracles) (71). Of the deacon's work, he wrote:

> The deacons of a congregation should constitute its financial board to plan and supervise the raising of all moneys necessary for all purposes. They should look after and care for the widow and orphan, the needy, the sick, the dying, the dead. When the deaconship shall be brought up to a proper efficiency, we will no more be compelled to witness the humiliating sight of Christians seeking avenues for systematic benevolence through the various human organizations. (80)

Also appearing in 1888 was Thomas Munnell's *The Care of All the Churches*, possibly the first Disciples' book dedicated to polity:

> As the Levites had charge of the Tabernacle in the wilderness and all its furniture, and of the outside business department of Jewish worship, so it seems Christian deacons ought to be charged with all those ministries that related to the business of the church - the collection and disbursement of its funds, the care of the church property, attention to the wants of the poor, waiting on the congregation with the elements of the Lord's Supper, seating the people and making strangers feel welcome and at home in the pews. (114+)

He held that the Seven were the first deacons and that the office of deacon continued in the Jerusalem church from that day forward (118+).

Carroll Kendrick's *Live Religious Issues of the Day* (1890) is a collection of thirty-one lessons on a wide variety of matters. In his chapter on "The Divine Government" he relates overseers and deacons to synagogue leaders and compares the deacons to the "almoners who collected alms and distributed to the poor." He refers to the Seven as deacons. "They were a special class, selected for a special work, which is permanent in its nature, and not miraculous." A plurality of bishops and deacons makes up the "perfected system" of "permanent organization." He strongly opposes missionary societies and such related congregational confederations (374+). An interesting concept of Kendrick's is that bishops and deacons:

> ... were elders (seniors) with certain peculiar qualifications before they were made bishops and deacons. ... Of course they were elders still, and it is not surprising if we sometimes find them afterwards called elders, though elder means age, and not office. ... It is strange that we so often confound elder and office. Elder no more means bishop than it means evangelist. ...

He believes that deacons are servants, not rulers or teachers (388+).

Benjamin B. Tyler, historian and regular contributor to the *Christian Standard*, wrote "Organization" in *The Old Faith Restated, Vol. II* (1891). He viewed the Seven as a temporary committee, while they also marked the beginning of organization in the Christian church. He stated that they probably marked the beginning of the diaconate, but were "not called deacons by the Holy Spirit. ... The modern deacon in the modern Christian Church is not a descendant of the first martyr. ... At first the apostles... had charge of everything pertaining to the life of the new-born church" (358+). In his paper, Tyler traced the gradual development of leadership functions in the church, demonstrating how people were chosen to fill special needs as they developed, and pointing out that there were not uniform titles in the early development of these offices.

Like some of his contemporaries, Tyler defends the practice of having only one elder in small churches. The number required should be determined by the size of the congregation and the number of qualified men for the work (362). He concludes his remarks by stating:

> There is no divine legislation for the organization of the churches of Christ. The New Testament is not a statute book; it is a book of principles. The nature of Christianity and the work which it proposes require that certain men, qualified by nature, culture and grace, shall give themselves entirely to the ministry of the Word, while others are detailed to have a care for the temporal concerns of each church of Christ, or congregation of Christians. (364)

W. L. Hayden wrote *Church Polity* in 1894. He interpreted the Seven as deacons, spoke favorably of celibate deacons, and saw a role for deaconesses. Deacons' duties, according to Hayden, included caring of the house of worship, administering the Lord's Supper, looking after the needy, and raising the necessary finances "for the support of the pastor and the general enterprises of the church." The work of the almoner was thoroughly developed by Hayden. He also advocated that:

> ... an apportionment should be made as nearly equitable as may be the judgment of the deacons, assigning to each member such portion of the needed expenditures that the congregation has decided upon as accords with his proportionate ability.

His benevolent concern was so strong that he believed that in a properly organized church "there would be no occasion for members to unite with worldly societies to make provision for themselves in the event of sickness or misfortune. . . ." He further advocated that "the board of deacons should consist of three to nine persons" elected in accordance with civil law with a tenure of office, suggested to be three years (66+).

J. M. Barnes agreed with Sewell. Writing in the *Advocate* (1895) he discussed with contempt the inconsistency of translating διακονος as minister in every place but 1Ti. 3 and Tit. 1:4 [sic]:

> There is too much of this title business. If there is one titled dignitary in the New Testament it is Jesus, but not Paul, Peter, Timothy, Titus, or other preachers. Why can we not be satisfied with being in the company of such worthies as those above. If they could go along through the world humbly, without prefixes, suffixes, adds on ends, why now we. . . ? Those who love the praise of men were least esteemed by Christ. It is commonplace and a condescension for the man who has the attention of angels, Christ, and God almighty to be fishing about for the adulation of professional praisers, or allowing himself feebly honored by abbreviated signs of the beast plastered over and about his name like a country store all meshed with show papers. ("To J. F." 311)

> Do the work of an evangelist. Make full proof of thy ministry (*diakonia*), "deaconry," "deaconship," "deaconate." Here is a big lesson. Here is much room

for study. You see again that the evangelist must do the work of the deacon - that is the *diakonia*. ("To J. F." 323)

John T. Brown, Editor of the *Christian Companion*, wrote *Churches of Christ* in 1904 as a historical, biographical, and pictorial history of Churches of Christ. In nearly seven hundred pages Brown traced the development of the churches of Christ in their first hundred years including biographies of its pioneers, college presidents and key preachers, and detailing the growth of the church state by state. This publication came at the time of the separation of the Churches of Christ from the Christian Church. Brown reflectd more of the liberal view, although he put little emphasis on that difference.

Brown provided no philosophy toward deacons in his book. However, in talking about various churches of the period, he often mentioned deacons by name. He cited a number of congregations which had only one elder, but a number of deacons. These included: Union, S.C., in 1836; Hewletts, S.C., in 1837; Walnut Hills, Cincinnati, OH, in 1884; First Church of Christ, Louisville, KY in 1891; and the Mississippi Avenue church in Memphis in 1890; and several others. Other forms of government besides "elders and deacons" were also noted, including the Third church in Memphis which had an "Official Board" that included seven men and a woman. P. Y. Pendleton who co-authored with J. W. McGarvey is noted as minister of the Walnut Hills church which had one elder (280+).

1906 - 1948

1906 is the beginning point of a new era. It is the census of this date that first lists the non-instrumental Churches of Christ as a different group from the instrumental Disciples. In the years that follow, one can trace developments through the *Christian Standard* as representative of the Disciples and the *Gospel Advocate* as representative of the Churches of Christ. Though other papers exist, these two have detailed indexes and accessible microfilm files. Because this book is concerned primarily with Churches of Christ, the *Advocate* receives the most thorough examination.

S. S. Lappin, editor of the *Christian Standard* (1909-1917), wrote *The Training of the Church* in 1911. He considered deacons as the ministers of the practical. He cited Ac. 6 as the pattern for their selection and the rationale for their existence. Their work was: to attend to the property of the congregation; to direct the material ministries of the church; and to look after financial matters (133).

M. M. Davis, writing in the *Christian Standard* of the same period (1916), quoted W. L. Hayden's *Church Polity* concerning deacon qualifications, "Reference is given to married persons having but one wife, but not as excluding those who are unmarried and otherwise qualified, when circumstances demand their service" ("Deaconesses" 711).

A. B. Lipscomb, writing in the *Advocate* of 1916 and reprinted in 1920 wrote:

> I like the New Testament idea . . . . It does not prescribe or limit the duties of the deacon. It makes him a servant, or minister, and it does not matter whom or what he serves, just so it is honorable and good. The fact is, no one is given an official designation in the New Testament. . . . The New Testament glorifies the work to be done rather than the title.

He saw the qualifications of the Seven as relating to elders and deacons, and was critical of appointing to the leadership successful businessmen without regard for their spirituality (58).

W. N. Abernathy answered the question "Should all churches have deacons?" He replied (1923):

> The necessity for deacons arises when it becomes needful to relieve the elders of the business affairs of the church that they may look more closely to spiritual matters. . . . Sometimes the work of the deacon is only temporary, as when some special duties are to be performed.

He also reminded his readers that "there are men who make good deacons, but would make poor elders." He gave the churches on Crete as examples of churches for which elders were important but deacons were not mentioned (539).

In the 1928 *Advocate*, C. R. Nichol explained Ac. 6 as a reference to deacons. He stated, "I am driven to the view that the work of the deacon is not necessarily a specific work, but that they are to be servants in any and every kind of work for which they are qualified" ("Deacon" 363).

R. C. Harding wrote a *Handbook for Elders and Deacons* in 1932. His view was that, "the bishops or elders assumed the spiritual, and the deacons and deaconesses the material responsibilities" (92). His structure of a board of deacons was detailed and more formal than that found in most Churches of Christ, reflecting the development of the Disciples (96).

One problem of the 30's was that some deacons were claiming too much authority. An articles in the 1937 *Advocate* by D. H. Hadwin was illustrative: "Deacons are in no sense overseers. . . . It is thought by some that elders are the spiritual overseers and that deacons are the temporal overseers. . . . This impression is manifestly wrong" (743).

R. L. Whiteside (1938) viewed deacons as "any one appointed to a special service," including Paul, Timothy, and Apollos. He did not make a distinction between these men and the servants of the local church:

> It would depend on the nature of the work and the time required to do it as to how long a deaconship, or the diaconate, lasted. Hence, those in a church who were appointed to a permanent work would, therefore, be referred to as the deacons of the church. ("Deaconesses" 799)

> Deacons are not rulers, but servants. The notion that some have hatched up that the elders have nothing to do with the financial affairs of the church is manufactured out of thin air. ("Queries" 564)

In addressing the method of selection, he responded negatively to the popular vote. However, he also did not know a practical way to achieve his ideal, that "only the godly and intelligent members - members who knew the necessary qualifications and the men to be voted for - were allowed to vote" ("Queries" 564).

A. L. Deveny (1941) in his appendix on the deaconate, attacked the situation that existed. Deacons were being:

> . . . regarded as on a par with the eldership. . . . That elders and deacons meet together as a regular custom to discuss matters pertaining to the spiritual upbuilding of the congregation is a travesty upon the divine plans. . . . Deacons are ordained in the congregation to minister to the physical necessities of the widows and orphans and any other members of the body.

He saw the Seven as the first deacons, but said that they, "cannot serve as a precedent for selecting and appointing deacons subsequent to the withdrawal of the Holy Spirit from the active direction of the affairs of the church." Deveny also believed that, "Paul has indicated unmistakably that the office of deacon is a necessary part of every congregation." Ro. 12:7 is cited as plainly dealing with the office of deacon (169+).

During this same period, A. W. Dicus wrote his often quoted text, *Church Leadership.* His chapter on deacons attacked the apparent position of authority that deacons had achieved. He stated that the scriptures give no indication that deacons attended business meetings; their judgment should not enter into the affairs of the church. Deacons were not chosen or elected by popular vote and should not operate as a board or unit. Elders were required by the Holy Spirit of every church, but deacons were not (43+).

H. Leo Boles (1941) was uncertain if the Seven were deacons ("Deacons" 292). When asked if a church could have deacons without having elders, he responded that nothing in the Bible prevented that situation, and, if the Seven were deacons, the Jerusalem church did have deacons before it had elders. On the other side, he also reminded his readers that Paul and Barnabas appointed elders in all the churches, but nothing is said about appointing deacons in every church ("Questions" 5). He summarized their duties:

> Deacons are expected to be leaders in the financial affairs and take the oversight of the expenses of the church. They may look after the church building and all needed repairs; they should see that the church house is kept comfortable for all public services. . . . The deacons should be good businessmen. They should know how to use in the most economical way the funds of the church. ("Deacons" 293)

John Paul Gibson, M.D., authored *The Church at Work* in 1947 with a chapter on "The Work of Elders and Deacons." His presentation represented the usual interpretation in churches to the current time. The elders taught and ruled while the deacons served in material affairs (6).

That deacons are primarily responsible for finances is expressed by H. H. Gray, Jr. (1947), "The financial success of the church rests in the hands of the deaconship" (38).

Every congregation should have a plurality of deacons, according to R. P. Cuff (1948). He held that no church could have deacons without first having elders, and that the deaconship should exist, "so long as his church should remain in the world." He believed that Phoebe was a deacon in the official sense, and called the church to, "provide for its own infirm and indigent members instead of leaving their benevolent care to some nonchurch agency" (738+).

1949 to 1988

In 1950, Herbert Winkler published a mammoth book (402 pages) entitled *The Eldership*. In his single chapter on deacons, he refered to Acts 6 as the example. He wrote, "There will ever be the need of deacons to look after the temporal affairs of the church under the direction of the elders who have the oversight of the whole flock." He continued by stating, "I affirm that these 'young men' mentioned in the matter of Ananias and Sapphira were the deacons or ministers of the church at Jerusalem" (165+).

J. Roy Vaughan (1951) spoke of the power struggle between elders and deacons. Deacons in his understanding were not to take the authority of elders. He did not see the elders as over the spiritual while the deacons were over the material work. Everything was under the oversight of the elders, and the deacons were to do whatever was assigned to them. He was critical of elders who failed to delegate work to the deacons, and agreed with and cited Lipscomb against calling elders and deacons "officers of the church" (594).

George Dehoff (1953) felt, "It is possible for a congregation to operate without elders and deacons, but every congregation should look forward to developing, selecting and appointing men to fill these places." In defining that appointment process, he saw nothing magical about the laying on of hands and prayer. Some public appointment was necessary for the good of the church (281+).

G. C. Brewer (1957) is candid in *The Model Church* by saying, "we are not given any undisputed history of their [deacon's] origin and but little information with regard to their function" (95). After discussing Ac. 6 and the contrast mentioned in chapter 2 between πρεσβυτερος and νεοτερος, he reminds the reader that the information is inconclusive. He summarizes that: "... they looked after all the temporal affairs that were necessary. All the things mentioned above must be done today in order to have system, comfort, and decency; and it seems that the deacons should attend to such matters" (101).

The *Advocate* published an article on deacons by E. Claude Gardner in 1959. He saw deacons as assistants to the elders:

> It is essential for a congregation to select deacons when it is properly and adequately organized. . . . Since deacons serve under the bishops, deacons obviously should not be selected when elders have not been ordained. . . . The idea in the minds of some that elders are in charge of the spiritual affairs of the church, whereas deacons are responsible for the temporal matters is erroneous. The Bible teaches that elders have the responsibility for both phases of the work. . . . Let it be understood that deacons do not have control over the church. (392)

L. R. Wilson (1959) emphasized the business ability of the deacons. "It ought to be clearly understood that the deacons are to look after the business of the church." He did clarify that they were accountable to the elders. One of the weaknesses he saw in the diaconate was that "men have been appointed. . . who had no more business ability than a child." Deacons should be appointed to "individual duties of a permanent nature" (54+).

Cleon Lyles (1962, rev. 1971) wrote a practical book on church leadership that typically reflected Church of Christ concepts. In his *Bigger Men for Better Churches* he stated:

> The misconstrued idea that the elders are appointed to look after the spiritual

affairs of the congregation while the deacons are to oversee the temporal management of business is erroneous and unsubstantiated by the Word of God. The elders have complete oversight of all work. . . . (85)

When men are appointed to serve as deacons they should be instructed and fully understand that they are to work in the capacity of assistants under the direction, or oversight, of their elders, with no independent authority. (86)

The elders serving a church are in a more advantageous position to better know the men who would qualify in all respects, but the final selection should be made by the congregation. It is advisable for the elders to consider the men who are scripturally qualified, selecting those who are best adjusted to the work they are chosen to do for presentation to the membership of the church. (91)

In an *Advocate* lead article entitled "Deacons - Their Rank and Work" (1965), B. B. James wrote:

There must have been some particular reason for having deacons, otherwise Paul would not have ordered their appointment. . . . The elders. . . have the responsibility of overseeing the entire program of the church. . . . The deacon is a helper, an assistant, a minister. (425)

One of the few books specifically addressing deacons is J. D. Bales' *The Deacon and His Work* (1967). The majority of the book is dedicated to the qualifications. He assumes without discussion that mature churches have deacons. "Although there were temporary offices in the church, such as apostles and prophets, the permanent offices in the church are two: the eldership and the deaconship." "To function at its maximum capacity, the church needs to have elders and deacons." Only two paragraphs summarize the background and development of the diaconate following the first century (7+).

Bales poses the question:

Does the deacon occupy an office? He does not have authority over the church, but he does have an office for he has a position of trust, a ministry, or a service. Not everyone has his position; for not everyone is qualified or appointed to the work of a deacon. (6)

He states, "the Bible does not specify exactly what they are to do," and concludes: 1) "Any work that needs to be done in the congregation, which the elders can delegate to the deacons, and which is within the range of their qualifications, would be work for deacon;" 2) "They are not the overseers of the congregation, since they are not elders, but their qualifications are of such a nature that they are equipped to render a wide range of services;" and, 3) "They could serve the church in any capacity which was within their qualifications, and which did not usurp the authority of the elders" (63+).

A chapter is dedicated to "How are Deacons to be Selected?" His first sentence states, "The Bible does not tell us how deacons are to be

selected, and so one cannot affirm that there is only one way to do it."
The sixteen pages which follow suggest a procedure of teaching on the
subject, selection by the congregation, testing, voting, and appointing
with prayer, laying on of hands, and fasting (86+). He gives extended
attention to voting and to clarifying the non-miraculous laying on of
hands.

Ed Wharton published his text book, *The Church of Christ*, for the
Sunset School of Preaching in 1970. Wharton saw Phl. 1 and 1Tm. 3
as the only passages clearly referring to deacons, although he said the
Seven of Acts 6 "could be called deacons." "What the duties of this
group are must be learned from the original language. There is no
specific teaching in the New Testament regarding their duties" (77+).

Another lead article in the *Advocate* comes from Hugh Fulford
(1974). He emphasizes that, "a deacon that is one in name only and
not in service is not a deacon at all...." He sees the Seven as probably being deacons in the formal sense.

Guy N. Woods, associate editor of the *Advocate*, was asked about
appointing deacons in a church where there were no elders (1980).
He replied: "It seems to us absurd to conclude that men who meet the
qualifications of the scriptures as deacons should be regarded as in-
capable of serving because other men are not possessed of the
qualifications of elders." He held the Seven as deacons of the
Jerusalem church, noting his disagreement with Bales on this interpretation and citing Lipscomb's *Queries and Answers* in support of his
position ("Questions" 35).

Star Bible Publications produced an inexpensive paperback in
1981 designed for free distribution entitled *Introducing the Church of
Christ: Distinctive Features of the Church of Christ Discussed by over
Fifty of Her Ministers*. Ben S. Flatt wrote the chapter on deacons:

> Although the Bible has relatively little to say about deacons, sufficient
> information is given and adequate guidelines are defined to produce the logical
> conclusions concerning the authority of deacons, their qualifications, the process
> of selection, their assigned duties, and the performance of their duties. (81)

Such was an overstatement. He depended exclusively on Acts 6 for
the method of selection and description of duties and partly for the
qualifications.

Dan R. Owen wrote in the *Firm Foundation* (1982) criticizing the
creation of the word "deacon" for a purely religious vocabulary:

> It [*diakonos*] is rendered "minister" or "servant" in every case except Phl. 1:1 and

1Tm. 3:8-12. Why must we create a word for those passages and further cloud the issue?

Certainly, the ministers or servants talked about in Phl. 1:1 and 1Tm. 3:8-12 were officers of the church in some sense. They were chosen according to qualifications set forth by the apostle Paul. They were not, however, called by a different name than were other Christian servants. . . . Let these take care that they accept a task or ministry to perform and not simply an "office" or position to fill.

James Thompson (1986) spoke of leadership:

Our uncertainty over authority is exacerbated by the fact that our own background and experience predispose us to read the biblical evidence in a way that corresponds to our own experience of the way groups function. In our own society, we are naturally tempted to take the biblical titles "elder," "minister," and "deacon," superimposing a democratic or corporate model of authority. When this is done, we naturally read into the text ideas of representative government and decision-making that are foreign to it. Our own experience of authority thus conditions us to read the New Testament with our own assumptions.

The complexity of the modern situation, where the church holds property titles and has extensive programs and budgets, adds to the uncertainty about using the New Testament to discover the nature of authority in the church. Since ancient churches had no budgets or property titles, no one exercised authority in these matters. Thus our situation was not envisioned in the New Testament. (21+)

The use of participles rather than nouns to describe them [leaders, as in 1Th. 5:12] indicates that no fixed titles exist in the community. They are known for the functions which they perform. . . . Their legitimacy is not derived specifically from ordination or appointment, but from their commitment to a task and the church's recognition of their work. (26+)

His colleague at the Austin Institute of Christian Studies, Allan McNicol, continued the thought (1986):

There seems to be a basic incompatibility between the proclamation of the gospel and the perception of ministry (as it developed in Western Christendom) as a status, or *ordo*, perceived to function as somewhat akin to the old Roman senatorial system. (45)

Within the history of the Restoration Movement considerable exegetical effort has been expended in order to find an underlying formal pattern for church organization and ministerial offices in the New Testament church and to implement this pattern in the church of our time. But such an attempt is doomed to repeated frustration and failure. Try as we can it is very difficult to see that the churches of the New Testament period structured their ministry along the lines of conscious following of some revealed formal pattern of ministry. (52)

But from beginning to end leadership in the New Testament finds its basis in the spiritual rule of Christ in the lives of his followers who excel in sharing common obligation to sustain the weak and who show the αγαπη manifested by their lord. As their Lord, they elicit the flock to follow them by the power of their surrendered lives. This is the model for ministry we would commend to the church today. (56)

Dr. Jack Lewis, preaching on deacons, made a similar emphasis on function (1987):

> Rather than thinking in terms of deacons being church officials, we ought to think in terms of their being congregational servants. Rather than thinking in terms of deacons being appointed to a rank in the congregations, we should think of their being given a work and of their discharging that work. (4)

Carroll Osburn of the A. C. U. Bible faculty said at the 1988 Lectureship:

> There is no indication in the Biblical literature to my awareness where the deacons are authority figures. They are servants. And to put them a rung above and right below another group is a very, very bad model. A Deacon is not a stepping stone to anything. A Deacon is just a member of the church that has a specially designated task. And in the early church, whether he was a male or female, [he] just [had] a specially designated task, and he didn't have any kind of authority in the church.
>
> There is no evidence in the ancient church in the first century for this Roman stepping stone idea that there is the church over whom are the deacons over whom are the elders.

Great Britain

It is important to recognize that the American Restoration Movement had its roots in the British Isles. Although the movement in that country was effected by Campbell and Stone, the British restoration developed essentially independent of the American movement.

Prior to any records of the Restoration Movement in America, the Tottlebank Church of Christ was formed in the Lake District of England. The minute book of 1669 reported that this church of adult immersed believers practiced a congregational government with elders and deacons. One of the elders was the teaching elder and was supported financially by the church (Nisbet).

The periodical, *Old Paths* (1868), records, "The treasury is committed to deacons, chosen by the church of which they are members, and supplied by the freewill offerings of brethren only" (King 325).

David King has been called the Alexander Campbell of Britain. "He was an editor, publisher, debater, teacher, and evangelist, a kind of 'Bishop' over the 76 churches that he either founded or consolidated" (Garrett 451). In his Memoirs (1890) he wrote:

> Refuse to call them deacons if you please - call them ministers, servants, or whatever you find authority for calling them; but so long as you have a table to furnish, funds to take care of, poor to help, expenses to meet, some must have charge; the whole church cannot act; and those who act for the church must not be self-chosen. . . . The term deacon, in its special application to the custodians of the church treasury, seems to have been derived from the synagogue of the

Jews, where, usually, there were three persons set apart to collect and appropriate alms. They had charge of the poor-chest provided for Sabbath contributions, and also of the produce of the gleanings of cornfields and vineyards. (285)

The British brethren faced a split at the turn of the century much like that of the U. S. A. The discussions were numerous, but the liberal Cooperation of Churches of Christ wing was heavily influenced by Overdale College and professional ministers while the Old Path's brethren generally held to mutual ministry. The seeds of the division began around 1917 but were not fully developed until World War II. In both groups, many of the opinions were centered in personalities, not in the biblical text (Nisbet).

Fred Day, speaking at a national lectureship (1946), referred to the first century deacons as the almoners of the church for collecting and distributing alms just as servants ministered in the synagogue. However, he recognized that times change, and that contemporary deacons had little to do with the poor. This observation reflected the socialized economy of Britain. He suggested contemporary service in worship services, visitation, and the maintenance of physical facilities (45).

Summary

The development of the diaconate concept has been seen chronologically. In the nineteenth century, the discussions reflected the establishment of many young churches which had limited formal internal structure. These churches had heard of elders and deacons and were seeking a definition of terms and instructions on selection and appointment. The older churches which had deacons utilized them primarily as almoners and custodians of the Lord's Supper.

The questions of the early twentieth century concerned interpretations of the qualifications, the meaning of appointment or ordination, and the role of females. (See Chapter Five for differing views on qualifications.) The teachings of the mid twentieth century reflected a power struggle between the elders and deacons for control of the congregation and its money.

The most recent articles indicate a lack of utilization of the diaconate and a revival of the discussion of office versus function. Older churches are concerned about elderly non-functioning deacons. The role of deacons in the emerging "ministry system" is creating new questions.

Within the Restoration movement, a myriad of interpretations exist. Occasionally someone will say, "If your new understanding is valid, why is it that we have done things differently all these years?" It is not that new answers are being found, but that readers are ignorant of their heritage. Some of the words penned by past editors of publications probably would not make it to print in those same periodicals today, and if they did, the authors would risk attack as liberals and be questioned for their newfangled distortion caused by too much or too little education. But the teacher was right, "there is nothing new under the sun" (Ec. 1:9).

CHAPTER 11

Female Deacons in the Restoration Movement

Possibly the most surprising discovery to current Churches of Christ is the fact that most early restoration writers took the work of the female deacon for granted. They assume that restoration churches had deaconesses.

Alexander Campbell stated (1835), "From Ro. 16:1 as well as from 1Tm. 3:11 it appears that females were constituted deaconesses in the primitive church. Duties to females, as well as to males, demand this" ("Order" 507). "The Primitive church had also deacons. Such was Phebe, of Cenchrea" (1853) ("Organization 2" 185). He said "deaconesses" referred, "to those female public servants, who officiate amongst the females" (1829) ("Order XXXII" 17):

> Amongst the Greeks who paid so much regard to differences of sex, female deacons, or deaconesses, were appointed to visit and wait upon the sisters. (1826) ("Order XIX" 4)

> I say it [the church] is an organized body. Its organs are pastors or teachers, deacons and deaconesses; and for foreign missions and influence, evangelists or missionaries.... (1853) ("Organization 3" 247)

Robert Richardson wrote in the 1836 edition of the *Harbinger:*

> Doubtless the "showers of mercy" and the "distributors" were deacons, while the deaconess had for her peculiar department the care of sick and indigent females, and those duties which can be better and more appropriately performed by females. (519)

Walter Scott encouraged deaconesses. In a note in the 1840 *The Evangelist* he wrote:

> We could name a church in which the sisterhood is in the habit of assembling once a week at the house of one of the deaconesses to sew and make garments for the poor and needy; but to name the church is wholly unnecessary and it might be improper, as I mention it merely to recommend the charitable custom to the sisters of other churches, that they also may be fruitful in good works and adorn their holy profession by deeds of love and benevolence.... ("Letters" 72)

The minutes of the Chestnut Grove Church of Christ, dating from 1845, recorded the appointment of deacons and deaconesses in that church (see previous chapter for details). The notes of Ferguson and others indicated that the church was probably influenced by the Baltimore church which had deaconesses from about the time of Campbell's visits there in 1833 (239 n. 14). Two deaconesses were appointed in 1845, two more in 1846, three in 1860, two in 1864, and two in 1865. One reference to their duties was in an entry for April 30, 1865, in the context of the discipline of members, which reads, "They also asked the Deaconess to visit Sister Lizzie Ironsides the coming week and report" (239+).

W. K. Pendleton (1848) wrote several articles concerning deacons. He said:

> In the discharge of this duty [care for the poor], there would necessarily arise cases in which men could not with propriety act, especially in a country like the East where the social intercourse between the sexes was restricted by so many forms; and, therefore, we find that into this order females were introduced, evidently by apostolic sanction. Paul. . . speaks of Phoebe as a deaconess of the church at Cenchrea; . . . and in the Epistle to Timothy 3:11, 12, we interpret him as describing their qualifications for office. . . . It is generally regarded, among our brethren, as an essential element in the restoration of primitive order, to ordain, in every church, both deacons and deaconesses. ("Discipline" 292)

> Besides deacons, every church should have deaconesses, whose duty it is to perform such offices as cannot be so well performed by deacons, and especially such to females, as could not with delicacy and propriety be laid upon the deacons. ("Deacons" 54)

Robert Milligan (1855) assumed the work of deaconesses, while denying an official teaching ministry to them:

> But to teach, is no part of their office. Were it so, women would never have been made deaconesses. . . . It is still true, however, that intelligent, grave, and pious females may do much for the feeble, the sick, the poor, and the destitute, especially of their own sex. The Phoebes should, therefore, constitute a part of the *diakonoi* of every fully organized congregation. ("Deacons" 626)

> The Diaconate of the primitive Church was not confined to male members. Deaconesses were also appointed to attend to the wants of the sick and the needy, especially of their own sex. . . . The order was continued, in the Greek church, until about the beginning of the thirteenth century, and it is to be regretted that it was ever discontinued in any church. The poor and the needy will always be with us, and will require the attention of both Deacons and Deaconesses just as much as they did in the Churches of Jerusalem, Cenchrea, and Ephesus. (Redemption 343)

Tolbert Fanning (1859) also recognized the service:

> In the primitive churches there were also deaconesses, as Phoebe - the servant - deaconess in Cenchreae. ("Deacons" 83)

> The Sisters, beyond all question, were as legitimately deacons as the brethren. Paul said, "I commend to you Phoebe, our sister, who is a deacon/servant of the

church at Cenchrea." The Apostle, not only recommended the brethren at Rome to receive her as a deacon of her church as became saints, but to "assist her in whatsoever business she had need of them." . . . The ministering to the Savior by these Galilean women (Mt. 27:55) evinced the strongest faith and an earnestness of life seldom witnessed. They were deacons, or ministers, to Jesus Christ in the most expressive sense. ("History 8" 357+)

We have failed to learn that Elders, Bishops, Deacons, Deaconesses, Evangelists or other officers were made or constituted officers in the Apostolic churches by virtue of an election or ordination, or both together. ("Service" 724)

Elders, or seniors, are made by years and labor, deacons and deaconesses by servitude, preachers by labor, and bishops by overlooking the flock. ("Officers 3" 684)

Regarding the labor of both deacons and deaconesses it is clear that it is their business to relieve the needy, especially the sick, the widowed and orphans. (Cited by Stroop Restoration Ideas 215)

The Christian Standard (1867) was asked: "Does the New Testament teach that the Apostles in organizing the Church, introduced the office of deaconesses and was it their design to teach Christians to so continue that office to the present day in organizing the Church of Christ?" The reply from Isaac Errett included:

Sometimes women were employed as deaconesses or servants of the churches. . . . There is many an active ministration of benevolence and mercy for which women are better fitted than men. . . . There is a vast amount of wealth of mind, sympathy, and activities in our churches, lying unemployed; and many an earnest nature pining for suitable employment. When the church wakes up to her true mission, we shall have numbers of women like Phoebe, Euodia, and Syntyche, who, whether known officially as deaconess or not, will be serviceable helpers in the work of the Lord in suitable departments of activities. (Errett "Querists")

The *Philadelphia Inquirer* of September 2, 1868, reported an example of five ladies being ordained to the First Church of Christ in Philadelphia. The article stated:

Ladies would often be more forward in good and pious work than they are, were it not for the unkind and uncharitable insinuations often indulged by the captious to the effect that they desire to attract attention to themselves.

The speaker pointed out that the duties of the deaconess consist in part in attending female candidates for baptism, in visiting the sick of their own sex, in reporting cases of destitution to the board of deacons, in reading, talking and praying with the afflicted and dying, etc. ("Items from Correspondents" 301)

The debate over deaconesses must have been developing in this period. Right after Milligan wrote his *Scheme of Redemption* (1868), the *Christian Standard* cited him against "some of our 'sound' brethren" who "have recently been making themselves very merry over the subject of deaconesses." Milligan's stance supported the view of the *Standard* (Walk 379).

In 1873, the *Standard* ran a two part article in support of deaconesses in reaction to negative comments in the *Apostolic Times,* edited by Moses E. Lard. The article made it clear that the *Times* was against deaconesses. Concerning Phoebe the *Standard* stated, "The fact remains that a woman was appointed to serve the church; and had the approval of Paul in her official character." Schaff was cited for additional support as to the work of deaconesses:

> We are simply left to conclude that the office of deacon was inferior to that of bishop and hence to infer that as the bishop had charge of spiritual interests, the inferior order of ministers had more especial charge of temporal interests. . . . Churches are at liberty to appoint them to any ministry not forbidden to them in the New Testament, in which they can serve the church acceptably and profitably. (Errett 7 June 1873 180)

The second article addressed the texts in 1Tm. In connection with 1Tm. 5:9 and the enrollment of widows, Errett stated:

> The qualifications evidently point to a ministry involving the exercise of hospitality, the care of the afflicted, the training of children, and the instruction of younger women in the duties of life. Taking this as referring to deaconesses - and this seems to us the most reasonable interpretation - the text throws more light on the duties of their ministry than any other in the New Testament. It does not necessarily follow that all deaconesses were widows, but that among the widows supported by the church those possessing these qualifications could be profitably employed in this office. (Errett 14 June 1873 188)

He concluded with a statement concerning the natural evolution of the office of deacon (male and female) without concern for title or authority by those who sought to serve their Lord and His people.

Lard in his commentary on Ro. 16 written two years later (1875) agreed:

> Phoebe was a servant of the church in Cenchrea. This much is actually asserted. Was she appointed to the service by the church, or did she assume it of herself? The question is not material. For whether she assumed the service of her own accord, or was appointed to is, she performed it with the Apostle's sanction. This stamps it right. . . . I am therefore of the opinion that Phoebe was a deaconess in the official sense of that word.
>
> What the special duties were of this order of women, it would seem not difficult to conjecture. Their work consisted in serving the sisterhood. . . . In all churches there would be among the females, the poor, the sick, the untaught, the erring, the unfortunate. These would need attentions which no other persons could so delicately and successfully give as the deaconesses. . . . Even in the present day, wherever the necessities of the churches are such as to demand it, the order of the deaconesses should be re-established. They are often of as much importance to a church as the deacons, if not even more. (451+)

J. M. Barnes in the *Gospel Advocate* (1893) did a study of 1Tm. 3:8. He defended the translation of "deaconess" and then spoke of Phoebe:

> Was she not a *diakonos* different from the rank and file? It is obvious. . . . In this there were men and women. Does this surprise you? . . . If this does not mean the women among the deacons what is the apostles' doctrine on this subject? Why does the Holy Spirit give such specific instruction about the wives of deacons and not a word about the wives of elders? Why are the women put in here when wives of deacons are spoken of in the next verse? ("Deacons" 43)

E. G. Sewell (1893) said:

> Now the apostolic *ekklesia*. . . must have deacons, and these embrace men and women who perform a work, the *diakonia*, the ministering to the poor or unfortunate saints, the widows, and teaching the word. ("Apostolic Church" 121)

> Phoebe is called a "servant of the church" - that is, she served or helped the church in some way that was proper for women to serve. She was not an officer in the modern sense of the word "deacon" among religious denominations. ("Deaconesses" 761)

> All official authority in the church is from Christ, the great Head of the church, and not among the members. They have no official authority over each other. . . . The deacons were to simply serve in any capacity needed. The word "deacon" simply means service, not office. ("Deaconesses" 761)

Hayden (1894) interpreted deaconesses as wives of deacons and supported their ministry:

> Their wives, also, should have like dignity and prudence, that they may not injure the usefulness of their husbands, and may serve as deaconesses if called to render such service. Phoebe, our sister, was a deaconess of the church in Cenchrea. (66)

> Women may be deaconesses in the church and render valuable service in various kinds of loving helpful ministries. In work among the poor and neglected classes, among the degraded and outcast - especially of their own sex - in charitable work among the sick, suffering and dying in the hospitals, in zenana work and other ministrations in mission fields, there are activities which women can work more successfully than men. (85+)

> But let them not presume to partake of the forbidden fruit of official authority in teaching God's word and governing His church. (86)

The work of David Lipscomb edited and revised by J. W. Shepherd, as revealed in the *Commentary on I Timothy*, promotes an unusual interpretation. The commentary does not call the women in 1Tm. 3:11 deaconesses, but at the same time breaks the thought of deacons in the passage and talks about the qualities of women "who serve the church in looking after the wants of women." The interpretation is clearly that the women in 1Tm. 3:11 are not wives of deacons, but women who serve the church in a special way. The changing philosophies between Lipscomb's time and Shepherd's revision of

1942 may explain why Shepherd does not call the women deacons or deaconesses in the commentary (151).

Robert Mathews of Drake University (1897) said, "In the genuine sense of the word proof, the office of deaconess is seen to be strictly scriptural." The proof he cites is the reading of the Revised Version and the facts of post-Apostolic history. "In reforming the polity of the church, we may rest assured that any congregation which maintains the office of deaconess is occupying indisputable Scripture ground" (219).

Isaiah Boone Grubbs was Professor of Sacred Literature, College of the Bible, Lexington, Kentucky. In his commentary on Romans printed posthumously by the Gospel Advocate (1913), he stated of Phoebe, "She was a deaconess in the church at Cenchrea. Her work seemed to have been that of ministering to the saints whenever they needed help" (174).

It is important to note that deacons and deaconesses, as advocated by these early Disciples, were not decision makers, but servants in the most basic of definitions. Most disciples felt that deaconesses were not to teach males. Their work was primarily benevolent assistance to females and children.

John T. Brown's yearbook, *Churches of Christ* (1904), written from the view of the liberal wing of the movement, recorded many women in leadership roles, although only one church was specifically cited for its deaconesses. In 1874 the Christian Woman's Board of Missions was organized and established many churches in American and foreign lands (109, 163+). Local chapters of the C. W. B. M. were found in many congregations and their missionaries were both male and female.

In reporting on the work at various places, Brown mentioned the name of the minister and then an unmarried female who was his "helper." These were found in Cincinnati congregations: the Central church in 1896, Richmond St. in 1902, and Central Fairmont Church in 1902 (306+).

Brown included a photograph of the deacons of the Central church in St. Louis at the turn of the century - thirteen deacons and three deaconesses. The Central church had about 550 members. He also mentioned the Third church of Memphis as being led by "The Official Board" composed of seven men and one woman (348+).

Churches of Christ in the Twentieth Century.

J. W. McGarvey denied deaconesses, stating that "I am sure there was not" the office of a deaconess in the apostolic church. "Many a good woman then, and many a good one now, is a servant of the church without being appointed to an office" ("Deaconesses" (1902) 1616). In another article he said, "There is not even a hint" that Phoebe was a deacon. He cited correspondence with a brother who had served a church which had four deaconesses and found that they were usurping the powers of the deacons. He concluded by remembering the example of Euodia and Syntyche, suggesting that they were ambitious for offices ("Deaconesses" (1906) 166).

After McGarvey's death, Philip Y. Pendleton completed the Standard Bible Commentary on Romans which was begun by McGarvey. Concerning Ro. 16:1 he stated:

> The word "deaconess" is found only here; but this single reference with commendation stamps the office with apostolic sanction and approval, though the attempt to revive the office in our modern churches has not as yet met with any marked success. (545)

Daniel Sommer (1910) sees the women of 1Tm. 3 as deacons' wives. He states that:

> As we are unable to find the Scriptures which set forth the qualifications of a deaconess we should not appoint any for such office. . . . An elder can, at any time, request a suitable sister, or several sisters, in the church, to prepare the candidates, on their side of the house, for baptism, or do anything else that is appropriate for a woman only to do. (13)

His reference to the "side of the house" shows that the congregation he served segregated men and women in the worship assembly.

J. C. McQuiddy, while Managing Editor of the *Gospel Advocate* (1916), was asked if Phoebe was a deaconess and if deaconesses were deacon's wives. He answered:

> The Scriptures do not teach that a deacon's wife is a deaconess, any more than the wife of a preacher is a preacheress. Phoebe was a deaconess. . . . In the East, where women were so much secluded, deaconesses would be very necessary. ("Query" 494)

He continued by citing Adam Clark in support of deaconesses.

C. R. Nichol, the noted preacher in Texas, wrote a book entitled *God's Woman* (1938) and dedicated a chapter to the deaconess. After examining the texts, he summarized:

> It should be known in every congregation that Sister Phoebe, Sister Priscilla, and Sister Dorcas are deaconesses in the congregation, and that when their assistance is needed they are to be called. Many congregations are falling short of the work

that should be done, because they do not have women appointed to do certain work for the church. . . . As there was a need for the deaconess in the early days of the church, so there is now. (165)

R. L. Whiteside (1939), who co-authored the *Sound Doctrine* series with Nichol, disagreed with him on the subject of deaconesses. He stated, "I do not see how a woman could belong to this class of deacons." He did see Phoebe as being "appointed to do a special work by the church at Cenchrea" ("Deaconess" 799), but stated in his commentary on Romans, "*Diakonos* therefore had no official significance. . . . We let our minds run to officialism too much" (293).

H. Leo Boles (1941) took the position that special female servants worked in the early church, but that their office was not official in the same sense as that of elders and deacons ("Deaconess" 317).

The work by Deveny (1941) stated that:

Many good women in the church should be designated deaconesses. Oftentimes there is work that can best be done by a woman as a servant of the church. At least it would seem that Paul gave unqualified endorsement to one such woman [Phoebe]. . . . (172+)

Gray cites Robert Milligan, G. C. Brewer, and B. W. Johnson in support of the activity of deaconesses. He concludes that, "regardless of one's views on this subject, the fact remains that women do most of the work in the church" (45).

R. P. Cuff addressed "The Qualifications and Duties of Deacons" in the *Advocate* (1948):

That deacons in the primitive church had various temporal or physical duties is also supported by the reference to Phoebe (a servant of the church in Cenchreae) as a helper of many, including Paul himself. In the Greek language she is mentioned as a *diakonon*; the word is translated "deacon." (739)

Winkler's book (1950) contains two chapters on the deaconess, one by himself and one by Thomas C. Whitfield. Winkler states, "It is clear that the early churches had deaconesses in them" (169). He cites Phoebe as an example and holds that 1Tm. 3:11 is speaking of deaconesses:

There is, oftentimes, work for the poor, in the sick room and elsewhere that women can do much more effectively than men. It is my earnest conviction that the churches today should have two or three deaconesses to serve them in various duties. (169)

The churches, preachers and individual members need to be blasted out of their complacent indifference to the New Testament teaching, and the need, of a Scriptural eldership, or presbytery, the diaconate, including the deaconess, and membership. (179)

In discussing the qualifications for a deaconesses, he not only mentions 1Tm. 3, but also 1Tm. 2:9 + ; 5:13 + ; 1Pt. 3:4; and Tit. 2:3 + . He sees Euodia and Syntyche of Philippi as deaconesses (170).

Whitfield's chapter addresses the question, "Should We Have Deaconesses Today?" He states:

> The New Testament seems to clearly teach that there were deaconesses in the early church. . . . We might well reason therefore that if the church in Cenchrea appointed her [Phoebe] to this service and Paul did not condemn it, congregations today have the authority to do likewise. . . . The church today may and should have deaconesses when they are needed. (180)

Whitfield gives a number of arguments for the appointment of deaconesses: 1) women out number men in the church; 2) women are often more faithful and loyal than men; 3) women are better equipped to do some jobs; and, 4) women have more time available for volunteer work (181).

G. C. Brewer's *The Model Church* (1957) speaks of Philippians as being the earliest specific mention of deacons "unless we consider Phoebe an officer in the church, which is probable, but not certain" (96). Later in his work, he elaborates:

> It is a disputed point as to whether there was an order of deaconesses in the New Testament church, and there is probably no way definitely to decide the question. . . . There is nothing in the work that belongs to the deacons that a woman cannot do consistently with the inhibitions laid upon her by the Scriptures. On the contrary, there is a part of the work that women seem eminently better adapted to than men. In our present-day congregations the good women do most of this work, whether we call them "deaconesses" or something else or nothing. (101)

> The strongest indication that there were deaconesses in the early church is the language of 1Tm. 3:11. . . . To translate it "their wives," and thus make it apply to the wives of the deacons only, is a mistake, . . . If it is true that the churches had deaconesses in them, we would most naturally understand Phoebe to be a deaconess and not simply a servant. Indeed, the language concerning her seems to sustain the idea. . . . She [Phoebe] had succored many, and that is the very work that deacons are appointed to do. (102 +)

Don DeWelt, a professor in the Independent Christian Church's Ozark Bible College, in his commentary, workbook, and teaching manual (1959), calls Phoebe a deaconess. He then goes on to add: "Was Phoebe a servant of the church at Cenchrea in the official sense? We really cannot know. She performed her service with 'Apostle's sanction.' Whether such women are officially appointed or not, we need more of them" (Romans 242). DeWelt's commentary on 1 Tm., copywritten two years later states: "It must then refer either to female deacons or to the wives of the male deacons. The later conclusion is our preference. . . . All the deacons mentioned are men (unless we are to understand Phoebe was a deaconess in an official sense)" (69). He then quoted Guthrie who said: "The reference is too general to postulate with certainty a distinct order of deaconesses, but some feminine ministration was necessary in visitation and in attending to women candidates for baptism" (Timothy 69 +).

J. Ridley Stroop of the David Lipscomb faculty, wrote *The Church of the Bible* (1962) to question a number of traditional viewpoints in Churches of Christ. He said concerning deacons, "It has come to be applied to men only and the word or office apparently limited to men, which completely ignores Paul's statement in Ro. 16:1" (47).

In the Sweet *The Living Word* adult Bible school material, J. D. Thomas (Abilene Christian College, 1965) writes concerning Ro. 16, "There seems to be no reason to believe that she was not an official deaconess and so recognized because she helped much in this connection." Then speaking of the women in 1Tm. 3:11, he says:

> It seems unlikely that qualifications would have been given for a deacon's wife when none is given for the elder's wife; and, since qualifications for women, a certain group of women, are definitely given, and since they follow the qualifications of the deacon, it is likely that this should be understood as meaning "deaconess" in an official sense just the same as deacons are recognized in an official sense. . . . But it would no doubt be perfectly scriptural if there were reasons why any church should employ a woman (either with or without pay) to have a regular responsibility in this connection and for them to recognize her by this designation." (84)

In the same class literature, J. W. Roberts (Abilene Christian College, 1964) writes concerning I Tm 3:11, "To this writer the evidence seems strong for the existence of deaconesses in the New Testament church, yet it must be admitted that the question is not plainly answered" (37).

James Bales (Harding College, 1967) discusses deaconesses in his examination of the qualifications of deacons in 1Tm. 3. From the context, he states that: "Paul is not discussing women in general, any more than he is discussing men in general. . . . Whether the wives of deacons, or other female servants of the church, there would be certain work they could do that the men could not do" (73+). Bales goes on to give many arguments to support the interpretation that these were deaconesses, but he stops short:

> The author is not convinced that there was an office of deaconess in the church, but it is clear that there were female servants of the church. It is not necessary to prove that there was an office of deaconess in order to prove that there were women whom the church selected to do special work for the church. Thus, it is

unnecessary to settle the question as to whether technically there is such an office; for surely there is such work. (79)

He concludes that the women of 1Tm. 3 are "women who could assist the deacons and do the work which women were better fitted to do, either by training or because of the customs of the day" (83).

Roy H. Lanier, Sr., wrote "The Problem Page" in the *Firm Foundation* in 1967. In his article, "Are Deaconesses Scriptural?" he stated:

> I believe Paul intended for women to be servants (deaconesses) in the same way in which he intended for men to be servants (deacons) of the churches.

> Someone says he objects to this view of the matter because it elevates women to a position equal to men; especially does it give women servants a position equal to that of men who serve the church. This objection has weight only because we have usually elevated the position of deacon to the equal of the bishop in authority. . . . Deacons and deaconesses are simply men and women with special qualifications which fit them to serve the church in a peculiar way.

In the Sweet *Living Word Commentary* series, Richard A. Batey (Southwestern at Memphis, 1969) says concerning Phoebe: "Deaconess implies more of a function than an office in this context. While deacons are described elsewhere in the New Testament, this is the only mention of a deaconess. . ." (185).

In the companion commentary on 1Tm., Carl Spain (Abilene Christian College, 1970), states:

> The term likewise in verses 8 and 11 suggests that Paul is concerned with three special offices or ministries, one of which pertained to women. . . . The office of deacon did not involve oversight and authority over the church, so the appointment of certain women as special servants of the church introduces no contradiction with 2:9-15. . . . It seems more in harmony with the immediate context and with the general context of the Scriptures to translate vs. 11 "women," rather than "wives" of the deacons. The term deaconess (*diakonissa*) is not used in the New Testament and may not have come into use at the time Paul is writing, but Paul does use the word deacon in a feminine sense in his reference to Phoebe. (66 +)

Gus Nichols, in his regular *Gospel Advocate* article, answered a question about deaconesses in 1971. He stated:

> I believe women can and should serve in the church, and that a good sister, like sister Phoebe, may be a servant of the church. But I know of no Bible authority to have women fill some office in the church, in the sense that we think of the elders and deacons. There is nothing said of the selection and appointment of women to an official position in the church. No qualifications are recorded for such an appointment. (797)

He gets to the main problem as he continues, "If given such a position in the church, would they not be 'over' the men in the church?" He makes a definite distinction between appointment to serve and appointment to an office by saying: "Good Christian women may be employed by the church, or do good work in the church without charge, if they can do so, but where is the authority for having them selected and appointed to some office in the church" (798)?

Burton Coffman in his mammoth commentary series also discusses the question. Discussing Ro. 16:1 (1973), he says:

> Those who appoint deaconesses must do so without a clear mandate and without a scriptural list of what their qualifications should be. . . . Therefore, the proposition is rejected that would make Paul's reference here to Phoebe as a "servant of the church" as sufficient ground for the fantastic elaboration of this so-called office of deaconesses which abounds in some of the commentaries. (511 +)

Much of Coffman's argument is based on the fact that no feminine word for deaconess appears in the Scriptures. He sees 1Tm. 3:11 as describing the wives of both elders and deacons. He also states, "If churches were commanded to appoint women deacons, where is the record of it, either in the N. T. or in the custom of the historical church" (1 & 2 Timothy 184)?

In an address on *The Role of Women* to the Harding Graduate School of Religion (1978), Dr. Neil Lightfoot (Abilene Christian University) said concerning Phoebe:

> She is a deaconess in the sense that she is a servant or minister. To translate *diakonos* as "servant" is not a slight to her. . . . This shows clearly that certain women in the church were not passive but played active parts in the spreading of the word. They labored with Paul, and he with them. (18)

Later in a footnote, he stated, "whether 'deaconess' is a technical term is an open question" (49).

Dub McClish spoke at the Eighth Annual Spiritual Sword Lectureship (1983) concerning Phoebe, "I am not convinced that Phoebe or any other woman was ever a 'deaconess' in the official sense that certain men were deacons or bishops." He explained that Ro. 16:1 should not be translated as an official deaconess and that the women of 1Tm. 3 were wives of elders and deacons (237). In support of his position he cited Barclay, Whitesides, Coffman, and Lipscomb and Shepherd.

Guy Caskey in his booklet entitled *What the Christian Woman Can Do In the Church* concludes that, "She can be a servant of the Church." He goes on to use Phoebe as an example and says:

> The form of the Greek word is deaconess, here applied to Phoebe; and it means that she was the kind of servant who executed the commands of God and ministered to others unselfishly, voluntarily, out of love and always for the benefit

of other people. It says, "she has been a great help to many people." The term employed is *prostatis*. The lexicons define it: one who stands in front or before; a leader; a protector; a patroness. From this, and other passages, one may deduce that a Christian woman's role is one of leadership. We have learned before, however, that she cannot teach over or be head over or exercise dominion over man, but there is that sphere, circle of service and operation in which she stands before others and is their patroness as she renders help to many people. (10)

Dr. Thomas Olbricht (1987), chairman of the Religion Department at Pepperdine University, wrote:

> I have examined several commentaries, read the relevant text in the Greek several times and it is my judgment that the use of *diakonos* in Romans 16:1 is as much a title or label as the same word employed in 1 Timothy or Titus. To me it is not a foregone conclusion that the word in the two latter letters speaks of an office, but in the context such seems likely. In fact, I'm not sure that office is the correct word in the case of either elders or deacons. We might better express the New Testament meaning by calling them ministries or services to the churches. (Letter)

Dr. Jack Lewis stated (1987):

> . . . I would argue that Phoebe was one who served the church there [Cenchreae] rather than being a female appointee in the church organization. If one translates the term, she was a "deaconess" in the service sense, but was not in my opinion a church officer. (2)

> Hence, in 1Tm. 3:11, *gune* could designate a female "deacon," but in my opinion does not since there is no passage in the New Testament that indisputably provides for them. (3)

Lewis discussed the *ministrae* of Pliny as women who served the congregation just as Phoebe did, but not as officers of the congregation. Later he stated that male deacons should not think of themselves as office holders, but as "assistants to aid in any work. . . ." In his opinion female deacons did not appear until the third century (3+).

Speaking at the 1988 A. C. U. Lectureship, Carroll Osburn of the Bible faculty stated:

> I do not believe that the women in the early church were ever in a position of leadership. But I do believe they were servants, and that is what the word διακονος definitely is all about. They went on into the second century church and women were very active in roles, especially with regards to the relief of the poor, especially with regard to taking care of the sick, and so on.

> The deacon is just a member of the church that has a specially designated task. In the early church, whether he was a male or female, [the deacon] just [had] a specially designated task, and he didn't have any kind of authority in the church.

Oliver Howard, teaching a class at the Pepperdine Lectureship in 1988, polled his 450 member audience concerning matters of faith and matters of opinion. Of his respondents, thirty-nine percent said the exclusion of women from the diaconate was a matter of faith, while sixty-one percent considered it a matter of opinion.

Many authors of the past few decades who wrote on church leadership or the identity of the church, have either not mentioned women at all, or have denied to them any titled ministry in the church (i.e. Baird, Lyles, Wharton).

One Church that Tried

The Church of Christ, White Horse Pike, W. Collingswood, NJ, appointed deacons and deaconesses in 1958. Ralph Graham was the minister at the time.

The congregation studied the question of church leadership, including deaconesses, long and carefully. Graham wrote, "It is difficult to see how a church can be scripturally organized that declines to elect Christian women to serve in this important New Testament church office of deaconess" (Fellowship 10 Nov. 1957). When the majority were in agreement, six deaconesses were appointed. Apart from a few individuals who objected, the major portion of the congregation was in harmony on the matter. These were the most productive years in the history of the congregation. One week before the deacons were appointed, the first elders were also ordained to the church (Fischer and Milmanow).

With the laying on of hands, they were ordained. Sadly, one of the deaconesses reported, "At the time of the ordination service, many old friends in other congregations were invited, but none came. From that time on we were ostracized and our services boycotted" (Milnamow).

The duties of the deaconesses were similar to those of the deacons, often in partnership with them, and generally in areas that were more appropriate to female talents. The elders supervised all the duties, and no deaconess ever performed a duty conflicting with the doctrinal norms, such as teaching or supervising adult men or participating in worship in assigned positions (Ficher).

Elders and leaders from area congregations and Northeastern Christian College were displeased. "It was never a frontal attack on the Biblical position because they felt defeat there, but it was always 'go slow, study further, and permit us to counsel you and sit down with you to arrive at a consensus.'" Collingswood soon joined the "one-cuppers, Sunday schoolers, kitchen-in-the-building and congregational cooperation churches" as those to be avoided (Ficher).

Collingswood was a mission church in many ways and received financial support from a church in Texas. Leaders of that congregation traveled to Collingswood to check on the situation. When Collingswood would not do away with deaconesses, support was discontinued. Collingswood refused to yield and would not allow Graham to do so either. The church became an island; other congregations refused fellowship. Graham later described the situation:

> Looking back, I can see clearly how my studies, working experiences, and association with believers of different denominations led me gradually into a deeper and broader Christian commitment than the restricted liberty afforded me in the Churches of Christ. Being quite outspoken in my preaching, talk, and writings, I found the restrictions placed on my freedom of expression intolerably frustrating. I and my congregation became subjected to a West Berlin-type of isolation because of my views. (Ralph Graham 130)

When Graham left in 1962, the church had a bad experience with another minister which resulted in a split. One side sought to become a "Community Church" while the other wanted to remain a "Church of Christ." Since that time the church has had no elders and has been governed by a committee system due to a shortage of permanently located qualified men.

The road to respectability was hard:

> Only in 1968 were we reunited and "taken back" into the "mainstream" when we secured a very "conservative" minister, with the help of others. . . . Since Ralph left we have been taught the "party line" by good, well-meaning men, but who are truly "conservative" or are afraid to be "free" and reveal their innermost convictions. (Milnamow)

Graham went on to leave the Church of Christ (May, 1964) and began preaching for the Christian Church (Disciples) where he hoped to find a more expanded theology. He found no Eden there either and finally retired from preaching to sell real estate. "Christianity lost a great student and thinker of the type we sorely need" (Ficher).

Heinz Ficher, one of the original elders, and Lois Milnamow, one of the deaconesses, are hurt by the experiences of the past. Their writings demonstrate a disappointment in the traditional church, its violation of autonomy, its exclusivism, and the influence of preachers, papers, and Christians colleges which restricted the local church, yet both are still members at Collingswood in spite of all the problems.

Mark Finn became minister in 1986 and has led a regeneration of the church in numerical and spiritual growth. Ficher states:

> Whether we will be willing to go the "full mile" again in the future and elect deaconesses is a matter of conjecture at this point. It will take education anew, we are a completely different group now, but I question whether it will be worth the price if it results in internal rupture. . . . Our women today are not as eager to accept such a role. In fact some would reject it, unfortunately, from fear.

British Churches of Christ

Even though British churches of Christ do not have deaconesses today, noted restorationist David King (1890) recognized their value:

> Deaconesses should be ordained in every church as soon as practicable. . . . That women filled this honorable office is apparent. . . . With us, although not so absolutely necessary, many cases occur which can only be investigated and relieved by female agency; and, therefore, deaconesses should be ordained wherever practical. . . . (285+)

Evangelist Albert Brown, speaking at the annual conference of Churches of Christ in 1919, spoke in favor of freedom for women to minister. This lecture came on the heels of the first World War which caused women to step out into jobs that were previously taboo, including activities in the church in the absence of its male soldiers.

> Phoebe is named by the Apostle Paul as a deacon. . . . The word is the same as is used of men-ministers, and whatever kind of service it denotes it must mean that she was in some way recognized as an accredited servant of the Church. (29)

> There was evidently a recognized class of women deacons in the church of Apostolic days, for Paul names to Timothy the qualifications which they should possess (1Tm. 3). . . . Although this scripture tells nothing except what may be inferred from the qualifications about the kind of ministry in which these women deacons engaged, it does mark them out equally with the men as chosen by the Church for service. (31)

He also discussed the possibility of widows being an official group:

> We cannot believe that the church would refuse to relieve the need of destitute widows who did not fulfill those qualifications. Therefore we can only conclude that these instructions refer to a class of ministers in the Church who were probably supported while doing the work allotted to them. (32)

Fred C. Day spoke at the venerable Hindley Bible School in 1946 on church government. This annual event was a nationally recognized lectureship among British "Old Paths" churches. In a section on deaconesses he presented Ro. 16:1 and 1Ti. 3:11 as validating the work of deaconesses. He advocated these women serving other women and added, "As men do not require to give up their employment to become deacons, neither do women require to give up their business to become deaconesses" (45).

Albert Winstanley, respected leader among churches of Christ in Britain (1987) and former instructor at the British Bible School, gave a commentary on King's teaching:

> The quotation regarding deaconesses from David King's memoirs represented the generally held view among Churches of Christ in the United Kingdom in his day. It became quite common for churches in "the co-operation" to appoint deaconesses. . . . Subsequently many churches broke away from the co-operation

regarding it as a digressive organization. The digression included the following factors: 1) unscriptural organization - supplanting the autonomy of the local congregations, 2) unscriptural teaching - modernism through Overdale College had become rampant, and 3) unscriptural practice. It is this third point which concerns the question of deaconesses. Some of these travelled about the country and were in fact "women ministers" who regularly preached at Sunday services.

It seems that most of the "old paths" brethren (as they were called by the modernists) associated the idea of deaconesses with such unscriptural practices, and consequently threw out the baby with the bath water. Whenever the subject comes up nowadays people who oppose the idea of deaconesses usually regard others who are for them as having been influenced by or arguing for the co-operation's unscriptural practice in this area.

My own view is that David King was right. (Letter)

Frank Worgan, another veteran preacher, reported that a number of churches in the Cooperation of Churches of Christ had deaconesses, including the Rodney St. church in Wigan and the Coplay St. church in Glasgow. The church in Hindley discussed having them, and there was no argument against them, but no one was in a hurry to make appointments.

Disciples of Christ in the Twentieth Century.

In the previous sections of this chapter, the more liberal part of the Restoration Movement, the Christian Church (Disciples of Christ), has been overlooked. The separation of the Disciples from the Churches of Christ was in progress as Brown authored his yearbook, and it is from the Disciples perspective that Brown writes. As will be discussed in detail later, the northern half of the Restoration Movement was much more receptive to the service and leadership of women.

S. S. Lappin in his lesson on deacons wrote:

In the early church women as well as men were made members of the diaconate (Ro. 16:1). . . . They were considered as peculiarly adapted to such duties as the care of the sick and needy, especially when women and children were in need of tender ministries. . . . That they were appointed to such services in the early church may account for Paul's remark, "Women in like manner must be grave. . ." when giving the qualifications a deacon should possess. (133)

M. M. Davis writing in the *Christian Standard* (1916) quotes Milligan and W. L. Hayden in support of deaconesses. He then cautions:

We would suggest that in matters of this kind, where the teachings of the Book seem not to be absolutely clear, leaving good and wise men holding diverse views, that sanctified common sense, coupled with Christian love and forbearance, be the main factor in the settlement of the difference. While the question is important, it is not fundamental. . . . (711)

In the same period, Mrs. Ellie K. Payne wrote a pamphlet on *Women in the Early Church*. She stated:

> A wise man wrote that with all of its great discoveries, the greatest discovery of the nineteenth century was woman. (3)

> As mothers who trained for the church its standard bearers, as deaconesses in the service of mercy, as martyrs who vied with men for the immortal crown, serving everywhere, praying, toiling, enduring, women shared with men in the great conflict, and to them surely in no small degree is the victory due. (7)

J. B. Briney in the *Christian Standard* (1927) wrote to answer the question, "Do we have any Scripture authority for calling women to the official board to act as deacons?" Answering in reference to Phoebe he said:

> Dogmatic assertion would be out of place under the circumstances, but the context seems to indicate that the word is to be taken in its official sense, and, if so, it gives apostolic sanction to the appointment of women as deacons. ... From the foregoing Scriptures, it appears that sex did not cut any figure in the matter of church work, and, other things being equal, that women were eligible for any position in such work for which they were qualified. (318)

Three years later that answer is questioned by A. B. Sneed who asks why διακονος is not uniformly translated. His concept is that if God intended to have women deacons, he would have made it plain and there would be no need to guess about it. He sees the women in 1Tm. as being wives of elders and deacons (891).

R. C. Harding's *Handbook for Elders and Deacons* (1932) states that every church should have a board of elders and a board of deacons and deaconesses. He continues, "It seems clear from the Scriptures that there must have been at least some of the churches with female servants or deacons" (95).

The question came up in the *Standard* again in 1936 as Dan J. Ottinger stated that there could not be any female deacons according to the Scriptures and referred to 1Tm. 3. A later issue included a letter from I. H. Beckholt seeking to correct him by saying that "Paul wanted the church at Rome to give Phoebe adequate recognition fitting to her official position at Cenchrea, which position was a deaconess" (635). Ottinger then came back a few issues later to straighten out the question:

> I did say that a woman could not be a deacon, for 1Tm. 3:11 speaks of a deacon's wife. A lady can't have a wife! ... There were deaconesses in the early church, and Phoebe was one. However it could never have been considered a distinct church office, for no New Testament qualifications are given. ("Misread" 71)

In the following years, the attitudes of the Christian Church and the Churches of Christ have polarized strongly on a number of issues. The Christian Church has accepted women in all forms of ministry, commonly takes political stands, uses instrumental music, and leads in many ecumenical efforts.

The General Assembly of the Christian Church, meeting in Cincinnati in 1973, passed resolutions to increase the number of women in ministry. One resolution was that a single order of diaconate be implemented, representing men and women equally. Congregations which had called women as pastors were commended. The General Assembly also strongly endorsed the Equal Rights Amendment (Howe 146+).

Women are now serving on all the governing boards of the major units of the Christian Church and on all the regional boards. Percentages range from twelve to fifty percent. In 1980 the Church Finance Council, which collects and distributes all finances for the denomination, had a woman president (Howe 148).

Nineteenth Century Cultural Factors

Everyone's theology has been affected to some degree by his own cultural experience. Two questions haunted this author throughout this study: "In the formative Nineteenth Century, why were deaconesses only found in northern churches when such restoration giants as Alexander Campbell, Walter Scott, Robert Milligan, Tolbert Fanning, Isaac Errett, W. K. Pendleton, Moses Lard, J. M. Barnes, E. G. Sewell, W. L. Hayden, Robert Mathews, Isaiah Boone Grubbs, Philip Y. Pendleton, and J. C. McQuiddy advocated their appointment? Why did female deacons disappear from the Churches of Christ?"

In looking at the articles reviewed, the first hint of an anti-deaconess sentiment surfaced in the 1868 *Christian Standard* when David Walk cited Milligan who supported deaconesses against "some of our 'sound' brethren" who "have recently been making themselves very merry over the subject of deaconesses" (Walk 379). Moses Lard had denied deaconesses in his *Apostolic Times* articles, but changed his views to strong support by 1875 (Romans 451).

The only major nineteenth century leader discovered in this study who denied female deacons was J. W. McGarvey. His argument centered on translating the word διακονος as "servant." He stated, "The original word means a servant and should never be translated deacon, except where the context shows plainly that the reference is to that office" ("Deaconess" 166). However, a further paragraph may have revealed a cultural bias which also influenced his position:

You will meet with men now and then who imagine that all women are angels,

> especially all that are in the church. This is a very serious mistake. Euodia and Synteche in the church at Philippi, although they labored with Paul in the gospel, had fallen out with each other after Paul left there, so that in his Epistle he begged them to be of the same mind, and begged some good brethren there to help them come to an agreement.

> Exhort the good women in the church, and the men, too, to make themselves servants of the church, but not to be ambitious for offices and especially for offices unknown to the apostles. ("Deaconess" 166)

It is most remarkable that McGarvey wrote these words in the pages of the *Standard*. Thus the first strong attack on deaconesses came at the same time that Disciples were solidifying thought and making official a split which had been developing between conservatives, moderates, and liberals for nearly half a century.

Is the absence of female deacons in twentieth century Churches of Christ the result of biblical or cultural forces? The following material will shed some light on that question. The author is indebted to Dr. Fred Bailey, historian and sociologist at Abilene Christian University, for suggesting this line of research.

American Women in the Nineteenth Century

The Colonial woman had more power in her society than did her nineteenth century counterpart. In the early years of our country, men outnumbered women, a situation which worked to the woman's advantage. This was especially true in frontier areas. Wives often worked outside of the home and won social approval for their resourcefulness. They were found in virtually every kind of employment including butchers, gunsmiths, jail keepers, journalists, and the medical professions (Lerner 183). As the frontiers stabilized, the sexual balance shifted. Victorian influences, religious movements and revivalism of the early nineteenth century tended to produce a male dominated society with a subsequent loss of female visibility. Women's work outside of the home no longer met with approval.

In 1800, the North and South were agriculturally based. Only six percent of the population lived in towns of 2,500 or more and only two cities, New York and Philadelphia, had more than fifty thousand inhabitants. Households were self supporting, producing internally all items essential for life. This was illustrated by the census of 1810 with the fact that ninety-six percent of all wool cloth was homespun - produced at home. The rapid developments of the northern industrial revolution changed this so that by 1830 middle class women of the Northeast were more interested in purchasing finished garments than in making cloth (Douglas 50+). The South, however, remained virtually unchanged. The Industrial Revolution did not come to the South until the close of the century.

The female social/philosophical/religious situation became known as "The Cult of True Womanhood." It held that women were judged by four cardinal virtues - piety, purity, submissiveness, and domesticity. Religion or piety was at the core (Welter 152). Female education was seen as primarily religious, and the irreligious female was most revolting (Welter 154). Whatever societal change a women desired, was made within the framework of her true womanhood, or she faced rejection by all.

The North. In the 1820-1860 period, the attitudes of the North and South and the activities of women in the two regions developed differently. The North was characterized by transcendentalism: rugged individualism, freedom from restraint, equality of sexes and breakdown of class structures (Bailey interview). The North urbanized faster than the agricultural South. As Douglas put it, by the 1850's, "women no longer married to help their husbands get a living, but to help them spend their income" (50). As families moved to the cities, traditional family ties were broken. Dependence in times of crisis was centered on friends and neighbors. In the industrial areas, sexual segregation encouraged gender-identification, and women sought purposeful social roles.

Douglas reported that the nineteenth century northern minister moved in a world of women. He preached mainly to women, and they formed the main body of mission and charity workers of the church. With the disestablishment of religion and the development of voluntary societies, he became very reliant on an increasingly active, assertive, and feminine congregation (97). During the Second Awakening (1795-1830), women, primarily under the age of thirty, comprised two-thirds of those joining New Jersey Presbyterian, New England Congregationalists, and Southern evangelical churches (Blauvelt 1). Women were considered naturally religious. It was a part of society's expectation for a woman to be the spiritual leader in the home. Because of propriety, women were compelled to recruit primarily female converts perpetuating female dominance in the church (Blauvelt 9).

These independent middle-class women developed networks: literary societies, orphan concerns, cultural societies, temperance movements, etc. They often spent their free time in humanitarian pursuits, including the abolition of slavery which was the life blood of the South. The church recognized the worth of its women because they often had the free time to do good works and provided the main work force for the church. Women were honored as spiritual leaders within the family by such expressions as, "mother's Bible." The men hardly had time for feminine religion (Bailey interview).

More women became involved in missionary activities after the Civil War than all other areas of social reform combined. Women formed foreign missionary societies in thirty-three denominations and home mission groups in seventeen denominations between 1861 and 1894:

> Women saw in the dedication of deaconesses, who ministered to the neediest and lowliest at home and abroad, a reflection of the ministry of Christ. By 1894, the thirty-three foreign mission societies had sent one thousand female missionaries abroad, most of whom were trained in deaconess homes of Protestant denominations. They served as teachers, evangelists, and physicians in schools, churches, and hospitals on every continent. A major focus of deaconesses' ministry in this country was to Christianize and Americanize the immigrants who crowded the inner cities. They also started schools, industrial homes, agricultural projects, and chapels on Indian reservations, in prairie towns, and in backwood settlements. (Keller 243)

Between 1870 and 1900, over one hundred forty deaconess homes were opened in the United States representing most of the major denominations. Some were interdenominational. After the Civil War, in addition to foreign mission work, deaconesses became very significant in immigrant ministries. The foreigners were branded "unchristian and ignorant masses" who threatened the stability of the country. Deaconesses were the key to evangelize and Americanize them, thereby saving the cities of the north (Keller 247).

The South. On the other hand, the South was an agricultural society following a patriarchal structure. Large areas were settled by related families which created unique kinship networks. One's neighbors who were often located some distance away were one's kin, and the factors of distance and family limited women's choices of relationships. When crisis hit, one relied on kin (Friedman 10). Since women were not rigidly segregated in the agrarian economy, the development of feminine culture was restricted. The woman's concern was for her family, not her own personal development (Friedman xii):

> Women's reform evolved much later in the South because modernization with its attendant women's culture, occurred in the later part of the nineteenth century. Rapid, intense economic growth did not figure in the preindustrial South; gradual self-sufficiency marked southern development. Because the South continued what was essentially an older agrarian and family oriented structural pattern, homosocial networks, or same-sex interaction, did not evolve and therefore southern antebellum women were deprived of a social basis for reform. Family

and kinship bonds, drawn tightly together in the local evangelical church, assumed primary importance in defining human relationships. (Friedman 7)

Churches were centered in rural farming communities where the patriarchs were also the church leaders. Southern churches were patriarchal, while northern churches were matriarchal. Southern husbands tended to view clergy as competitors for the allegiance of their spiritually minded wives. This sometimes created resentment of female religiosity (Blauvelt 5). Male control of evangelical family churches insured a double standard of church discipline which reinforced traditional sexual roles and deterred formation of independent women's organizations. Most religious associations were either sexually integrated or all male. Even the antebellum reform associations were primarily male (Friedman 9+):

> Because female association tended to follow the development of the market system, women's societies did not penetrate much beyond the port cities of the South and a few scattered towns in its interior. Even within the cities, community disapproval, as well as anti-abolition attitudes associated with feminism, limited the advance of systematic organization. For the most part, rural evangelical discipline controlled the role, attitude, and behavior of southern women.

> Outside the cities, the absence of an organized female network made women even more vulnerable to the frustrations and demands of traditional sex roles. (Friedman 32)

Anne Scott's *The Southern Lady* demonstrated the wide variation between the mythical romantic lady in the antebellum mansion and the harsh reality of plantation leadership. The wife alone was responsible for the happiness or misery of her husband:

> She must resolve at the outset never to oppose her husband, never to show displeasure, no matter what he might do. A man had a right to expect his wife to place perfect confidence in his judgment and to believe that he always knew best. (6)

> No matter what secret thoughts a woman might have about her own abilities, religion confirmed what society told her - namely, that she was inferior to men. (13)

Southern pulpits relied on Paul's writings to add scriptural support to this inferiority.

Obedience and subordination were key ideas to southern life. A man's children, servants, and wife were to respect him as the head of the household and bow to his wishes. In many situations he was a law unto himself with a different set of standards to live by than his household. The subordination of women and slaves often were considered in the same context. It should not be suprising that the most articulate spokesmen for slavery were also exponents of the subordination of women. The counter is also true - many of the strongest proponents of abolition were women (Scott Lady 17+). The orator, George Fitshugh, made it clear that he considered any change in the role of women or in slavery would result in the downfall of the family and the demise of society (Scott Lady 21).

The southern lady was responsible for the affairs of a complex household which often included slaves. Although the planter's wife did not work in the fields like the wife of the small farm owner, she did much of the spinning, weaving, and sewing. The son of a South Carolina slaveholder wrote of his mother:

> My mother spun, wove cloth, cooked and occasionally went to the cow pen to milk the cows, father plowed and drove the wagon, made shoes and did other work. My mother always seed to her cooking and did a good deal of it, had her spinning and weaving done for the whole plantation white and black, no cloth or negro shoes were bought whilst father and mother lived, father made his own negro shoes and mother made the clothes. (David Gavin Diary quoted in Scott Lady 30)

The mistress was expected to understand all of this plus gardening, care of poultry, care of the sick, and everything related to putting food on the table. She supervised the hog butchering, dried the fruits and vegetables for the winter, and made her own yeast, lard, and soap. And if this was not enough, she frequently arbitrated disputes between slaves and supervised their labor (Scott Lady 30+).

Working class women worked side by side with their husbands in the field and followed domestic jobs from planting through the completed product. Since slavery and class were important to economics, humanitarian concerns before the Civil War were self-defeating for those women who had time for outside activities. The elite women spent their time in parties, crafts, and other non-political pursuits (Bailey interview).

Women were encouraged to be teachers which was seen as an extension of the domestic function. They were considered more fitted for such a work than men. In 1888, sixty-three percent of all teachers were women, while the figure increased to ninety percent in urban areas (Lerner 189).

The key at the end of the century for the development of female activity was mission work. Although denominations generally fought the formation of women's missionary societies, their proven ability to raise money finally overcame the objections. By that time women were increasingly being accepted as foreign missionaries sponsored by women. The cry of "Women's Work for Women" became acceptable among the major denominations so that major cities develop women's aid societies, ladies benevolent and missionary societies, and similar groups (Friedman 113). The denominations encouraged women to be active in benevolent causes, but strongly opposed women's rights in any form. The Baptists agreed to female involvement in temperance crusades as long as they avoided feminist agitation and politics (Scott Lady 138). An interesting situation developed where women could report on their mission works from the pulpit, but were forbidden to preach. Of course this liberty led to abuse (Boles Interview). Most female groups originated in the North and were slowly accepted in major southern cities at the end of the century.

Another group which encouraged women's networks was the Women's Christian Temperance Union. Begun in the North many years earlier, the movement began to develop in the South in the 1880's. By this time some women in urban areas had the resources to work for reform. The W. C. T. U. promoted a broad spectrum of public work for women, including welfare, temperance education, and prison and almshouse reform. From these areas the reform spread to educational opportunities for women and children (Friedman 119). Suffrage societies also tapped into the network of the W. C. T. U. in the 1880's, but it was not until 1910 that suffrage gained full respectability in the South. Even then, the strongest argument was not for an improved status for women, but for a larger white vote (Friedman 120+).

Nineteenth Century Disciples Women

Bailey in his unpublished dissertation, *The Status of Women in the Disciples of Christ Movement, 1865-1900*, presented a glimpse of women in the Restoration Movement. This was the period when women could not vote, but were fighting for that right. In general, women's suffrage was not an issue in the movement and was not publicly supported.

Women began to gain admission to colleges and universities during this period, with David Lipscomb changing his mind during the period from being totally against female advanced education to encouraging it. Lipscomb, speaking at Daughters College in Waco, Texas, 1881, called coeducation "an experiment of doubtful propriety." In 1875 he stated that boys and girls should never be brought together "when they are large enough for the development of the animal or sexual impulses" (Bailey Status 188). In 1891, Lipscomb and James Harding opened the Nashville Bible School (now David Lipscomb College) and advertised that anyone, male or female, could attend. However, the classes for men were to train them in public ministry while the classes for females were to help them be better mothers. To him, females were designed by God to be the mistress of the classroom and mother in the nursery (Bailey Status 192).

Although not universally accepted, the Disciples' first female minister was Clara Babcock who began preaching for several small Illinois congregations in 1888 (Bailey Status 32). David Lipscomb wrote, "The habit of women preaching originated in the same [northern] hot bed with easy divorce, free love, and the repugnance to child bearing" ("Women Preach" 486). This statement was also a slap on the "Yankeeism" that the southern church came to detest. Although Lard wrote in favor of deaconesses, he solidly condemned women preaching (Lard "Speak" 1). When McGarvey was unsuccessful in banning women from his classes at Lexington Theological Seminary, he stipulated that they arrive after all the male students were seated, sit quietly on the back row, ask no questions, speak to no one, and leave before the rest of the class was dismissed (Stevenson 125 +).

In 1874 the Christian Woman's Board of Missions was organized and established many churches in American and foreign lands (Brown Churches 109, 163 +). These works paralleled the works of denominations during the same period.

Although Bailey's dissertation does not mention deacons or deaconesses, he certainly demonstrates that women would not be accepted in any kind of leadership role in the southern conservative wing of the movement. Women were to bear children, serve in domestic ways, and leave leadership and business to the male. Lipscomb stated (1892), "Women must teach their own children; must visit the sick, the afflicted, the needy, and in these quiet ministrations, teach the word of truth" ("Woman's Work" 756 +). He also affirmed (1874) that wives could teach their husbands and men as individuals privately, and should "teach those misguided women, who refused to bear children" ("Woman's Work" 305):

> Although they universally praised the potential of woman's maternity, liberal and conservative Disciples differed widely in the application of their beliefs. At century's end, church liberals embraced women preaching, casting the ballot, and engaging in various extradomestic reform projects. Conservatives looked upon each of those activities as a cancer threatening the destruction of the home. Essentially their differing interpretations of Alexander Campbell's restoration plea largely accounted for their dichotomous view of woman's role in society. (Bailey "Superiority" 156)

In the early days of the Restoration Movement, women did serve in a variety of capacities, including as deaconesses.   From this moderate position, the northern and southern churches moved in two opposing directions.   The northern churches gradually adopted an "anything goes" attitude while the southern churches restricted women from most activities except accepted domestic and teaching roles.

The Baptists, as a typical southern church, experienced the same withdrawal of women from service that the Disciples experienced. The earliest Baptists held an extreme doctrine of personal liberty and congregational autonomy which resulted in women preaching and serving as deaconesses. This was especially true in the 1600's (Martin 160).   As that denomination adapted to the Victorian culture and American way of life, the roles of women became less and less. Deaconesses were still active in the 1700's, but declined in the nineteenth century as the role of deacons changed to a primarily administrative function which required female submission (Deweese "Deaconess" 55). The Baptists' split in the 1800's as did most major religious groups, and southern Baptist women were often held with restraint because of their activism on abolition and suffrage (Martin 162). Deaconesses were a topic of controversy from the time of reconstruction until after the beginning of the twentieth century. A handful of deaconesses were mentioned in Texas, but their office was not comparable to the male deacon. They did not have congregation-wide leadership. The Baptist papers of the 1880's and 1890's de-emphasized the official nature and considered deaconesses to be the wives of deacons. Another view was that since women were already functioning in service areas, there would be no benefit in ordaining them as deaconesses (Martin 182+). This situation was not only true in Texas, but in Louisiana and Mississippi during the same period (Larry James). The woman's place was in the home, with submission and piety. The neglect of domestic duties was against her place in "true womanhood."

Female activities were restricted after the split between the northern and southern Methodist churches. With considerable debate, the Southern Methodist General Conference authorized a Woman's Board of Foreign Missions in 1878. This group rapidly grew so that twelve years later it owned property worth $200,000 and led ten boarding schools, thirty-one day schools, and a hospital. In 1902 that same board petitioned the General Conference to create the office of deaconess which was already successfully in use in northern and European branches of the denomination. After lengthy and acrimonious debate, deaconesses became a reality (Scott Lady 138+).

Social Sources of Denominationalism

Niebuhr postulates, "In general it may be said that the sects divided on the slavery issue and the churches divided on the political issue." He goes on to illustrate that the Baptists and Methodists divided before the Civil War, while the Presbyterians, Lutherans, and Episcopalians divided when secession took place (191). Regardless of the timing, most religious groups experienced a north-south split in the nineteenth century. Churches of Christ were not unique. The same issues affected most other groups.

Colonial Baptists and Methodists were prejudiced against education, especially for ministers. It was not unusual for a southern minister to have just one or two years of formal education. This did not mean one or two years of college work, but one or two years in all of his life. Still they might rank above the majority of white southerners. The prejudice against education gradually softened so that the groups began establishing church colleges in the mid-nineteenth century. Most early colleges in the United States were church schools; however, many groups looked askew at the well educated minister. The North accepted education faster than the south as views toward success changed (Loveland 25).

In the 1830's:

> Baptists were critical of those who would introduce choir singing, and they agreed with Presbyterians in opposing the intrusion of instrumental music into the worship. Evangelicals criticized such innovations not only on the ground that they were unscriptural - substituting "the inventions of men for the precepts of divine truth" - but also because they debased "a devotional exercise" into "a mere performance" or "entertainment." (Loveland 96)

The issues of educated professional staff, fine buildings, and items such as organs also underlined the economic issues involved. The more prosperous northern churches could more easily afford such embellishments.

Slavery was also a major issue. Northern churchmen condemned the inhumane institution. Southern churches countered by linking religious instruction to the justification of slavery. After all, if the slaves had not been brought to the South, they would have never learned the Gospel and been brought into the manifest destiny of America (Loveland 227). To free the slaves would be to expose them to worse evils that to retain them under gospel influences. Preachers could quickly show that many of the Old Testament heroes were themselves slave owners, and Paul had given his sanction of slavery by writing Philemon:

> Given the southern evangelical's insistence that the Bible sanctioned slavery, it is not surprising that they more and more tended to view the sectional controversy as a conflict between those who acknowledged the authority of the Bible and those who repudiated it. (Loveland 261)

Most women who wrote on the subject opposed slavery and were glad when it ended. Many wrote of their desire to relocate in a free state. Slaves were a "troublesome property." The mistress was their supervisor, teacher, doctor and minister. There was no privacy for the mistress of the house. Freedom for slaves was freedom for women. The support of slavery was primarily from the male population. However, for a southern woman to express this feeling too loudly was to go against her position of subordination and obedience (Scott Lady 46 +).

In general, northern churches were involved in broad social concerns: community responsibility, serving and reforming society, and seeking a perfect America. In the South, evangelism was seen as an individual thing not designed to reform society. Going to church was an all day event where widely scattered individuals assembled to court, gossip, and generally socialize (Boles interview). The North was busy reforming its society; the South was defending its way of life. The North pursued the new, the modern, and was known for its "isms", while the South defended its purity.

Sectional Concerns Among Disciples

A number of excellent studies have been produced detailing the history of the Disciples. A two part series by Richard Hughes in the *Restoration Quarterly* annotated many of them. These histories pointed out some of the differences that produced the split among Disciples. Hughes showed that there was a theological rupture built into Disciples' theology from the start: the impossible combination of ecumenism and restoration ("Theology"). Humble contended that the dilemma of restoration versus unity was compounded by sectionalism, Civil War bitterness, and social and economic differences between urban and rural Christians. David Harrell's contributions were the most thorough in developing the social factors that led to the division. He stressed that some social issues were more significant than the doctrinal ones.

It is simplistic to say that the major issues that split the Disciples were instrumental music and missionary societies. These were also issues of contention in the denominations. The split developed over a long period of time concerning a variety of issues, and the above disputed practices were expressions of entirely different ways of looking at life. Those ways of viewing life could be summed up in two words: North and South.

When the split was formally recognized in 1906, the division was remarkably geographic. Eighty-three percent of the members of Churches of Christ lived in the eleven former confederate states. Only fourteen percent of the Christian Church membership lived in those same states. The only state north of the Ohio River which had a Church of Christ membership in excess of five thousand was Indiana, and the Christian Church membership outnumbered them ten to one (Harrell Sources 325).

Politics played a large part. The slavery issue was seen as a biblical issue by both groups, but with very different results. A critical event took place at the American Christian Missionary Society Convention in Cincinnati in 1863. The convention, in the absence of many southern leaders, passed a resolution declaring unqualified support for the Government of the United States. The northern church was undeniably unionist, and the southern church was seceding (Harrell "Sectional" 268). Lipscomb and a number of other influential preachers in the South were pacifist during the Civil War. Although the southern churches sought to stay out of politics, the North wanted to contribute Christian leadership for the government. The high point of its contribution was James A. Garfield, preacher, author and statesman, becoming the Republican candidate for president in 1880 (Harrell Sources 26 +).

The papers of the movement also illustrated the division. In 1866, Isaac Errett founded the *Christian Standard* in Cincinnati. Lipscomb stated that the *Standard* was founded so that "loyal brethren" could have an outlet to express themselves on "the duty of Christians to support the government in its war upon the rebellion, its duty to punish traitors, and to express themselves on the infamy of slavery" ("Truth" 436). The *Gospel Advocate*, on the otherhand, resumed publication in 1866 from Nashville after a four year wartime interruption. David Lipscomb and Tolbert Fanning, editors, denounced the northern church. Errett wrote that the *Advocate*:

> . . . commenced its new issue with an appeal to men of southern blood, and proposed cooperation among them only. It has constantly denounced the brethren of the North who shared in the military defense of the government. ("Advocate" 52)

These publications along with others further polarized the churches. Another illustrative quote comes from the *Christian Evangelist* (1892):

> We know the doctrine advocated by them [writers in the *Standard*] comes from the North. It is neither scriptural nor Southern, and is not suited to Southern people. But it is the determination of the *Standard* and its Northern allies. . . to force the new things upon the churches of this section. (Burnett 472).

James Thornberry remarked that, "Mormonism, adventism, sanctificationism, spiritualism, women's rights, free love, and all such, started north of the Mason and Dixon's line" (89). Lipscomb added, "New England and the North are tenfold more given to irreligion and infidelity than the South" ("Preachers" 398).

The economy of the North and South became very different in the nineteenth century, and both sides were proud of their differences. The South remained a cultural unit in part because of the farming economy. The hero was the simple farmer. In the North, the successful businessman was the hero; success and godliness were often equated. These distinctions translated into dollars. For southern Churches of Christ, the average value of church property in 1936 was less than $3,000. The average for the northern Christian Church was nearly $16,000 (Harrell Sources 335). Lipscomb wrote, "For our part, we would much prefer membership with an humble and despised bank of ignorant negroes, than with a congregation of the aristocratic and refined whites of the land" ("Race" 121). The northern church, however, had targeted the upper classes in an attempt to become a respectable denomination. Harrell pointed out:

> All of the doctrinal issues involved in the division of the movement - organized mission work, instrumental music, the pastor system - required congregations to make a decision that concerned no only their faith but also their finances. ("Sectional" 273)

> The rising middle-class within the movement did demand a more sophisticated and socially responsible denomination. The poorer classes still saw religious truths in the same old dogmatic framework. (Sources 344)

The congregations of the South desired plain church buildings. They should be functional, but not extravagant. The churches of the North decided that the church building was an attraction and an honor to the Lord. They began desiring the best building in town, to the glory of God. The northerners increasingly linked American national interests, and success with God's providence. The United States was the promised land (Harrell Sources 23).

The southern church reacted against educated professional

preachers as did other southern denominations. The northern churches established colleges. The southern church felt that educational responsibilities lay with the local congregation. One southern writer called Bible colleges one of the four leading departures from the faith. Even when Lipscomb founded his own school in 1891, he tried to clarify that it was not a theological school and it would not teach philosophy (Harrell Sources 338+). That attitude towards the words "theology" and "seminary" remain in christian education today. The links between money, the business world, urban life, and education were inseparable.

> Harrell summarizes the sectional differences:
>
> Conservative and liberal theological positions, Northern and Southern sectional feeling, urban and rural prejudices, and agricultural and middle-class economic views were all important ingredients in the nineteenth-century fracturing of the movement. Every Disciples periodical and every Disciples minister during these critical years represented not simply a theological position but a describable mixture of one or another of these clashing viewpoints. The twentieth-century Churches of Christ are the spirited offspring of the religious rednecks of the post bellum South. ("Sectionalism" 277)

Explanations

Considering the above material, several issues explain the absence of female deacons in Churches of Christ:

1. Deaconesses matched the sociology of the North. They did not fit the structure of the South. All American deaconess movements, reform movements, women's networks, and missionary societies originated in the North. The northern church was matriarchal while the southern church was patriarchal. When the split took place between the Christian Church and the Churches of Christ, deaconesses logically fell into the northern camp.

2. As with any divorce, lines were drawn over property rights, and new definitions of identity were formed. Since the Christian Church advocated reform and women's rights, the Churches of Christ reacted with rejection. Southerners threw the baby out with the bathwater. Had the split not forced a stand, attitudes may have remained more flexible.

3. The split was not only cultural, but hermeneutical. As B. J. Humble recognized, "the goals of unity and restoration, complementary in theory, proved to be antagonistic in practice" (22). The Christian Church accepted silence as liberty; Churches of Christ took silence as restrictive. The Christian Church sought unity; Churches of Christ sought purity. Since διακονος meant "servant" unless the con-

text indicated otherwise, the bias of southern culture made it virtually impossible to prove that the church should have deaconesses. Southerners knew that a woman's place was in the home, therefore Phoebe could not have been a deacon in the church. Since Phoebe could not have been a deacon, they found no example of a women being a deacon in the scripture. They reasoned that if God had wanted female deacons, He would certainly have given qualifications in scripture, but since 1Tm. 3:11 could not be those qualifications since women could not be deacons, qualifications do not exist. Since there were no deaconesses or qualifications in the scripture, there should be none in the pure restored church. Unfortunately the conclusion reached by this circular argument was also its major premise.

Scripture is usually interpreted through the eyes of culture. It was that way in the first century, and shall remain so as long as man lives. No man is totally objective, completely unbiased. Mike Casey's unpublished dissertation, The *Development of Necessary Inference in the Hermeneutics of the Disciples of Christ/Churches of Christ*, points out that the elevation of necessary inference to binding authority for doctrinal purposes with direct commands comes to the fore with the instrument and missionary society split as a means of justifying the position of non-instrumentalists. Campbell begins his movement denying the validity of inference, but later adopts it as the tensions between the inclusive idea of Christian union and the exclusive idea of Restoration grows. At the time of the split in the movement, both conservatives and moderates use inference to justify their positions, but with different beginning assumptions. The same cultural and rhetorical influence on restoration hermenteutics is visible in the question of the deaconess.

Thus a northern Christian, accustomed to the activity of women, saw female "deacons" as official. The southern Christian, not comfortable with women in the fore, could only see domestic duties in the lives of "servants." It is this writer's opinion that the absence of deaconesses in Churches of Christ is more a result of cultural reaction than of biblical exegesis.

The contemporary situation is almost a repeat of one hundred years ago. However, the sociological issues are divided between the urban and rural communities of the South. Many rural areas remain male dominated and family structured. Women frequently maintain domestic roles. The less educated offspring remain in the rural setting while the better educated move to the big cities. The major urban areas experience a greater equality of women. Many young women hold professional positions and are equally educated with their male co-workers. Domestic duties are handled between husband and wife with extended family ties being very disjointed. A disturbing number of families are single parent, and the provider is the mother. The social networks of the urban southern woman of today resemble the networks of the northern woman of the last century. The cries for women's equality and the renewed study of women's work in the church come primarily from the major urban centers. If history repeats itself, the next division will be between the urban and the rural sociological groups.

Summary

Like her religious neighbors, Churches of Christ have failed to distinguish between having female deacons and having female preachers. The memberships have generally confused the meaning of service with the authority of an office. It will be interesting to observe the debate that will continue to intensify among Churches of Christ over the two distinct but related issues of women's work and ecclesiastical authority. Hopefully the leaders will have the wisdom to avoid the same damaging splits of a century ago.

PART FOUR

CONTEMPORARY IMPLICATIONS

CHAPTER 12

Conclusions

In reading the New Testament, one gets the impression that Christians did not think in terms of clergy and laity, of sacred persons and sacred places. Everything is sacred, and every person was a minister, an integral part of a priesthood of believers. Titles of hierarchy and distinctions of primacy or rank are out of place. Submission to God and to one another is the frequent theme. The emphasis is on service, of which διακονος was the key word. Barnett describes the situation well:

> Most Christians today seem to have little sense of being an integral and important part of a community - a caring, loving family - which needs each one in all of his or her uniqueness to be whole. This means among much else that far fewer people are actively participating in the Church's work. Much of the Church's ministry goes undone. (Barnett 6)

> As Jesus himself had worked within the system, the primitive Church continued to do so. It regarded the whole system as essentially valid, continuing to worship in the Temple, attend the synagogues, and keep the Law. It formed no revolutionary party but saw its mission as being sent to call the whole of Israel into the Church, the true Israel of God. . . . It was only natural at the outset that the primitive Church was not greatly concerned with questions of organization and structure. . . . The answers to most questions about the nature of the ministry are not answered directly by the New Testament. (Barnett 7+)

> Making "sacred persons" of the clergy is not commensurate with the revelation in Christ wherein the distinctions between the sacred and the secular of the old Israel are abolished and the unity of all creation is affirmed. In like manner, the shift from a Church whose ministry encompassed all its people, each with a special function, like the organs of the body, for the good of the whole, to a Church whose ministry was one of ascending grades characterized by rank, status, and power is to be found wanting when tested by the revelation in Christ. (Barnett 10)

Schweizer agrees:

> Fundamentally the New Testament knows no distinction between ministry and office. . . . The concept of office is today even fuller than in New Testament times, and is laden with the content that it has acquired in the secular sphere. . . . Even the special designations of individual ministries were by no means uniform. Only in the case of "elders" and perhaps "bishops" was there a comparable ministry in the Jewish community; but neither has any ceremonial function, and both are also used in a non-technical sense. Other functions like "pastors," "evangelists," "catechists," are purely functional terms. (25a+)

Bromiley looks at leadership from a theological perspective. He sees a threefold service: The elder is primarily a minister of the word; the deacon is a minister of action; and the bishop is a minister of rule. He writes:

> What is essential and indispensable, however, is that the threefold work of the ministry should be done, that its exercise should take this threefold form, and that the orders adopted should be best calculated to provide a balanced and harmonious and effective, although always relative and reformable, concretion of the three basic aspects. (82)

> Diaconate covers the practical activity of the congregation in the provision of facilities, the financing of operations, corporate concern for the temporal needs of members, the undertaking of medical or general educational services where necessary and the contribution of the church to social well-being. . . . Much of the work will be relatively small and humdrum. . . . The particular structure of diaconate is not decisively important, and it may be adapted to varying needs and circumstances. (84)

> Only too often a scheme is allowed to grow out of date and thus to burden the church and its ministry with hampering archaisms. . . . The church is in many ways a stabilizing factor, and it does not seek change or novelty merely out of restlessness and dissatisfaction. It is a spiritual stability which gives it dynamic in relation to the externals upon which it does not need to rest. . . . It will always be quick to make the adjustments or even the radical rearrangements which are necessary to the discharge of its threefold ministry. (85)

Although the writer of this book is influenced by the application of the church fathers and historians, he is drawn back to the Scriptures for his primary conclusions. However, this complicates rather than clarifies the question at hand. The New Testament books are written over a period of forty years to a variety of cultures and to churches in various stages of development. Not all churches appear to have the same organization, and one must ask at what point in that development he wishes to stop and establish a reference for study? No deacons, male or female, (or any other "officers" unless you so define Apostles) are apparent on Pentecost when the church was established. The leadership structure evolves based on the spiritual gifts of early Christians and the needs of their assemblies. This is especially significant as the church spreads from Jerusalem and the apostles in time, distance, and culture:

> The difficulty comes really from forgetting that the early church was an organic growth: we are apt to expect to find already precisely formulated at a very primitive stage structures and offices that only developed gradually in response to circumstances and needs. It seems safer to start from the assumption that the diaconate developed gradually. (Nowell 40 +)

Likewise Robinson sums up the situation concisely:

> It was only after the lapse of some considerable time, when the need arose of

organizing and defining the different kinds of service which the church required, that the word διακονια became restricted to a special form of ministry, and those to whom such service was entrusted, whether men or women, were called Deacons. . . . The institutions of the church were not given to her ready made, but were developed gradually on certain great principles, in response to the needs of her corporate life. (3+)

The following is apparent for deacons in the New Testament:

1) In some churches a group of early Christian servants were recognized for their service by the word διακονος.

2) The group included male and female servants.

3) The servants were under the oversight/leadership of the elders/shepherds of the local church and may have been primarily assistants to those overseers. No job description was given.

4) Those "officially" recognized for their service were outstanding examples of Christian character (1Tm. 3).

5) No instructions were given for the method of selection, "ordination" or appointment, or tenure of this special group.

6) Evidence is insufficient to show that deacons were a recognizable group of special servants in every mature congregation.

7) Evidence is insufficient to illustrate that deacons were ordained to an office in the church; rather the emphasis was on function.

8) Current thoughts of celibacy and communal life for a clergy class were unknown in the New Testament.

Vischer wisely cautions:

The processes involved are too complicated and the sources too few for the exegete to speak with certainty. He remains true to his task only if, after completing a most thorough investigation, he expresses great reserve. (19)

Concerning the Seven in Jerusalem, this writer sees them as a unique group produced for a particular historical situation. They were neither elders nor deacons in a sense recognizable today.

By the middle of the second century, the diaconate developed into a church office. By A.D. 200 a pyramid structure had settled into the form of bishop, presbyter, and deacon, but, in the first century one did not see a well defined diaconate. Since the offices of the monarchial bishop and the deacon developed simultaneously, one should be very cautious in calling one essential and the other anathema.

In trying to make some conclusions, it is necessary to remember that a lot is not known. To quote Brown:

> Our knowledge of local supervision during Paul's lifetime is quite limited. Among the things we do not know are the following: Did the local leaders at the various Pauline churches differ in terms of the authority they exercised and the roles they played? Did they all have titles and were the titles uniform? Was theirs a true office held for a set or long period of time? What precisely did they do? Were they appointed by Paul, or were they elected by the local community, or did they come forward feeling themselves to be possessors of a charism? ... We do not know how such figures as prophets, teachers, and administrators were interrelated in the supervision of a community. ("επισκοπη" 329)

For some Christians, selecting women to the diaconate is against the concept of women being in subjection (1Tm. 2:12). It is not the purpose of this book to decide the role of women in the church, but an example of another female function in the church might be in order. The New Testament speaks of male and female prophets in the early church (Ac. 21:9), that is male and female spokespersons. A sign of the arrival of the kingdom is, "your sons and daughters will prophesy" (Ac. 2:17). Antioch is led by prophets and teachers, as if the work of a prophet has some official credibility. Philip, one of the Seven, has four daughters who were prophets. Paul in 1Co. 11 makes it clear that a female with the gift of prophesy is not freed from the limitations placed on women in her society. She is to exercise her function with the proper veiling and attitude to demonstrate her subjection. The Scripture recognizes male and female prophets, but cautions against abuses of their gifts that would render them ineffective.

The same situation existed for female deacons:

> The deacon is in the serving office, one not inherently involving teaching or ruling. Thus even if we grant that Phoebe was a church deacon, the New Testament has still not placed her in the ruling or teaching office. Many churches who hold to the apostolic prohibition on teachers and rulers have ordained women as deaconesses. (Knight 19)

> I believe a differentiation in the order is manifested, affected by a recognition of the prohibitions of 1Tm. and 1Co. When the order is essentially ministerial, then both women and men are naturally included. There is no restriction here. However, as the order takes on a specifically hierarchical character, then a differentiation is established in the order. (Rand 372)

> There has never been any mention of women filling strictly sacerdotal offices. We never see a woman offering the Eucharistic Sacrifice, or ordaining, or preaching in the Church. On the other hand, all Christian history - and particularly in the first centuries - shows that women have played a considerable part in missionary work, in worship and in teaching. (Danielou 7)

Throughout history, male and female deacons have the same function - serving - but with different groups and methods in mind. Patristic writers make it clear that women serve groups that men cannot, and vice versa. The consideration is how to serve most effectively. Early restoration writers teach the subjection of women alongside the need for deaconesses in the church. A need always exists for male and female servants of the church serving within the parameters which society, sex, and Scripture demonstrate most appropriate. Generally speaking, women have always been more limited in their ministry by society and scriptural interpretation.

Many Churches of Christ are currently studying the diaconate. One well known congregation in Texas has wrestled with the material and its elders have come to the following conclusion:

All of the eldership and staff were in basic agreement that:

1. There were certainly deaconesses in the New Testament period and for several centuries thereafter.

2. Since it has been largely unplowed ground for 1200 years, we probably cannot make any sudden moves without causing widespread consternation.

3. There is a troubling incongruity in our claiming to be people who "do Bible things in Bible ways, and call Bible things by Bible names" and yet finding ourselves unable to make the slogan a reality.

4. We cannot leave the matter unaddressed. Teaching must begin immediately at every level to change the perceptions of our brethren that what they regard as a dangerous "innovation" is, in fact, simply a return to the primitive church.

The elders requested anonymity at this time because of the sensitive nature of this study.

The final conclusion is that one cannot be dogmatic about deacons and deaconesses. If a church wants male deacons, have them. Philippi and Ephesus did. And those deacons can do whatever the elders feel proper since no definite guidelines are given. If the church does not want deacons, that is equally acceptable, as the majority of New Testament churches are not described as having them. However, it is a disservice to the word "deacon" (and to the church) to have deacons who are not serving - non-serving servants. The church does not need members wearing titles in order to conform to an apostolic pattern.

If the church wants female deacons or deaconesses, have them. Cenchrea and Ephesus, and possibly Philippi, did. Female deacons can do whatever the elders feel proper within the boundaries of female propriety. If the church does not want females as deacons, that is permissible too as most New Testament churches are not mentioned as having them. However, using a functional approach, it is inconsistent to recognize male servants without recognizing female servants.

Finally, if the church wants to use another designation for its servants, it should feel free to do so. It is sound translation to call them servants, ministers, stewards, waiters, or even more specific terms such as bakers, messengers, cooks, or maids, if the tasks warrant those designations. "Deacon" is burdened with a load of ecclesiastical baggage that requires translation for all inquirers, churched and unchurched alike.

A lot has been made of two passages where men are said to be deacons and two more passages where women serve in that capacity. Too many churches are overly concerned about finding and following a pattern of scriptural organization and too little concerned about catching the spirit of service.

The words of Isaac Errett in the *Christian Standard* of 1873 serve as a fitting conclusion:

> We come to the New Testament as if it were a book of positive laws and statutes on these questions, and expect to find all officers mentioned by name, with their duties carefully specified and the details of their official work minutely described. The truth is, that much we are seeking for is conveyed in the form of narrative - of history, and not of statute. There was not much that was formal and precise in the order of the primitive churches. The officer existed and the work was done before the office was formally recognized and named, and these officers come into notice rather casually, just as circumstances and emergencies require. It is altogether likely, therefore, that women (and men) ministered unofficially in the first place, as circumstances required; that the household of Stephanas were self-appointed to their ministry; that Phoebe had become, in a similar way, active in the service of the church to which she belonged; that there was no authoritative limitation to their duties, or special name for their office, but a devotion of their talents to any work of benevolence or necessity that did not war against existing apostolic instructions; and that after their work had grown into permanency the apostles gave instructions to regulate its performance. ("Deaconesses" 188)

The person who serves to become a deacon, serves for the wrong reason. The person who serves because he is a deacon, also serves wrongly. Worse yet is the person who does not serve because he is not a deacon. The only real deacons are the humble, unselfish, transparent servants who naturally imitate the loving ministry of their Lord.

The question is not, "Does this church have deacons?" It is rather, "Are the individuals who make up this body of believers serving in the name of Christ?"

CHAPTER 13

The New Testament Pattern

Churches of Christ teach that the New Testament reveals a pattern for the organization and operation of the church. This concept of "patternism" merits some examination. If a pattern is present, it should be followed. But what constitutes a pattern?

> Deacons are needed now because the office is an inseparable part of the New Testament church pattern. "New Testament pattern" is a phrase that should be particularly meaningful to us, who like to call our churches New Testament churches and assert that we would not hold membership in any other kind of church. It is our firm conviction that a church should discover its doctrines, determine its organization, define its procedures, and catch its commission in the pages of the New Testament. (Naylor 5)

Most readers would "amen" this quote which comes from the *The Baptist Deacon.* The problem is that the Baptist "pattern" is different from that of Churches of Christ even though based on the same scriptures.

The pattern that no church is complete without deacons resulted because two churches had deacons: Philippi and Ephesus. Whether that was sufficient evidence to establish a universal pattern is for the individual to decide. Other patterns of church organization did exist.

The Jerusalem church was led by apostles and elders. That was the group that met to discuss how to treat Gentile converts (Ac. 15:2, 4, 6, 22, 23; 16:4). Prophets led in Jerusalem (Ac. 11:27; 21:10), but they may not have had a decision-making position. When benevolent money was sent to Jerusalem, it was sent to the elders (Ac. 11:30), and this is after the discussion of the Seven. No mention was made of deacons in Jerusalem or the book of Acts. The letter which results from the Jerusalem conference may have indicated that the elders of Jerusalem had authority in a much wider geographic region. Some scholars have called them the Christian Sanhedrin (Schweizer 24i).

One must question what the role of James was within that church. James summarizes the Jerusalem conference after all have spoken (Ac. 15:13 +), and he is the one who composed the final ruling by stating, "It is my judgment, therefore. . ." (Ac. 15:19+). Paul refers to him as an Apostle (Ga. 1:19). Is James officially an Apostle, is he an elder, or does he hold some other special position in the church?

Antioch, which scholars assume was one of the better developed congregations outside of Jerusalem, was led by prophets and teachers (Ac. 13:1). It was this group that commissioned Paul and Barnabas to ministry.

It was Paul's usual pattern to appoint elders in the churches he established (Ac. 14:23; 20:17; Tit. 1:5). No mention was made of deacons in these key passages. Leaders were called elders in some churches and bishops in others. Possibly elders came from the Jewish background while bishops and deacons came from the Greek - a reaction to the existing cultural structures.

The exact role and authority of the evangelist is uncertain (Ac. 21:8; 2Tm 4:5) as is the role and authority of the prophet (Ac. 11:27; 13:1; 15:32; 21:9; 1Co. 12:28-29; 14:29-32, 37; Ep. 2:20; 3:5; 4:11). Some writers interpret the evangelist's authority as being superior to that of the elders (Tit. 1:5). One should question whether current preachers should presume to be evangelists in the same sense as those with apostolic appointment and charismatic gifts. Are the terms "prophet" and "evangelist" simply descriptive terms and not official titles?

1 Corinthians 12:28 + and Ep. 4:11 + give lists of gifted servants and leaders in the church. Elders and deacons appear in neither list, and those lists vary slightly from each other. It is difficult to state definitely that one group of leaders compose a pattern to be followed forever while the others are temporary positions or simply functions within the church.

How many of Churches of Christ accept the pattern in 1Tm. 5 of setting up a special group of widows over sixty who are supported by the church? Qualifications are given for those widows just as for elders and deacons. The early Christian documents demonstrate that such a group was common. Many people probably explain that this practice was custom, or that Social Security eliminates the need for enrolled widows. Can similar arguments be used to explain away deacons?

Hans Kung is right when he states: "Thus the New Testament community displays a great variety; the different offices are not yet clearly and strictly distinguished as they are today - a development that took place much later" (207).

Much of the "pattern" is based on an assumption that the contemporary church can "do Bible things in Bible ways and call Bible things by Bible names." But most churches would admit that they can not and do not want to re-live the life of the first century church. Our churches are far different from those of the first century and have a multiplicity of specialized church structures, outreach services, and modern technologies.

The early church in most communities met in homes. The congregations did not have sizable facilities, if any. Nor did they have located preachers. The members knew each other because they all lived in the same geographic community, probably within a one or two mile radius. Commuting twenty miles in a car and passing five other congregations in the process was unknown. The elders were the community patriarchs. Most of the members were related to one of those patriarchs because families stayed together to live on and work the same land. The situation was more akin to the rural South of the 1900's or third world lands today than to contemporary urban America.

When someone was a shut-in, a "Shut-in Ministry" was not needed because he was the relative of a number of members and lived with those members. Jerusalem was probably an exception because of its metropolitan nature and its religious significance which attracted the aging. The "Building and Grounds Ministry" did not exist, nor did the "Communications Ministry," "Computer Ministry," "Audio-Visual Ministry," etc. Finances were simple since budgets were not required to pay for insurance, mortgages, staff, advertising, or the myriad of other items required in the twentieth century. Much giving was probably in the form of sharing possessions and supplies directly with those in need rather than giving money to a common treasury. America's giving patterns have been affected greatly by tax laws. The leadership of the local church was tailored to the needs of that community and was adapted from cultural roles already in existence in civic and religious organizations.

The question for today is whether a normative pattern of polity can be discovered and frozen in time or whether the church is to remain flexible to its environment. History shows that the church in Rome froze the diaconate for centuries, limiting the number of deacons to seven according to the pattern they saw in Acts 6.

In the days before the Industrial Revolution, most people were general practicioners. However, the last 150 years has produced a society of specialists. Kitchens are getting smaller while fast food restaurants are springing up everywhere. Prepared microwave meals are flourishing. Home mechanics are turning their automobiles over to the "Quick Change" and "Tune Up" specialists. Institutions rear the family children. Reading is giving way to the video cassettes and computers for instruction and entertainment. Many activities are measured in neat brief blocks of time.

Ministry within the church has the same specialization. The days when there was an ever ready corps of unemployed female volunteers to do whatever is needed is gone. Long term weekly activities such as visitation groups or Wednesday classes compete with a myriad of community and home functions. Members serve in very specialized ways. They do not volunteer but must be drafted. They want to limit their service commitment to a specific, often brief, span of time. If the church is to tap its service potential, it must either change the attitudes of its members, or, more likely, adapt its ministry to the changes in society.

The ministry team concept added new qualifications to the diaconate, changing the pattern. First century deacons were, as the word derivation suggests, humble servants or table waiters. They were doers, not overseers.

Deacons in modern ministry team leadership should primarily be administrators, not doers. If the deacon in charge of the "Benevolent Ministry" does all the benevolent work, no teamwork is developed. The ideal team leader is one who can motivate and organize his team members to do the work and who can recruit others to join in that team's activities. A doer deacon/team-leader can kill a ministry team. Ministry team churches add new qualifications to those listed in 1Tm. 3: "A deacon must be an organizer, motivator, and recruiter." Often more authority is implied in the contemporary diaconate than in the New Testament example, and deacons are organized following current business practices. This adds complexity to the female deacon discussion that is not present in the original service orientation.

As the monarchial bishop developed through the first three centuries, the roles of deacons changed. Churches of Christ rejected most of those developments as unbiblical, while contemporary adaptations to culture (i.e. ministry teams) have been accepted.

The "pattern," if the strict traditional biblical understanding is accepted, would limit the diaconate to those in table service (fellowship ministry), shut-in ministry, or financial concerns. Deacons in charge of audio-visuals, Boy Scouts, building and grounds, communications, etc., must be considered "unbiblical" in light of the New Testament "pattern." However, if the "pattern" is an example and is flexible, then the extent of that adaptation is up to the individual congregation and will not be uniform in all settings.

This flexibility extends into what the servant is called. "Deacon" is a non-translation of the Greek word for "minister" or "servant." Congregations sometimes call their elders by other legitimate English translations: "shepherds" and "bishops." Few Churches of Christ refer to them as "presbyters," "poimens," or the "episcopacy," all of which are anglicized Greek words used of the elders' situation. So why should the church not have "ministers" or "servants" instead of "deacons?" The main reason is to maintain the identity of a unique ecclesiastical office. The more colloquial "minister" or "servant" more nearly conveys to us what διακονος would have conveyed to the first century world, yet even those translations might be outdated for contemporary urban vocabulary. A change in nomenclature could free the church to be more concerned about service and less concerned about the authority of an office, thereby catching the spirit of Jesus.

Looking back at the attempts in the 1830's to unite the movements of Campbell and Stone, these leaders held many things in common but differed on others. They disagreed on what name their adherents should wear and the nature of Jesus (or the doctrine of the Trinity). Campbell preferred "Disciples"; Stone preferred "Christians." Stone attacked Calvinistic Trinitarianism; the Campbells were pronounced Trinitarians:

> But happily they soon came to see that it was wholly a speculative matter that did not pertain either to human salvation or Christian living, and that it should not be made a test of fellowship among disciples of Christ, nor of controversy among brethren - that it should be relegated to the realm of opinion and every individual left free to hold such opinions on the subject as might seem to each one to be most in accord with Scripture teaching and human reason. (Brown Churches 79)

Both believed that Jesus Christ was the only begotten Son of God, that He died for our sins, was buried, and rose on the third day.

Stone and Campbell have set a real pattern, a pattern of unity in diversity without sacrificing the validity of the scriptures. In years to come, one congregation will have no deacons, another will have deacons, and another will have deacons male and female. Hopefully, these congregations will respect the autonomy of each other and the attempts of the leaderships to be true to the Word in their ministry for God. Hopefully, they all will be known for their loving service in the example of Jesus. Hopefully, their internal organization will not be an end in itself, but a transparent tool releasing the gifts of the Spirit for service.

"Jesus called them together and said, 'You know that those who are regarded as rulers of the Gentiles lord it over them, and their high officials exercise authority over them. No so with you. Instead, whoever wants to become great among you must be your διακονος, and whoever wants to be first must be slave of all. For even the Son of Man did not come to be served, but to serve, and to give his life as a ransom for many.'"

Mark 10:42+

APPENDICES

Διακονος **in the New Testament**

A. Church Office

Phl. 1 [1] Paul and Timothy, servants of Christ Jesus, To all the saints in Christ Jesus at Philippi, together with the overseers and *deacons*: [2] Grace and peace to you from God our Father and the Lord Jesus Christ.

1Ti. 3 [8] *Deacons*, likewise, are to be men worthy of respect, sincere, not indulging in much wine, and not pursuing dishonest gain. [9] They must keep hold of the deep truths of the faith with a clear conscience. [10] They must first be tested; and then if there is nothing against them, let them serve as deacons. [11] In the same way, their wives are to be women worthy of respect, not malicious talkers but temperate and trustworthy in everything. [12] A *deacon* must be the husband of but one wife and must manage his children and his household well. [13] Those who have served well gain an excellent standing and great assurance in their faith in Christ Jesus.

B. Διακονος **applied to Jesus**

Ro. 15 [7] Accept one another, then, just as Christ accepted you, in order to bring praise to God. [8] For I tell you that Christ has become a *servant* of the Jews on behalf of God's truth, to confirm the promises made to the patriarchs [9] so that the Gentiles may glorify God for his mercy.

Ga. 2 [17] "If, while we seek to be justified in Christ, it becomes evident that we ourselves are sinners, does that mean that Christ *promotes* sin? Absolutely not!

C. Διακονος **applied to Paul**

2Co. 3 [4] Such confidence as this is ours through Christ before God. [5] Not that we are competent to claim anything for ourselves, but our competence comes from God. [6] He has made us competent as *ministers* of a new covenant - not of the letter but of the Spirit; for the letter kills, but the Spirit gives life.

2Co. 6 [3] We put no stumbling block in anyone's path, so that our ministry will not be discredited. [4] Rather, as *servants* of God we commend ourselves in every way: in great endurance; in troubles, hardships and distresses; [5] in beatings, imprisonments and riots; in hard work, sleepless nights and hunger; [6] in purity, understanding, patience and kindness; in the Holy Spirit and in sincere love.

2Co. 11 [22] Are they Hebrews? So am I. Are they Israelites? So am I. Are they Abraham's descendants? So am I. [23] Are they *servants* of Christ? (I am out of my mind to talk like this.) I am more.

Ep. 3 [7] I became a *servant* of this gospel by the gift of God's grace given me through the working of his power. [8] Although I am less than the least of all God's people, this grace was given me: to preach to the Gentiles the unsearchable riches of Christ, [9] and to make plain to everyone the administration of this mystery, which for ages past was kept hidden in God, who created all things.

Col. 1 [23b] This is the gospel that you heard and that has been proclaimed to every creature under heaven, and of which I, Paul, have become a *servant*. [24] Now I rejoice in what was suffered for you, and I fill up in my flesh what is still lacking in regard to Christ's afflictions, for the sake of his body, which is the church. [25] I have become its *servant* by the commission God gave me to present to you the word of God in its fullness.

D. Διακονος applied to specific individuals (not Paul or Christ)

Ro. 16 [1] I commend to you our sister Phoebe, a *servant* of the church in Cenchrea. [2] I ask you to receive her in the Lord in a way worthy of the saints and to give her any help she may need from you, for she has been a great help to many people, including me.

1Co. 3 [5] What, after all, is Apollos? And what is Paul? Only *servants*, through whom you came to believe - as the Lord has assigned to each his task.

Ep. 6 [21] Tychicus, the dear brother and faithful *servant* in the Lord, will tell you everything, so that you also may know how I am and what I am doing.

Col. 1 [6] All over the world this gospel is producing fruit and growing, just as it has been doing among you since the day you heart it and understood God's grace in all its truth. [7] You learned it from Epaphras, our dear fellow servant, who is a faithful *minister* of Christ on our behalf, [8] and who also told us of your love in the Spirit.

Col. 4 [7] Tychicus will tell you all the news about me. He is a dear brother, a faithful *minister* and fellow servant in the Lord. [8] I am sending him to you for the express purpose that you may know about our circumstances and the he may encourage your hearts.

1Th. 3 [1] So when we could stand it no longer, we thought it best to be left by ourselves in Athens. [2] We sent Timothy, who is our brother and God's *fellow worker* in spreading the gospel of Christ, to strengthen and encourage you in your faith, [3] so that no one would be unsettled by these trials.

1Tm. 4 [6] If you point these things out to the brothers, you will be a good *minister* of Christ Jesus, brought up in the truths of the faith and of the good teaching that you have followed.

E. Διακονος as model of all Christians

Mt. 20 [25] Jesus called them together and said, "You know that the rulers of the Gentiles lord it over them, and their high officials exercise authority over them. [26] Not so with you. Instead, whoever wants to become great among you must be your *servant*, [27] and whoever wants to be first must be your slave - [28] just as the Son of Man did not come to be served, but to serve, and to give his life as a ransom for many."

Mt. 23 [10] Nor are you to be called 'teacher,' for you have one Teacher, the Christ. [11] The greatest among you will be your *servant*. [12] For whoever exalts himself will be humbled, and whoever humbles himself will be exalted.

Mk. 9 [35] Sitting down, Jesus called the Twelve and said, "If anyone wants to be first, he must be the very last, and the *servant* of all."

Mk. 10 [42] Jesus called them together and said, "You know that those who are regarded as rulers of the Gentiles lord it over them, and their high officials exercise authority over them. [43] No so with you. Instead, whoever wants to become great among you must be your *servant*, [44] and whoever wants to be first must be slave of all. [45] For even the Son of Man did not come to be served, but to serve, and to give his life as a ransom for many."

Jn. 12 [23] Jesus replied, "The hour has come for the Son of Man to be glorified. [24] I tell you the truth, unless a kernel of wheat falls to the ground and dies, it remains only a single seed. But if it dies, it produces many seeds. [25] The man who loves his life will lose it, while the man who hates his life in this world will keep it for eternal life. [26] Whoever serves me must follow me; and where I am, my *servant* also will be. My Father will honor the one who serves me.

F. Misc. use of Διακονος

Mt. 20 at the parable of the wedding banquet, [13] "Then the king told the *attendants*, 'Tie him hand and foot, and throw him outside, into the darkness, where there will be weeping and gnashing of teeth.'"

Jn. 2 [5] His mother said to the *servants*, "Do whatever he tells you." [6] Nearby stood six stone water jars, the kind used by the Jews for ceremonial washing, each holding from twenty to thirty gallons. [7] Jesus said to the servants, "Fill the jars with water"; so they filled them to the brim. [8] Then he told them, "Now draw some out and take it to the master of the banquet." They did so, [9] and the master of the banquet tasted the water that had been turned into wine. He did not realize where it had come from, though the *servants* who had drawn the water knew.

Ro. 13 [3] For rulers hold no terror for those who do right, but for those who do wrong. Do you want to be free from fear of the one in authority? Then do what is right and he will commend you. [4] For he is God's *servant* to do you good. But if you do wrong, be afraid, for he does not bear the sword for nothing. He is God's *servant*, an agent of wrath to bring punishment on the wrongdoer.

2Cor. 11 [13] "For such men are false apostles, deceitful workmen, masquerading as apostles of Christ. [14] And no wonder, for Satan himself masquerades as an angel of light. [15] It is not surprising, then, if his *servants* masquerade as *servants* of righteousness. Their end will be what their actions deserve."

Deacons in Post New Testament Literature

(Arranged in Chronological Order)

I Clement (of Rome, c. A.D. 100, 42), "And thus preaching through countries and cities, they appointed the first fruits (of their labors), having first proved them by the Spirit, to be bishops and *deacons* of those who should afterward believe. Nor was this any new thing, since indeed many ages before it was written concerning bishops and *deacons*. For thus saith the Scripture in a certain place, 'I will appoint their bishops in righteousness, and their *deacons* in faith.'" (The quote is a modification of Isa. 60:17, from the Septuagint)

Didache (c. A.D. 100, 15), "Elect therefore for yourselves bishops and *deacons* who are worthy of the Lord, men who are meek, not lovers of money, true and tested. For they minister to you the service of the prophets and teachers. Do not look down on them, for they are your honored men along with the prophets and teachers."

Ignatius (A.D. 107, *Ephesians* 2), "As to our fellow-servant Burrhus, your *deacon* in regard to God and blessed in all things, I pray that he may continue blameless for the honor of the Church and or your most blessed bishop."

Ignatius (A.D. 107, *Philadelphians* 4), "For there is one flesh of the Lord Jesus Christ; and His blood which was shed for us is one; one loaf also is broken to all, and one cup is distributed among them all: there is but one altar for the whole Church, and one bishop, with the presbytery and *deacons*, my fellow servants. . . . Let governors be obedient to Caesar; soldiers to those that command them; *deacons* to the presbyters, as to high priests; the presbyters, and *deacons*, and the rest of the clergy, together with all the people, and the soldiers, and the governors, and Caesar (himself), to the bishop; the bishop to Christ, even as Christ to the Father. And thus unity is preserved throughout."

Ignatius (A.D. 107, *Philadelphians* 7), "For when I was among you, I cried, I spoke with a loud voice - the word is not mine, but God's - give heed to the bishop, and to the presbytery and *deacons*."

Ignatius (A.D. 107, *Polycarp* 6), "Give heed to the bishop in order that God may also to you. I am devoted to those who are submissive to the bishop, presbyters, and *deacons*, and may I have a part with them in God."

Ignatius (A.D. 107, *Trallians* 2), "It behooves you also, in every way, to please the *deacons*, who are *ministers* of the mysteries of Christ Jesus; for they are not ministers of meat and drink, but servants of the Church of God. They are bound, therefore, to avoid all grounds of accusation, as they would a burning fire. Let them, then, prove themselves to be such."

Ignatius (A.D. 107, *Trallians* 3), "Likewise all are to respect the *deacons* as Jesus Christ, even as the bishop is a type of the Father, and the presbyters are as the council of God and as the college of apostles. Apart from these it is not called a church."

Ignatius (A.D. 107, *Trallians* 7), "And do ye also reverence your bishop as Christ Himself, according as the blessed apostles have enjoined you. He that is within the altar is pure, wherefore also he is obedient to the bishop and presbyters: but he that is without is one that does anything apart from the bishop, the presbyters, and the *deacons*. Such a person is defiled in his conscience, and is worse that an infidel."

Ignatius (A.D. 107, *Smyraeans* 8), "All of you follow the bishop, as Jesus Christ does the Father, and the presbytery as the apostles, and respect the *deacons* as the commandment of God. No one should do anything which pertains to the church without the bishop."

Ignatius (A.D. 107, *Smyrnaeans* 10), "Ye have done well in receiving Philo, and Gaius, and Agathopus, who, being the *deacons* of Christ, have followed me for the sake of God, and who greatly bless the Lord in your behalf, because ye have in every way refreshed them."

Ignatius (A.D. 107, *Smyrnaeans* 12), "I salute your most worthy bishop Polycarp, and your venerable presbytery, and your Christ-bearing *deacons*, my fellow-servants, and all of you individually, as well as generally, in the name of Christ Jesus, and in His flesh and blood. . . ."

Ignatius (A.D. 107, *Smyrnaeans* 13), "Greetings to the families of my brethren, including their wives and children, and to the virgins who are enrolled among the widows."

Ignatius (A.D. 107, *Magnesians* 2), "Since, then, I have had the privilege of seeing you, through Damas your most worthy bishop, and through your worthy presbyters Bassus and Apollonius, and through my fellow-servant the *deacon* Sotio, whose friendship may I ever enjoy, in as much as he, by the grace of God, is subject to the bishop and presbytery, in the law of Jesus Christ."

Ignatius (A.D. 107, *Magnesians* 6), "Since therefore I have, in the persons before mentioned, beheld the whole multitude of you in faith and love, I exhort you to study to do all things with a divine harmony, while your bishop presides in the place of God, and your presbyters in the place of the assembly of the apostles, along with your *deacons*, who are most dear to me, and are entrusted with the ministry of Jesus Christ."

Ignatius (A.D. 107, *Magnesians* 7), "As therefore the Lord does nothing without the Father, for says He, 'I can of mine own self do nothing,' so do ye, neither presbyter, nor *deacon*, nor layman, do anything without the bishop. Nor let anything appear commendable to you which is destitute of his approval."

Ignatius (A.D. 107, *Magnesians* 13), "Study, therefore, to be established in the doctrines of the Lord and the apostles, that so all things, whatsoever ye do, may prosper, both in the flesh and spirit, in faith and love, with your most admirable bishop, and the well compacted spiritual crown of your presbytery, and the *deacons* who are according to God. Be ye subject to the bishop, and to one another, as Christ to the Father."

Pliny (A.D. 112, *Letters*, Book 10:96:8, addressed to the Emperor Trajan), "I judged it so much the more necessary to extract the real truth, with the assistance of torture, from two female slaves, who were styled *deaconesses*; but I could discover nothing more than depraved and excessive superstition."

Hermas (c. A.D. 120, *Visions* 3:5), "The stones which are square, white, and fit into their joints are the apostles, bishops, teachers, and *deacons*, who walked according to the holiness of God and did the work of overseeing, teaching, and *serving* the elect of God purely and piously."

Hermas (c. A.D. 120, *Visions* 2:4), "You will write therefore two books, and you will send the one to Clemens and the other to Grapte (a *deaconess*). And Clemens will send his to foreign countries, for permission has been granted to him to do so. And Grapte will admonish the widows and the orphans."

Hermas (c. A. D. 120, *Similitude* 9:26), "And they who believed from the ninth mountain, which was deserted, and had in it creeping things and wild beasts which destroy men, were the following: they who had the stains as *deacons*, who discharged their duty ill, and who plundered widows and orphans of their livelihood and gained possessions for themselves from the ministry which they had received."

Polycarp (c. A.D. 155, *Philippians* 5), "Likewise the *deacons* are to be unblameable before his righteousness as *servants* of God and Christ and not of men. They are not to be slanderers, double tongued, nor lovers of money, but self-controlled in all things, compassionate, attentive, walking according to the truth of the truth of the Lord, who became the *servant* of all. . . . Wherefore it is necessary that. . . you be subject to the elders and *deacons* as to God and Christ. . . ."

Polycarp (c. A.D. 155, *Philippians* 4), "Widows are to observe discretion as they practice the Lord's faith; they should make constant intercession for everyone, and be careful to avoid all tale-bearing, spiteful tittle-tattle, false allegations, overeagerness for money, or misconduct of any description. They are to recognize that they are an altar of God, who scrutinizes every offering laid on it."

Justin Martyr (A.D. 155, *Apology* 1:67, speaking of the Lord's Supper observance), "Next we all rise together and send up prayers. And, as I said before, when we cease from our prayer, bread is presented and wine and water. The president in the same manner sends up prayers and thanksgivings according to his ability, and the people sing out their assent saying the 'Amen.' A distribution and participation of the elements for which thanks have been given is made to each person, and to those who are not present it is sent by the *deacons*."

Clement of Alexandria (A.D. 180-200, *Instructor* 3:12:97), "Innumerable such commands have been written in the holy books with reference to chosen persons, some to presbyters, some to bishops and *deacons*, others to widows."

Clement of Alexandria (A.D. 180-200, *Miscellanies,* 6:13:106; 107), "It is possible even now for those who have exercised themselves in the Lord's commandments and have lived perfectly and knowingly according to the Gospel to be enrolled in the elect body of the apostles. Such a person is truly a presbyter of the church and a true *deacon* of the will of God, if he do and teach the things of the Lord. He has not been ordained by men, nor regarded righteous because a presbyter, but enrolled in the presbyterate because righteous. . . . The grades here in the church, of bishops, presbyters, *deacons*, are in my opinion imitations of the angelic glory."

Clement of Alexandria (A.D. 180-200, *Miscellanies* 3:12:90), "Indeed Paul altogether accepts the man who is husband of one wife, whether he be presbyter, *deacon*, or layman, if he conducts his marriage unblameably."

Clement of Alexandria (A.D. 180-200, *Miscellanies* 7:1:3), "Similarly also in the church the elders preserve the most excellent part and the *deacons* the ministerial."

Clement of Alexandria (A.D. 180-200, *Stromata* 3:6:53), "The women whom. . . the apostles. . . took around with them were not wives but, as befitted the apostles' dedication to an undistracted preaching ministry, sisters, fellow ministers to the women who kept house. So the Lord's teaching made its way into the women's quarters too, and in a manner above reproach; for we know what the honorable Paul in one of his letters to Timothy prescribed regarding *female deacons*."

Irenaeus (c. A.D. 185, *Against Heresies*, 1:26:3), "The Nicolaitanes are the followers of that Nicolas who was one of the seven first ordained to the *diaconate* by the apostles."

Irenaeus (c. A.D. 185, *Against Heresies*, 3:12:10) "And still further, Stephen, who was chosen the first *deacon* by the apostles, and who, of all men, was the first to follow the footsteps of the martyrdom of the Lord, being the first that was slain for confessing Christ, speaking boldly among the people, and teaching them, says. . . . "

Tertullian (A.D. 208-217, *On Monogamy*, 11), "Grant, now, that you marry 'in the Lord,' in accordance with the law and the apostle - if, notwithstanding, you care even about this - with what face do you request (the solemnizing of) a matrimony which is unlawful to those of whom you request it: of a monogamist bishop, of presbyters and *deacons* bound by the solemn engagement, of widows, whose order you have in your own person refused?"

Tertullian (A.D. 208-217, *On Prescription against Heretics* 41:5), "And the women of these heretics, how wanton they are! For they are bold enough to teach, to dispute, to enact exorcism, to undertake cures - maybe even to baptize."

Tertullian (A.D. 208-217, *On the Veiling of Virgins* 9:1), "It is not permitted to a woman to speak in church. Neither may she teach, baptize, offer, nor claim for herself any function proper to a man, least of all the sacerdotal office."

Tertullian (A.D. 208-217, *On the Veiling of Virgins* 9:2-3), "I know plainly that in a certain place a virgin less than twenty years old has been placed in the order of widows! Whereas if the bishop has been bound to accord her any relief, he might, of course, have done it in some other way without detriment to the respect due to discipline, that such a miracle, not to say monster, should not be pointed at in the church, a virgin-widow! The more portentous, indeed, that not even as a widow did she veil her head, denying herself either way: both as a virgin, in that she is counted a widow, and as widow, in that she is styled a virgin. By the authority which licenses her sitting in that seat uncovered is the same which allows her to sit there as a virgin: a seat to which not merely 'single husbanded' (women) - that is, married women - are at length elected, but mothers to boot, yes, and educators of children; in order that their experimental training in all the affections may, on the one hand, have rendered them capable of readily aiding all others with counsel and comfort, and that, on the other, they nonetheless have traveled down the whole course of probation whereby a female can be tested. So true it is that, on the ground of her position, nothing in the way of public honor is permitted to a virgin."

Tertullian (A.D. 208-217, *Exhortation to Chastity* 13:4), "How many men and how many women in ecclesiastical 'orders' owe their position to the practice of continence! They have preferred to be wedded to God; they have restored their flesh in its first dignity and have already dedicated themselves as sons of the other world by slaying in themselves desire, the fruit of lust, in everything which could not be admitted within Paradise. . . . How detrimental to faith, how obstructive to holiness second marriages are, the discipline of the church and the prescription of the Apostle declare when he does not allow men twice married to preside (over a church), when he would not grant a widow admittance into the order unless she had been the wife of only one man."

Hippolytus (c. A.D. 215, *Apostolic Tradition* 9), "But the *deacon*, when he is chosen according to those things that were said above, the bishop alone in like manner laying his hands upon him, as we have prescribed. When the *deacon* is ordained, this is the reason why the bishop alone shall lay his hands upon him: he is not ordained to the priesthood but to serve the bishop and to carry out the bishop's commands."

Hippolytus (c. A.D. 215, *Apostolic Tradition* 11), "When a widow is appointed, she is not ordained but she shall be chosen by name. But if she lost her husband a long time previously, let her be appointed. But if she lately lost her husband, let her not be trusted. And even if she is aged, let her be tested for a time, for often the passions grow old with him who give place for them in herself. Let the widow be instituted by word only and let her be reckoned among the (enrolled) widows. But she shall not be ordained, because she does not offer the oblation nor has she a (liturgical) ministry. But the widow is appointed for prayer, and this is of all Christians."

Hippolytus (c. A.D. 215, *Apostolic Tradition* 21), "At the hour set for the baptism the bishop shall give thanks over oil and put it into a vessel: this is called the 'oil of thanksgiving.' And he shall take other oil and exorcise it: this is called 'the oil of exorcism.' A *deacon* shall bring the oil of exorcism, and shall stand at the presbyter's left hand; and another *deacon* shall take the oil of thanksgiving, and shall stand at the presbyter's right hand. Then the presbyter, taking hold of each of those about to be baptized, shall command him to renounce, saying: 'I renounce thee, Satan, and all thy servants and all thy works.' And when he has renounced all these, the presbyter shall anoint him with the oil of exorcism, saying: 'Let all spirits depart from thee.' Then, after these things, let him give him over to the presbyter who baptizes, and let the candidates stand in the water, naked, a *deacon* going with them likewise."

Hippolytus (c. A.D. 215, *Apostolic Tradition* 25-27, speaking of the Lord's Supper), "And if the faithful should be present at a supper without the bishop, but with a presbyter or *deacon* present, let them similarly partake in orderly fashion. But let every one be careful to receive the blessed bread from the hand of the presbyter or *deacon*."

Clement (A.D. 220, *To James* 12), "Moreover let the *deacons* of the church, going about with intelligence, be as eyes to the bishop, carefully inquiring into the doings of each member of the church ascertaining who is about to sin, in order that, being arrested with admonition by the president, he may haply not accomplish the sin. Let them check the disorderly, that they may not desist from assembling to hear the discourses, so that they may be able to counteract by the word of truth those anxieties that fall upon the heart from every side, by means of worldly casualties and evil communications; for if they long remain fallow, they become fuel for the fire. And let them learn who are suffering under bodily disease, and let them bring them to the notice of the multitude who do not know of them, that they may visit them, and supply their wants according to the judgment of the president. Yea, though they do this without his knowledge, they do nothing amiss. These things, then and things like to these, let the deacons attend to."

Didascalia Apostolorum (A.D. 220-240, 2:26), "Let the bishop. . . be honored by you as God, the *deacon* is with you as a type of Christ, so let him be loved by you. Let the *deaconess* be honored by you as a type of the Holy Spirit. Let the presbyters be looked on by you as a type of the apostles."

Didascalia Apostolorum (A.D. 220-240, 2:28), "But let them [the people] have free access to the *deacons*, and let them not be troubling the head at all times, but making known what they require through the ministers, that is through the *deacons*. For neither can any man approach the Lord God Almighty except through Christ. All things therefore that they desire to do, let them make known to the bishop through the *deacons*, and then do them."

Didascalia Apostolorum (A.D. 220-240, 2:28), "But how much silver is given to one of the widows, let the double be given to each of the *deacons* in honor of Christ, twice two-fold to the leader for the glory of the Almighty. But if anyone wish to honor the presbyters also, let him give them a double portion as to the *deacons*."

Didascalia Apostolorum (A.D. 220-240, 2:44), "Let the bishops and the *deacons*, then, be of one mind; and do you shepherd the people diligently with one accord. For you ought both to be one body, father and son; for you are in the likeness of the Lordship. And let the *deacon* make known all things to the bishop, even as Christ to His Father. But what things he can, let the *deacon* order, and all the rest let the bishop judge. Yet let the *deacon* be the hearing of the bishop, and his mouth and his heart and his soul; for when you are both of one mind, through your agreement there will be peace also in the Church."

Didascalia Apostolorum (A.D. 220-240, 2:57), "But of the *deacons* let one stand always by the oblations of the Eucharist; and let another stand without by the door and observe them that come in; and afterwards, when you offer, let them minister together in the church. And if anyone be found sitting out of his place, let the *deacon* who is within reprove him and make him to rise up and sit in a place that is meet for him. . . so likewise in the Church ought those who are young to sit apart, if there be room, and if no to stand up; and those who are advanced in years to sit apart. And let the children stand on one side, or let their fathers and mothers take them apart; but if there be no room, let them stand up behind the women. . . . And let the *deacon* see that each of them on entering goes to his place, that no one may sit out of his place. And let the *deacon* also see that no one whispers, or falls asleep, or laughs, or makes signs."

Didascalia Apostolorum (A.D. 220-240, 3:8), "Widows ought then to be modest, and obedient to the bishops and the *deacons*, and to reverence and respect and fear the bishop as God. And let them not act after their own will, nor desire to do any thing apart from that which is commanded them, or without counsel to speak with any one by way of making answer, or to go to any one to eat or drink, or to fast with any one, or to receive aught of any one, or to lay hand on and pray over any one without the command of the bishop or the *deacon*. . . . But if you obey not the mind of the bishops and *deacons*, they indeed will be quit of your offenses, but you shall render an account of all that you do of your own will, whether men or women."

Didascalia Apostolorum (A.D. 220-240, 3:12), "Those that please thee [bishop] out of all the people thou shalt choose and appoint as *deacons*: a man for the performance of the most things that are required, but a woman for the ministry of women. For there are houses whither thou canst not send a *deacon* to the women, on account of the heathen, but mayest send a *deaconess*. Also, because in many other matters the office of a *woman deacon* is required. In the first place when women go down into the water, those who go down into the water ought to be anointed by a *deaconess* with the oil of anointing; and where there is no woman at hand, and especially no *deaconess*, it is not fitting that a woman should be seen by men: but with the imposition of hands do thou anoint the head only. . . . And when she who is being baptized has come up from the water, let the *deaconess* receive her, and teach and instruct her how the seal of baptism ought to be (kept) unbroken in purity and holiness. For this cause we say that the ministry of a *woman deacon* is especially needful and important. For our Lord and Savior also was ministered unto by women ministers, Mary Magdalene, and Mary the daughter of James and mother of Jose, and the mother of the sons of Zebedee, with other women beside. . . . And thou also have need of the ministry of *deaconess* for many things; for a *deaconess* is required to go into the houses of the heathen where there are believing women, and to visit those who are sick and to minister to them in that of which they have need, and to bathe those who have begun to recover from sickness."

Didascalia Apostolorum (A.D. 220-240, 3:13), "Now the *deacons* shall be like in their conversation to the bishop: but laboring yet more shall they labor, far more abundantly than he. And they shall not be lovers of filthy lucre; but they shall be zealous in ministration: and according to the number of the multitude of the people of the church, so shall the *deacons* be that they may be able to distribute and relieve every one; so that to aged women that are infirm, and to brothers and sisters that are in sickness, to every one of them they shall provide the ministration that is right for him. But a woman the rather shall be zealous in the ministration to the women, and a man *deacon* in the ministration to the men. And let him be ready to obey and to submit himself to the command of the Bishop; and to any place that he is sent to minister not to say anything to any man, let him be laboring and toiling. For it is necessary that everyone one should know his place and be zealous to fill it. And be you of one counsel and of one purpose, and one soul dwelling in two bodies. And know what the ministry is, according as our Lord and Savior said in the Gospel: Whoso among you desireth to be chief, let him be your servant: even as the Son of Man came not to be ministered unto, but to minister and to give his life a ransom for many. So ought you the *deacons* also to do, if it fall to you to lay down your life for your brethren in the ministry which is due to them. . . . If then our Lord did thus, will you, O *deacons*, hesitate to do the like for them that are sick and infirm, you who are workmen of the truth, and bear the likeness of Christ. Do you therefore minister with love, and neither murmur nor hesitate; otherwise you will have ministered as it were for men's sake and not for the sake of God, and you will receive your reward according to your ministry in the day of judgment. It is required of you *deacons* therefore that you visit all who are in need, and inform the bishop of those who are in distress: and you shall be his soul and his mind; and in all things you shall be taking trouble to be obedient to him."

Origen (c. A.D. 240, *Romans* 10:17, commenting on Ro. 16:1-2), "This text teaches with the authority of the apostle that even *women* are instituted *deacons* in the Church. This is the function which was exercised in the church of Cenchreae by Phoebe, who was the object of high praise and recommendation by Paul. . . . And thus this text teaches at the same time two things: that there are, as we have already said, *women deacons* in the Church, and that women, who have given assistance to so many people and who by their good works deserve to be praised by the Apostle, ought to be accepted in the *diaconate*."

Cyprian (A.D. 249, *Epistle* 41:1, 4), "We have read, dearest brother, asking and desiring us to write again to you, and say what we thought of those virgins who, after once determined to continue in their condition, and firmly to maintain their continency, have afterwards been found to have remained in the same bed side by side with men; of whom you say that one is a *deacon;* . . . you have acted advisedly and with vigor, dearest brother, in excommunicating the *deacon* who has often abode with a virgin; and moreover, the others who had been used to sleep with virgins."

Cyprian (A.D. 249, *Epistle* 64:3, to Rogatianus, concerning the deacon who contended against the bishop), "But *deacons* ought to remember that the Lord chose apostles, that is, bishops and overseers; while apostles appointed for themselves *deacons* after the ascent of the Lord into heaven, as ministers of their episcopacy and of the Church. But if we may dare anything against God who makes bishops, *deacons* may also dare against us by whom they are made; and therefore it behoves the *deacon* of whom you write to repent of his audacity, and to acknowledge the honor of the priest, and to satisfy the bishop set over him with full humility. For these things are the beginnings of heretics, and the origins and endeavors of evil-minded schismatics.

Cyprian (A.D. 250, *On the Lapsed*, 25), "When, however, the solemnities were finished and the *deacon* began to offer the cup to those present, and when, as the rest received it, its turn approached, the little child by the instinct of the divine majesty, turned away its face, compressed its mouth with resisting lips and refused the cup. Still the *deacon* persisted and, although against her efforts, forced on her some of the sacrament of the cup."

Council of Elvira (A.D. 305, Canon 33), "Bishops, presbyters and *deacons* - indeed, all clerics who have a place in the ministry (of the altar) - shall abstain from their wives and shall not beget children - this is a total prohibition: whoever does so, let him forfeit his rank among the clergy."

Council of Arles (A.D. 314, Canon 18), "Concerning the city *deacons*, that they take not so much upon themselves but preserve to the presbyters their order, that they do nothing without the presbyters' knowledge."

*Council of Neo-Caesare*a (A.D. 315, Canon 15), "The *deacons* ought to be seven in number, according to the canon, even if the city be great. Of this you will be persuaded from the Book of Acts."

Eusebius (A.D. 324, *Ecclesiastical History* 2:1), "First, then, in the place of Judas the traitor, Matthias was chosen by lot, who, as was shown above, was also one of the disciples of the Lord. There were appointed also, with prayer and the imposition of hands, by the apostles, approved men, unto the office of *deacons,* for the public service; these were those seven of whom Stephen was one."

Eusebius (A.D.324, *Ecclesiastical History* 6:43), writing about a large council called by Novatus, around A.D. 250, "A very large council being held on account of this, at which sixty indeed of the bishops, but a still greater number of presbyters and *deacons* were present."

Eusebius (A.D.324, *Ecclesiastical History* 6:43), speaking of the church in Rome c. A.D. 250, under Pope Cornelius, "This assertor of the Gospel then did not know that there should be but one bishop in a catholic church. In which, however, he well knew (for how could he be ignorant?) that there were forty-six presbyters, seven *deacons*, seven *sub-deacons*, forty-two acoluthi (clerks), exorcists, readers, and janitors, in all fifty-two: widows, with the afflicted and needy, more than fifteen hundred; all which the goodness and love of God doth support and nourish."

Isodorus (June 6, 324, legal petition cited by Judge), "To Dioskorus Kaiso, superintendent of the fifth district, from Isodorus, son of Ptolemaios from the village of Karanis in your district. The livestock of Pamounis and Harpalos trampled down | a crop I have and moreover their cow grazed a second time in the same place so that my work became useless. I seized the cow and was leading it to the village when they met me in the | fields with a large stick, knocked me to the ground, beat me up and took away the cow, as the injuries on me show, and if I had not (by chance) found help from Antonios, *diakon*, | and Isak, *monachos,* who came along, they would probably have done me in. I therefore lodge this document asking for them to be brought before you and both in respect of the crop and of the assault for my claim to be kept for the | prefectural count. . . ."

Aurelius Besis (c. A.D. 325, deacon contract with bishop, cited in Horsley 80), "T o Ammonotheon, bishop. . . , greetings. Since today I was ordained [into your] | diaconate and made a public profession to you that I should be inseparable from your bishopric, because of this I agree by this document [not] to forsake you, nor to transfer [to the service of another?] bishop or presbyter or [cleric], | [unless] you assent to it because of my [making the agreement] on these terms. If I want to leave [without your consent] and/or without a written [release, let me be unable] to retain the diaconate [under you, but merely] hold lay fellowship with dignity (?). [I have arranged] | this document with you for [security] and - may it not happen - if I do this I [will be] liable to the matters determined between us. And in answer to the question, [I have agreed]. And I am not allowed to share in [the eucharist?]. . . unless. . . | to the aforesaid. . . I, Aurelius Besis, the aforesaid, have had the aforesaid document made and agreed as aforesaid. [I] Aurelius Hierakion [wrote] on his behalf [since he is illieerate]. Mesore 12th."

First Council of Nicaea (A.D. 325, Canon 3), "The great Synod has stringently forbidden any bishop, presbyter, *deacon*, or any one of the clergy whatever, to have a *subintroducta* dwelling with him, except only a mother, or sister, or aunt, or such persons only as are beyond all suspicion."

First Council of Nicaea (A.D. 325, Canon 18), "It has come to the knowledge of the holy and great Synod that, in some districts and cities, the *deacons* administer the Eucharist to the presbyters, whereas neither canon nor custom permits that they who have no right to offer should give the Body of Christ to them that do offer. And this also has been made known, that certain *deacons* now touch the Eucharist even before the bishops. Let all such practices be utterly done away, and let the *deacons* remain within their own bounds, knowing that they are the ministers of the bishop and the inferiors of the presbyters. Let them receive the Eucharist according to their order, after the presbyters, and let either the bishop or the presbyter administer to them. Furthermore, let not the *deacons* sit among the presbyters, for that is contrary to canon and order. And if, after this decree, any one shall refuse to obey, let him be deposed from the *diaconate.*"

First Council of Nicaea (A.D. 325, Canon 19), "Concerning the Paulianists who have flown for refuge to the Catholic Church, it has been decreed that they must by all means be rebaptized; and if any of them who in past time have been numbered among their clergy should be found blameless and without reproach, let them be rebaptized and ordained by the Bishop of the Catholic Church; but if the examination should discover them to be unfit, they ought to be deposed. Likewise in the case of their *deaconesses,* and generally in the case of those who have been enrolled among their clergy, let the same form be observed. And we mean by *deaconesses* such as have assumed the habit, but who, since they have no imposition of hands, are now to be numbered only among the laity."

Epiphanius of Salamis (A.D. 350, *Panarion* 79:3), "If women had been appointed to act as priests on behalf of God, or to perform official liturgical acts in the church, it must surely have come about that Mary herself, who received the privilege of carrying in her bosom the Sovereign King, the heavenly God, God's Son, would in the New Testament have exercised the priestly office. But she did not judge such action to be right. She was not even entrusted with the bestowal of Baptism, since the Christ himself was baptized not by her but by John."

Epiphanius of Salamis (A.D. 350, *Panarion* 79:4), "Never has a woman been appointed amongst bishops and priests. But someone will say, there were the four daughters of Philip, who prophesied. Yes, but they did not exercise the priestly office. Although there is an Order of *deaconesses* in the Church, yet it is not for priestly service, not to undertake anything of the sort, but on account of the modesty of the female sex with a view to either the occasion of Baptism, or of inspection of illness, or of suffering and when the woman's body is bared, so that it may not be seen by the men officiating, but by the *deaconess*, who is directed by the priest to see to the woman when her body is bared. . . they are only women-elders, not priestesses in any sense, that their mission was not to interfere in any way with Sacerdotal functions, but simply to perform certain offices in the care of women. . . . Women had never been allowed to offer sacrifices, as the Collyrideans presume to do, but were only allowed to minister. Therefore, there were only *deaconesses* in the church."

Canons of Basil (A.D. 370, Canon 24), "A widow put into the catalog of widows, that is, a *deaconess* being sixty years old, and marrying, is not to be admitted to communion of the Good Thing, till she cease from her uncleanness; but to a widower that marries no penance is appointed, but that of digamy. If the widow be less than sixty, it is the bishop's fault who admitted her *deaconess*, not the woman's."

Testament of Our Lord (c. A.D. 375), cites the proclamation of the *deacon*, "Let us arise; let each know his own place. Let the catechumens depart. See that no unclean, no careless person is here. Lift up the eyes of your hearts. Angels look upon us. See, let him who is without faith depart. Let no adulterer, no angry man be here. If anyone be a slave of sin let him depart. See, let us supplicate as children of the light. Let us supplicate our Lord and God and Savior Jesus Christ."

Apostolic Constitutions (c. A.D. 375, 2:25), "For these (bishops) are your high priests, as the presbyters are your priests, and your present *deacons* instead of your Levites; as are also your readers, your singers, your porters, your *deaconesses*, your widows, your virgins, and your orphans: but He who is above all these is the High Priest."

Apostolic Constitutions (c. A.D. 375, 2:26), "For let the bishop preside over you as one honored with the authority of God, which he is to exercise over the clergy, and by which he is to govern all the people. But let the *deacon* minister to him, as Christ does His Father; and let him serve him unblameably in all things, as Christ does nothing of Himself, but does always those things that please His Father. Let also the *deaconess* be honored by you in the place of the Holy Ghost, and not do or say anything without the *deacon;* as neither does the Comforter say or do anything of Himself, but gives glory to Christ by waiting for His pleasure. And as we cannot believe on Christ without the teaching of the Spirit, so let not any woman address herself to the *deacon* or bishop without the *deaconess*."

Apostolic Constitutions (c. A.D. 375, 2:28), "But let them not on all occasions trouble their governor [bishop], but let them signify their desires by those who minister to him, that is, by the *deacons*, with whom they may be more free. For neither may we address ourselves to Almighty God, but only by Christ. In the same manner, therefore, let the laity make known all their desires to the bishop by the *deacon*, and accordingly let them act as he shall direct them."

Apostolic Constitutions (c. A.D. 375, 2:30), "For now the *deacon* is to you Aaron, and the bishop Moses. If, therefore, Moses was called a god by the Lord, let the bishop be honored among you as a god, and the *deacon* as his prophet. For as Christ does nothing without His Father, so neither does the *deacon* do anything without his bishop; and as the Son without His Father is nothing, so is the *deacon* nothing without his bishop; and as the Son is subject to His Father, so is every *deacon* subject to his bishop; and as the Son is the messenger and prophet of the Father, so is the *deacon* the messenger and prophet of his bishop. Wherefore let all things that he is to do with anyone be made known to the bishop, and be finally ordered by him."

Apostolic Constitutions (c. A.D. 375, 2:44), "And let the *deacon* refer all things to the bishop, as Christ does to His Father. But let him order such things as he is able by himself, receiving power from the bishop, as the Lord did from His Father the power of creation and of providence. But the weighty matters let the bishop judge; but let the *deacon* be the bishop's ear, and eye, and mouth, and heart, and soul, that the bishop may not be distracted with many cares, but with such only as are more considerable, as Jethro did appoint for Moses, and his counsel was received."

Apostolic Constitutions (c. A.D. 375, 2:57), "When thou (bishop) callest an assembly of the Church as one that is the commander of a great ship, appoint the assemblies to be made with all possible skill, charging the *deacons* as mariners to prepare places for the brethren as for passengers with all due care and decency. And first, let the building be long, with its head to the east, with its vestries on both sides at the east end so it will be like a ship. In the middle let the bishop's throne be placed, and on each side of him let the presbytery sit down; and let the *deacons* stand near at hand, in close and small girt garments, for they are like the mariners and managers of the ship. . . . Let the porters stand at the entries of the men, and observe them. Let the *deaconesses* also stand at those of the women, like shipmen. . . . let the *deacon* oversee the people, that nobody may whisper, nor slumber, nor laugh, nor nod; for all ought in the church to stand wisely, and soberly, and attentively, having their attention fixed upon the word of the Lord. . . . As to the *deacons*, after the prayer is over, let some of them attend upon the oblation of the Eucharist, ministering to the Lord's body with fear. . . ."

Apostolic Constitutions (c. A.D. 375, 2:58), "If any brother, man or woman, come in from another parish, bringing recommendatory letters, let the *deacon* be the judge of that affair, inquiring whether they be of the faithful and of the church. . . . Nay, if a poor man, or one of a mean family, or a stranger, comes upon you, whether he be old or young, and there be no place, the *deacon* shall find a place for even these, and that with all his heart; that instead of accepting persons before men, his ministration towards God may be well-pleasing. The very same thing let the *deaconess* do to those women, whether poor or rich, that come unto them."

Apostolic Constitutions (c. A.D. 375, 3:7), "The widows therefore ought to be grave, obedient to their bishops, and their presbyters, and their *deacons*, and besides these to the *deaconesses*, with piety, reverence, and fear; not usurping authority, nor desiring to do anything beyond the constitution without the consent of the *deacon*; as, suppose, the going to any one to eat or drink with him, or to receive anything from anybody."

Apostolic Constitutions (c. A.D. 375, 3:11), "We do not permit presbyters to ordain *deacons*, or *deaconesses*, or readers, or ministers, or singers, or porters, but only bishops; for this is the ecclesiastical order and harmony."

Apostolic Constitutions (c. A.D. 375, 3:15), "For which reason, O bishop, do thou ordain thy fellow-workers, the laborers for life and for righteousness, such *deacons* as are pleasing to God, such whom thou provest to be worthy among all the people, and such as shall be ready for the necessities of their ministration. Ordain also a *deaconess* who is faithful and holy, for the ministrations towards women. For sometimes he cannot send a *deacon*, who is a man, to the women, on account of unbelievers. Thou shalt therefore send a woman, a *deaconess*, on account of the imaginations of the bad. For we stand in need of a woman, a *deaconess*, for many necessities; and first is the baptism of women, the *deacon* shall anoint only their forehead with the holy oil, and after him the *deaconess* shall anoint them; for there is no necessity that the women should be seen by the men; but only in the laying on of hands the bishop shall anoint her head."

Apostolic Constitutions (c. A.D. 375, 3:16), "After that, either thou, O bishop, or a presbyter that is under thee, shall in the solemn form name over them the Father, and Son, and Holy Spirit, and shall dip them in the water; and let a *deacon* receive the man, and a *deaconess* the woman, that so the conferring of this inviolable seal may take place with a becoming decency."

Apostolic Constitutions (c. A.D. 375, 3:19), "Let the *deacons* be in all things unspotted, as the bishop himself is to be, only more active; in number according to the largeness of the Church, that they may minister to the infirm as workmen that are not ashamed. And let the *deaconess* be diligent in taking care of the women; but both of them ready to carry messages, to travel about, to minister, and to serve. . . . If, therefore, our Lord and Master so humbled Himself, how can you, the laborers of the truth, and administrators of Piety, be ashamed to do the same to such of the brethren as are weak and infirm? . . . It is your duty who are *deacons* to visit all those who stand in need of visitation."

Apostolic Constitutions (c. A.D. 375, 3:20), "But a presbyter and a *deacon* are to be ordained by one bishop and the rest of the clergy. Nor must either a presbyter or a *deacon* ordain from the laity into the clergy; but the presbyter is only to teach, to offer, to baptize, to bless the people, and the *deacon* is to minister to the bishop, and to the presbyters, that is, to do the office of a ministering *deacon*, but not to meddle with the other offices."

Apostolic Constitutions (c. A.D. 375, 3:22), "The *deacons*, doers of good works, searching about everywhere day and night, neither despising the poor nor regarding the person of the rich, shall acknowledge the oppressed, and not exclude him from a share in the collections of the congregation, but compel those having possessions to lay up for good works, in consideration of the words of our teacher:

'Ye saw me hungry, and did not feed me;' for those who have been *deacons* of good report and blameless purchase to themselves the pastorate."

Apostolic Constitutions (c. A.D. 375, 6:17), "Let the *deaconess* be a pure virgin; or, at the least, a widow who has been once married, faithful, and well esteemed."

Apostolic Constitutions (c. A.D. 375, 8:17-19, concerning the Ordination of Deacons - The Constitution of Philip), "Concerning the ordination of *deacons*, I Philip make this constitution: Thou shalt ordain a *deacon*, O bishop, by laying they hands upon him in the presence of the whole presbytery, and of the *deacons*, and shalt pray, and say:" (The Form of Prayer for the Ordination of a Deacon) "O God Almighty, the true and faithful God, who art rich unto all that call upon Thee in truth, who art fearful in counsels, and wise in understanding, who art powerful and great, hear our prayer, O Lord, and let Thine ears receive our supplication, and 'cause the light of Thy countenance to shine upon this Thy servant,' who is to be ordained for Thee to the office of a *deacon*: and replenish him with Thy Holy Spirit, and with power, as Thou didst replenish Stephen, who was Thy martyr, and follower of the sufferings of Thy Christ. Do Thou render him worthy to discharge acceptably the ministration of a *deacon*, steadily, unblameably, and without reproof, that thereby he may attain an higher degree, through the mediation of Thy only begotten Son, with whom glory, honor, and worship be to Thee and the Holy Spirit for ever. Amen."

Apostolic Constitutions (c. A.D. 375, 8:19-20, concerning the Deaconess - The Constitution of Bartholomew), "Concerning a *deaconess*, I Bartholomew make this constitution: O bishop, thou shalt lay thy hands upon her in the presence of the presbytery, and of the *deacons* and *deaconesses*, and shalt say:" (The form of Prayer for the Ordination of a Deaconess) "O Eternal God, the Father of our Lord Jesus Christ, the Creator of man and of woman, who didst replenish with the Spirit Miriam, and Deborah, and Anna, and Huldah; who didst not disdain that Thy only begotten Son should be born of a woman; who also in the tabernacle of the testimony, and in the temple didst ordain women to be keepers of Thy holy gates, - do Thou now also look down upon this Thy servant, who is ordained to the office of a *deaconess*, and grant her Thy Holy Spirit, and 'cleanse her from all filthiness of flesh and spirit,' that she may worthily discharge the work which is committed to her to Thy glory, and the praise of Thy Christ, with whom glory and adoration be to Thee and the Holy Spirit for ever. Amen."

Apostolic Constitutions (c. A.D. 375, 8:28), " A *deacon* does not bless, does not give the blessing, but receives it from the bishop and presbyter: he does not baptize, he does not offer; but when a bishop or presbyter has offered, he distributes to the people, not as a priest, but as one that ministers to the priests. But it is not lawful for any one of the other clergy to do the work of a *deacon*. A *deaconess* does not bless, nor perform anything belonging to the office of presbyters or *deacons*, but only is to keep the doors, and to minister to the presbyters in the baptizing of women, on account of decency. A *deacon* separates a *sub-deacon*, a reader, a singer, and a *deaconess*, if there be any occasion, in the absence of a presbyter. It is not lawful for a *sub-deacon* to separate either one of the clergy or laity; nor for a reader, nor for a singer, nor for a *deaconess*, for they are the ministers to the *deacons*."

Theodotian Code (A.D. 390, 16), "No woman should be admitted to the office [*deaconess*] except they had children and were above sixty years old according to the express rule of St. Paul."

Fourth Council of Carthage (A.D. 398, Canon 12), "Widows and dedicated women who are chosen to assist at the baptism of women, should be so well instructed in their office as to be able to teach aptly and properly unskilled and rustic women how to answer at the time of their baptism to the questions put to them, and also how to live godly after they have been baptized."

Pelagius (c. A.D. 400, *Commentary on 1 Timothy*), "'The women likewise must be chaste.' He commands that they must be chosen in the same way as *deacons*. One may deduce from this that he is talking about those who still live today in the East are called 'deaconesses.'"

Pelagius (c. A.D. 400, *Commentary on Romans*), "'. . . a *deaconess* of the church at Cenchreae.' Just as now, in the Eastern regions, one sees women *deaconesses* ministering to those of their sex at baptism or in the ministry of the word; for one finds women who have taught in private, like Priscilla, whose husband was called Aquila."

Chrysostom(c. A.D. 400, *Homily 14 on Acts 6*), "It is also a subject of wonder, how it was that the multitude was not divided in its choice of the men [the Seven], and how it was that the Apostles were not rejected by them. But what sort of rank these bore, and what sort of office they received, this is what we need to learn. Was it that of *Deacons*? And yet this is not the case in the Churches. But is it to the Presbyters that the management belongs? And yet at present there was no Bishop, but the Apostles only. Whence I think it clearly and manifestly follows, that neither *Deacons* nor Presbyters is their designation: but it was for this particular purpose that they were ordained."

Chrysostom (c. A.D. 400, *Homily 2 on 2 Corinthians*), "Therefore church law enjoins that there be prayers for the catechumens as well as for the faithful, for when the *deacon* says, 'Let us pray earnestly for the catechumens,' he stirs up the whole assembly of the faithful to pray for them."

Chrysostom (c. A.D. 400, *Homily 3 on 2 Thessalonians*), "For when the lector stands up and says: 'This is the Word of the Lord,' and when the *deacon* stands and imposes silence on all, he does not do so to confer an honor on the lector, but on Him who speaks to all through him."

Chrysostom (c. A.D. 400, *Homily 3.4 on Ephesians*), "You hear the *deacon* stand up and say: 'As many as are penitents, all pray.' As many as do not partake are in penitence. Why, then, does he say, 'Depart, you who are not qualified to participate?' Staying for the prayers is as forbidden to them as actually partaking of the Eucharist."

Chrysostom (c. A.D. 400, *Homily 30 on Romans*), "See how many ways he takes to give her [Phoebe] dignity. For he has both mentioned her before all the rest, and called he sister. And it is no slight thing to be called the sister of Paul. Moreover, he has adder her rank, by mentioning her being 'deaconess.'"

Chrysostom (c. A.D. 400, *Homily 11 on Timothy*), "Some have thought that this is said of women generally; but it is not so, for why should he introduce anything about women to interfere with the subject? He is speaking of *women* who hold the office of *deacon*."

Sozomen (A.D. 425, *Ecclesiastical History*, 7:19, reporting on the traditions in various churches), "Again, there are even now but seven *deacons* at Rome, answering precisely to the number ordained by the apostles, of whom Stephen was the first martyr; whereas, in other churches, the number of *deacons* is a matter of indifference."

Council of Orange (A.D. 441), "*Deaconesses* are absolutely not to be ordained; and if there are still any of them, let them bow their head under the benediction which is given to the congregation."

Theodoret of Cyrus (c. A.D. 450, *Commentary on 1 Timothy*), "'The women likewise,' i.e. the (*women*) *deacons*, 'must be serious, no slanderers, but temperate, faithful in all things.' What he prescribes for the men, he prescribes also and in about the same terms for the women. Since he says that the *deacons* must be 'serious,' he also says that the woman must be 'serious.' Just as he forbids the men to be 'double-tongued,' so too he forbids the women to be 'slanderers.' And, as he forbids the men to be addicted to much wine, so also he commands the women to be 'temperate.'"

Council of Chalcedon (A.D. 451, Canon 15), "A woman shall not receive the laying on of hands as a *deaconess* under forty years of age, and then only after searching examination. And if, after she has hands laid on her, and has continued for a time to minister, she shall despise the Grace of God and give herself in marriage, she shall be anathematized and the man who is united to her."

Council of Epaone (A.D. 517, Canon 21), "The consecration of widows, whom they call *deaconesses*, we wholly abrogate from all our region; the benediction of penitence alone being laid upon them if they desire to be converted."

Second Council of Orleans (A.D. 533, Canon 17, 18), "*Women* who up to time, contrary to the interdictions of the canons, have received the benediction of the *Diaconate*, if they are proved to have turned again to marriage, are to be expelled from the communion; but if, when admonished by the Bishop, they recognize their error and break off intercourse of this kind they may return to the grace of communion, after having done penance. . . . Moreover we determine, that to no *woman* hereafter shall the *Diaconal* benediction be entrusted, by reason of the frailty of this sex."

Council of Toledo (A.D. 633, Canon), "*Deacons* are not to raise themselves above the presbyters, and stand in the first choir whilst the priests are in the second."

St. Isidore of Seville (c. A.D. 650, *To Leudefredus*, 83:895), "To the *deacon* it belongs to assist the priests and to serve in all this done in the sacraments of Christ, in baptism, to wit, in the *hoy chrism*, in the paten and chalice, to bring the oblation to the altar and to arrange them, to lay the table of the Lord and to drape it, to carry the cross, to declaim the Gospel and Epistle, for the charge is given to lectors to declaim the Old Testament, so it is given to *deacons* to declaim the New.

To him also pertains the office of prayers and the recital of the names. It is he who gives warning to open our eyes to the Lord, it is he who exhorts with his cry, it is he also who announces peace."

Council in Trullo (A.D. 692, Canon 7), "Since we have learned that in some churches *deacons* hold ecclesiastical offices, and that hereby some of them with arrogancy and license sit daringly before the presbyters: we have determined that a *deacon*, even if in an office of dignity, that is to say, in whatever ecclesiastical office he may be, is not to have his seat before a presbyter, except he is acting as representative of his own patriarch or metropolican in another city under another superior, for then he shall be honored as filling his place. But if anyone, possessed with a tyrannical audacity, shall have dared to do such a thing, let him be ejected from his peculiar rank and be last of all of the order in whose list he is in his own church. . . ."

Council in Trullo (A.D. 692, Canon 14), "Let the canon of our holy God-bearing Fathers be confirmed in this particular also; that a presbyter be not ordained before he is thirty years of age, even if he be a very worthy man, but let him be kept back. For our Lord Jesus Christ was baptized and began to teach when he was thirty. In like manner let no *deacon* be ordained before he is twenty-five, nor a *deaconess* before she is forty."

Council in Trullo (A.D. 692, Canon 16), "Since the book of the Acts tells us that seven *deacons* were appointed by the Apostles, and the synod of Neo-caesarea in the canons which it put forth determined that there ought to be canonically only seven *deacons*, even if the city be very large, in accordance with the book of Acts; we, having fitted the mind of the fathers to the Apostles' words, find that they spoke not of those men who ministered at the Mysteries but in the administration which pertains to the serving of tables." (He then quotes John Chrysostom interpreting his quote to say that *deacons* did not yet exist at the time of Acts 6. The Canon then continues), "But on this account therefore we also announce that the aforesaid seven *deacons* are not to be understood as *deacons* who served at the Mysteries, . . . but that they were those to whom a dispensation was entrusted for the common benefit of those that were gathered together, who to us in this also were a type of philanthropy and zeal towards those who are in need."

Council in Trullo (A.D. 692, Canon 40), "For although the great Basil in his holy canons decreed that she who willingly offers to God and embraces virginity, if she has completed her seventeenth year, is to be entered in the order of virgins: nevertheless, having followed the example respecting widows and *deaconesses*, analogy and proportion being considered, we have admitted at the said time those who have chosen the monastic life. For it is written in the divine Apostle that a widow is to be elected in the church at sixty years old: but the sacred canons have decreed that a *deaconess* shall be ordained at forty. . . ."

Qualities of Elders and Deacons

QUALITIES OF ELDERS

Greek	Elder 1 Tm	Elder Tit	D'con 1 Tm	D'ess 1 Tm	Definition
φιλοξενος	3:2	1:8			Hospitable
διδακτικος	3:2	1:9			Apt at teaching, skillful in teaching
παρακαλεω		1:9			(Able to) exhort, encourage, urge, appeal to, implore
μη πληκτης	3:3	1:7			Not a striker, violent, bully
επιεικης	3:3				Forbearing, gentle, kind, yielding
αμαχος	3:3				Uncontentious, peaceable, not quarrelsome
μη οργιλος		1:7			Not passionate, quick-tempered, inclined to anger
μαρτυρια καλος	3:7				A good witness from outsiders
μη ασωτια		1:6			Not (accused) profligacy, wild, debauchery
μη ανυποτακτος		1:6			Not unruly, disobedient, rebellious, undisciplined
μη αυθαδης		1:7			Not self pleasing, arrogant, overbearing, stubborn
φιλαγαθος		1:6			Lover of good
δικαιος		1:6			Just, upright, righteous
οσιος		1:6			Holy, pleasing to God, devout

QUALITIES OF DEACONS

Greek	Elder 1 Tm	Elder Tit	D'con 1 Tm	D'ess 1 Tm	Definition
μη διλογος			3:8		Not double tongued, talking out of both sides of mouth
μη διαβολος				3:11	Not slanderer

QUALITIES OF ELDERS AND DEACONS

Greek	Elder 1 Tm	Elder Tit	D'con 1 Tm	D'ess 1 Tm	Definition
ανεπιλημπτος	3:2				Without (above) reproach
ανεγκλητος		1:6,7	3:10		Irreproachable, blameless
σωφρων	3:2	1:8			Sensible, self controlled, prudent, thoughtful, (of women: chaste, modest)
κοσμιος	3:2				Honorable, orderly, modest (dress), respectable
εγκρατες		1:8			Self controlled, disciplined
σεμνως			3:8	3:11	Grave, worthy of respect or honor, noble, dignified,
μη παροινος	3:3	1:7			Not an excessive drinker, temperate, drunken
μη προσεχω			3:8		Not adicted (to much wine), pay attention to, devote to
νηφαλιος	3:2			3:11	Temperate, sober
αφιλαργυρος	3:3				Not avaricious, not lover of money, not greedy
μη αισχροκερδης		1:7	3:8		Not fond of base gain
εχοντας το μυστηριον της πιστεως εν καθαρα συνειδησει			3:9		Having the mystery of the faith with clean conscience
αντεχομενον του κατα την διδαχην πιστου λογου		1:9			Holding fast to the faithful word
πιστας εν πασιν				3:11	Faithful in all things
μιας γυναικος ανδρα	3:2	1:6	3:12		Husband of one wife
προιστημι	3:4		3:12		Ruling (his own household well), manage, conduct, direct, be at head of
υποταγη τεκνον	3:4				Children in subjection, obedience, subordination
πιστος τεκνον		1:6			Believing children, faithful,
μη νεοφυτος	3:6				Not a recent convert, newly planted
δοκιμαζω			3:10		Tested, examined, proved

Bibliography

A. Biblical Greek Texts

Nestle, Eberhard, Ed. *Novum Testamentum Graece.* Stuttgart, W. Germany: Wurtemberg Bible Society, 1965.

United Bible Societies. *The Greek New Testament.* Stuttgart, W. Germany: Wurtemberg Bible Society, 1966.

B. Bible Translations

Conybeare, W. J. *The Epistles of Paul.* Baker.

King James Version. 1611.

New English Bible. Cambridge: University, 1961.

New International Version. New York: International Bible Society, 1984.

Phillips, J. B. The New Testament in Modern English. MacMillan, 1958.

Revised Standard Version. New York: Division of Christian Education of the National Council of Churches of Christ in the United States, 1946.

Taylor, Kenneth N. *Living Bible.* London: Coverdale, 1971.

Weymouth, Richard Francis. *Weymouth's New Testament in Modern Speech*. London: James Clarke.

Williams, Charles B. *The New Testament: A Translation in the Language of the People.* Bruce Humphries, 1937.

C. Ancient Writers and Church Fathers

Ambrosiaster. *Quaestiones Veteris et Novi Testamenti 127.* Trans. Alexander Souter. *Corpus Scriptorum Ecclesiasticorum Latinorum*, Vol. 50. New York: Johnson, 1963. 193 +.

Apostolic Constitutions. Trans. James Donaldson. *The Ante-Nicene Fathers*, Vol. 8. Grand Rapids: Eerdmans, 1981. 391 +.

Chrysostom, John. *The Homilies on the Acts of the Apostles.* Trans. H. Browne, J. Sheppard, George B. Stevens and J. Walker. *The Nicene and Post-Nicene Fathers,* Vol. 11. Grand Rapids: Eerdmans, 1980. 1 +.

---. The Homilies on Romans. Trans. J. B. Morris, W. H. Simcock, and George B.

Stevens. *The Nicene and Post-Nicene Fathers*, Vol. 11.   Grand Rapids: Eerdmans, 1980. 335 + .

---. *The Homilies on Timothy, Titus, and Philemon*. Trans. James Tweed. *The Nicene and Post-Nicene Fathers*, Vol. 13. Grand Rapids: Eerdmans, 1980. 407 + .

Clement. *First Epistle of Clement to the Corinthians*. Trans. Alexander Roberts and James Donaldson. *The Ante-Nicene Fathers*, Vol. 1. Grand Rapids: Eerdmans, 1981. 5 + .

Clement of Alexandria. *The Instructor*. Trans. W. L. Alexander. *The Ante-Nicene Fathers*, Vol. 2. Grand Rapids: Eerdmans, 1981. 209 + .

---. *The Stromata*, or *Miscellanies*. Trans. W. L. Alexander. *The Ante-Nicene Fathers*, Vol. 2. Grand Rapids: Eerdmans, 1981. 299 + .

The Council of Chalcedon. Ed. Henry R. Percival. *The Nicene and Post-Nicene Fathers*, Second Series, Vol. 14. Grand Rapids: Eerdmans, 1979. 267 + .

Council of Elvira. A New Eusebius: Documents Illustrative of the Church to A. D. 337. Ed. J. Stevenson. New York: Macmillan, 1957. 307 +

The Council of Laodicea. Ed. Henry R. Percival. *The Nicene and Post-Nicene Fathers*, Second Series, Vol. 14. Grand Rapids: Eerdmans, 1979. 125 + .

The Council of NeoCaesarea. Ed. Henry R. Percival. *The Nicene and Post-Nicene Fathers*, Second Series, Vol. 14. Grand Rapids: Eerdmans, 1979. 79 + .

The Council of Trullo. Ed. Henry R. Percival. *The Nicene and Post-Nicene Fathers*, Second Series, Vol. 14. Grand Rapids: Eerdmans, 1979. 359 + .

Cyprian. *The Epistles of Cyprian*. Trans. Ernest Wallis. *The Ante-Nicene Fathers*, Vol. 5. Grand Rapids: Eerdmans, 1981. 275 + .

---. *The Treatises of Cyprian*. Trans. Ernest Wallis. *The Ante-Nicene Fathers*, Vol. 5. Grand Rapids: Eerdmans, 1981. 421 + .

Didache [The Teaching of the Twelve Apostles]. Trans. Isaac H. Hall and John T. Napier. *The Ante-Nicene Fathers*, Vol. 7. Grand Rapids: Eerdmans, 1981. 377 + .

Didascalia Apostolorum. Trans. R. Hugh Connolly. Oxford: Clarendon, 1969.

Epistle of Clement to James. Trans. Thomas Smith. *The Ante-Nicene Fathers*, Vol. 8. Grand Rapids: Eerdmans, 1981. 218 + .

Eusebius. *The Ecclesiastical History of Eusebius Pamphilus*. Trans. Christian Frederick Cruse. Grand Rapids: Baker, 1966.

The First Council of Nicea. Ed. Henry R. Percival. *The Nicene and Post-Nicene Fathers*, Second Series, Vol. 14. Grand Rapids: Eerdmans, 1979. 8 + .

Hefele, Charles Joseph. *A History of the Councils of the Church*, in 5 Volumes. Trans.

William R. Clark and Henry Nutcombe Oxenham. Edinburgh: T. & T. Clark, 1895.

Hemmer, C. J. "17. The Cities of the Revelation." *New Documents Illustrating Early Christianity*, Vol. 3, 1978. N. Ryde, NSW, Australia: Macquarie Univ., 1983. 51+.

Hermas. *The Shepherd*. Trans. F. Crombie. *The Ante-Nicene Fathers*, Vol. 2. Grand Rapids: Eerdmans, 1981. 3+.

Hippolytus. *Apostolic Traditions of Hippolytus*. Trans. Burton Scott Easton. Cambridge: University, 1934.

---. *The Refutation of All Heresies*. Trans. J. H. MacMahon. *The Ante-Nicene Fathers*, Vol. 5. Grand Rapids: Eerdmans, 1981. 9+.

Horsley, G. H. R. "69. "οικονομος." *New Documents Illustrating Early Christianity*, Vol. 4, 1979. N. Ryde, NSW, Australia: Macquarie Univ., 1987. 160+.

---. "79. Women office-holders in the Church." *New Documents Illustrating Early Christianity*, Vol. 1, 1976. N. Ryde, NSW, Australia: Macquarie Univ., 1981. 121.

---. "80. A deacon's work contract." *New Documents Illustrating Early Christianity*, Vol. 1, 1976.. N. Ryde, NSW, Australia: Macquarie Univ., 1981. 121.

---. "82. Nuns as lessors of property." *New Documents Illustrating Early Christianity*, Vol. 1, 1976. N. Ryde, NSW, Australia: Macquarie Univ., 1981. 126+.

---. "109. Maria the *diakonos*." *New Documents Illustrating Early Christianity*, Vol. 2, 1977. N. Ryde, NSW, Australia: Macquarie Univ., 1982. 193.

---. "113. An *archisynagogos* of Corinth." *New Documents Illustrating Early Christianity*, Vol. 4, 1979. N. Ryde, NSW, Australia: Macquarie Univ., 1987. 213.

---. "122. Sophia, the 'second Phoibe'." *New Documents Illustrating Early Christianity*, Vol. 4, 1979. N. Ryde, NSW, Australia: Macquarie Univ., 1987. 239+.

Ignatius. *The Epistle of Ignatius to the Magnesians*. Trans. Alexander Roberts and James Donaldson. *The Ante-Nicene Fathers*, Vol. 1. Grand Rapids: Eerdmans, 1981. 59+.

---. *The Epistle of Ignatius to the Philadelphians*. Trans. Alexander Roberts and James Donaldson. *The Ante-Nicene Fathers*, Vol. 1. Grand Rapids: Eerdmans, 1981. 79+.

---. *The Epistle of Ignatius to the Smyrnaeans*. Trans. Alexander Roberts and James Donaldson. *The Ante-Nicene Fathers*, Vol. 1. Grand Rapids: Eerdmans, 1981. 86+.

---. *The Epistle of Ignatius to the Trallians*. Trans. Alexander Roberts and James Donaldson. *The Ante-Nicene Fathers*, Vol. 1. Grand Rapids: Eerdmans, 1981. 66+.

Irenaeus. *Against Heresies*. Trans. Alexander Roberts and James Donaldson. *The Ante-Nicene Fathers*, Vol. 1. Grand Rapids: Eerdmans, 1981. 315 + .

Jerome. *Letter 146.* Trans. S. L. Greenslade. *Early Latin Theology*, Vol. 5. Philadelphia: Westminster, 1956.

Josephus, Flavius. *The Works of Flavius Josephus*. Trans. William Whiston. Grand Rapids: Associated Publishers.

Judge, E. A. "81. The earliest attested monk." *New Documents Illustrating Early Christianity*, Vol. 1, 1976. N. Ryde, NSW, Australia: Macquarie Univ., 1981. 124 + .

Justin. *Dialogue with Trypho. Trans. Alexander Roberts and James Donaldson. The Ante-Nicene Fathers*, Vol. 1. Grand Rapids: Eerdmans, 1981. 194 + .

---. *The First Apology of Justin*. Trans. Alexander Roberts and James Donaldson. *The Ante-Nicene Fathers*, Vol. 1. Grand Rapids: Eerdmans, 1981. 163 + .

Paulinus. *Life of St. Ambrose.* Trans. John A. Lacy. *The Fathers of the Church*, Vol. 15. New York: Fathers of the Church, 1952.

Pelagius. *Pelagius' Exposition of the Thirteen Epistles of St. Paul.* Ed. J. Armitage Robinson. Cambridge: University, 1922.

Plinius [Pliny], Caecilius Secundus. *The Letters of the Younger Pliny*. Trans. Betty Radice. New York: Penguin, 1963.

Polycarp. *The Epistle of Polycarp to the Philippians*. Trans. Alexander Roberts and James Donaldson. *The Ante-Nicene Fathers*, Vol. 1. Grand Rapids: Eerdmans, 1981. 33 + .

Sozomen, Salaminius Hermias. *Ecclesiastical History.* Trans. Chester D. Hartranft. *The Nicene and Post-Nicene Fathers*, Second Series, Vol. 2. Grand Rapids: Eerdmans, 1979. 239 + .

Tertullian. *On Baptism.* Trans. S. Thelwall. *The Ante-Nicene Fathers*, Vol. 3. Grand Rapids: Eerdmans, 1981. 669 + .

---. *Exhortation to Chastity.* Trans. S. Thelwall. *The Ante-Nicene Fathers*, Vol. 4. Grand Rapids: Eerdmans, 1981. 50 + .

---. *To His Wife.* Trans. William P. LeSaint. *Ancient Christian Writers.* Westminster, MD: Newman, 1956. 10 + .

---. *The Prescription Against Heretics.* Trans. Peter Holmes. *The Ante-Nicene Fathers*, Vol. 4. Grand Rapids: Eerdmans, 1981. 243 + .

---. *On Veiling of Virgins.* Trans. S. Thelwall. *The Ante-Nicene Fathers*, Vol. 4. Grand Rapids: Eerdmans, 1981. 27 + .

D. Word Studies

Arndt, William F., and F. Wilbur Gingrich. *A Greek-English Lexicon of the New Testament.* Chicago: University of Chicago, 1957.

Beyer, Hermann W. "διακονεω." *Theological Dictionary of the New Testament,* Vol. 2. Grand Rapids: Zondervan, 1970. 81 + .

Bietenhard, Hans. "Satan, Beelzebul, Devil, Exorcism." *Dictionary of New Testament Theology,* Vol. 3. Grand Rapids: Zondervan, 1975. 468.

Bertram, Georg. "συνεργος." *Theological Dictionary of the New Testament,* Vol. 7. Grand Rapids: Zondervan, 1971. 871 + .

Brown, Colin. "Conscience." *Dictionary of New Testament Theology,* Vol. 1. Grand Rapids: Zondervan, 1975. 350 + .

---. "Vine, Wine." *Dictionary of New Testament Theology,* Vol. 3. Grand Rapids: Zondervan, 1975. 922.

---. "Woman." *Dictionary of New Testament Theology,* Vol. 3. Grand Rapids: Zondervan, 1975. 1055 + .

Brown, Raymond E. "*Episkope* and *Episkopos*: The New Testament Evidence." *Theological Studies* 41.2 (1980): 322 + .

Budd, Philip J. "Sober, Drunken." *Dictionary of New Testament Theology,* Vol. 1. Grand Rapids: Zondervan, 1975. 515.

Carpenter, H. J. "Minister, Ministry." *Theological Word Book of the Bible.* Ed. Alan Richardson. New York: MacMillan, 1959.

Coenen, Lothar. Bishop, Presbyter, Elder." *Dictionary of New Testament Theology,* Vol. 1. Grand Rapids: Zondervan, 1975. 192.

Cranfield, C. E. B "*Diakonia in the New Testament.*" *Service in Christ: Essays Presented to Karl Barth on his 80th Birthday.* Ed. J. I. McCord and J. H. L. Parker. London: Epworth, 1966. 37 + .

Finkenroth, Gunter. "Secret, Mystery." *Dictionary of New Testament Theology,* Vol. 3. Grand Rapids: Zondervan, 1975. 505.

Gunther, Walther. "Godliness, Piety." *Dictionary of New Testament Theology,* Vol. 2. Grand Rapids: Zondervan, 1975. 95.

Haarbeck, Hermann. "Tempt, Test, Approve." *Dictionary of New Testament Theology,* Vol. 3. Grand Rapids: Zondervan, 1975. 808.

Hahn, Hans-Cristoph. "Conscience." *Dictionary of New Testament Theology,* Vol. 1. Grand Rapids: Zondervan, 1975. 350 + .

---. "Openness, Frankness, Boldness." *Dictionary of New Testament Theology,* Vol. 2. Grand Rapids: Zondervan, 1975. 736.

---.   "Work." *Dictionary of New Testament Theology*, Vol. 3. Grand Rapids: Zondervan, 1978. 1147+.

Hess, Klaus. "Servant." *Dictionary of New Testament Theology*, Vol. 3.   Grand Rapids: Zondervan, 1978. 544+.

Jeremias, Joachim. "παισς θεου." *Theological Dictionary of the New Testament*, Vol. 5. Grand Rapids: Eerdmans, 1968. 654+.

Liddell, Henry George, and Robert Scott. *A Greek-English Lexicon*.   Oxford: Clarendon, 1890.

Michel, Otto. "Faith, Persuade, Belief, Unbelief." *Dictionary of New Testament Theology*, Vol. 1. Grand Rapids: Zondervan, 1975. 604.

---.   "οικονομος." *Theological Dictionary of the New Testament*, Vol. 5.   Grand Rapids: Eerdmans, 1968. 149+.

---.   "Son." *Dictionary of New Testament Theology*, Vol. 3. Grand Rapids: Zondervan, 1978. 607+.

Moulton, James Hope, and George Milligan. "διακονος." *The Vocabulary of the Greek Testament.* Grand Rapids: Eerdmans, 1930. 149.

Oepke, A. "γυνη." *Theological Dictionary of the New Testament*, Vol. 1.   Grand Rapids: Eerdmans, 1970. 776+.

Porter, Livingston. "The Word επισκοπος in Pre-Christian Usage." *Anglican Theological Review* 21 (1930-31): 103+.

Reicke, Bo. "προιστημι." *Theological Dictionary of the New Testament*, Vol. 6. Grand Rapids: Eerdmans, 1969. 700+.

Rengstorf, Karl Heinrich. "δουλος." *Theological Dictionary of the New Testament*, Vol. 2. Grand Rapids: Eerdmans, 1964. 261+.

---.   "υπηρετης." *Theological Dictionary of the New Testament*, Vol. 8.   Grand Rapids: Eerdmans, 1972. 530+.

Schonweiss, Hans. "Firm, Foundation, Certainty, Confirm." *Dictionary of New Testament Theology*, Vol. 1. Grand Rapids: Zondervan, 1975. 660.

Schrage, Wolfgang. "συναγωγη." *Theological Dictionary of the New Testament*, Vol, 7. Grand Rapids: Eerdmans, 1971. 798+.

Shepherd, Jr., Massey H. "Deacon." *Interpreter's Dictionary of the Bible*, Vol. 1. New York: Abingdon, 1962. 786.

Siede, Burghard. "Recompense, Reward, Gain, Wages." *Dictionary of New Testament Theology*, Vol. 3. Grand Rapids: Zondervan, 1975. 137.

Strathmann, H. "λειτουργος." *Theological Dictionary of the New Testament*, Vol. 4. Grand Rapids: Eerdmans, 1967. 229+.

Wahrisch, Hans. "Virtue, Blameless." *Dictionary of New Testament Theology*, Vol. 3. Grand Rapids: Zondervan, 1975. 924.

E. Commentaries - Non-Disciples

Arrington, French L. *Maintaining the Foundations*. Grand Rapids: Baker, 1982.

Barclay, William. *The Letter to the Romans. The Daily Study Bible*. Edinburgh: Saint Andrew, 1957.

---. *The Letters to Timothy, Titus and Philemon. The Daily Study Bible*. Edinburgh: Saint Andrew, 1965.

Barlow, George. *I - II Timothy, Titus, Philemon. The Preacher's Complete Homiletic Commentary*. New York: Funk & Wagnalls.

Barmby, J. *Romans. The Pulpit Commentary*, Vol. 18. Grand Rapids: Eerdmans, 1950.

Barnes, Albert. *Notes on the New Testament*. London: Blackie. Vols. 4, 8.

Barnhouse, Donald Grey. *Romans*. Grand Rapids: Eerdmans, 1964.

Barrett, C. K. *The Epistle to the Romans. Harper's New Testament Commentaries*. New York: Harper & Row, 1957.

---. *Pastoral Epistles. New Clarendon Bible*. Oxford: Clarendon, 1963.

Bernard, J. H. *The Pastoral Epistles*. Cambridge: University, 1899.

Best, Ernest. *Romans. Cambridge Bible Commentary*. Cambridge: University, 1967.

Bigg, Charles. *Epistles of St. Peter and St. Jude. International Critical Commentary*. Edinburgh: T. & T. Clark, 1902.

Black, Matthew. *Romans. New Century Bible*. Greenwood, SC: Attic, 1973.

Blackman, Edwin Cyril. "The Letter of Paul to the Romans." *Acts and Paul's Letters. Interpreter's Concise Commentary*. Nashville: Abingdon, 1983.

Blaiklock, E. M. *The Pastoral Epistles*. Grand Rapids: Zondervan, 1972.

Boylan, Patrick Canon. *St. Paul's Epistle to the Romans*. Dublin: M. H. Gill, 1934.

Briscoe, D. Stuart. *Romans. The Communicators Commentary*. Waco, TX: Word, 1982.

Bruce, F. F. *1 & 2 Thessalonians. Word Biblical Commentary*. Waco, TX: Word, 1982.

---. *Romans. The Tyndale New Testament Commentaries*. Grand Rapids: Eerdmans, 1963.

Burrows, W. *Romans. The Preacher's Complete Homiletic Commentary*. New York: Funk & Wagnalls.

Calvin, John. *Commentaries on the Epistle to the Romans*. Trans. John Owen. Grand Rapids: Eerdmans, 1959.

---. *Timothy, Titus, and Philemon*. Trans. by William Pringle. Grand Rapids: Eerdmans, 1959.

Childs, Brevard S. *The Book of Exodus*. *The Old Testament Library*. Philadelphia: Westminster, 1974.

Clarke, Adam. *Clarke's Commentary*, Vol. 6. New York: Abingdon, 1832.

Cragg, Gerald R. *Romans*. *The Interpreter's Bible*, Vol. 9. New York: Abingdon, 1954.

Cranfield, C. E. B. *Romans, A Shorter Commentary*. Grand Rapids: Eerdmans, 1985.

Croskery, T. *I Timothy*. *The Pulpit Commentary*, Vol. 2. Grand Rapids: Eerdmans, 1950.

Demarest, Gary W. *1, 2 Thessalonians, 1, 2, Timothy, Titus*. *The Communicator's Commentary*. Waco, TX: Word, 1984.

Dibelius, Martin and Hans Conzelmann. *The Pastoral Epistles*. Trans. Philip Buttolph and Adela Yarbro. Philadelphia: Fortress, 1972.

Dodd, C. H. *Epistle of Paul to the Romans*. *Moffatt New Testament Commentary*. London: Hodder and Stoughton, 1932.

Driver, S. R. *Notes on the Hebrew Text and Topography of the Books of Samuel*. Oxford: Clarendon, 1913.

Earle, Ralph. *1 & 2 Timothy*. The Expositor's Bible Commentary. Vol. 11, Grand Rapids: Zondervan, 1978.

Easton, Burton Scott. *The Pastoral Epistles*. New York: Scribner, 1947.

Enslin, Morton S. *Letters to the Churches: 1 and 2 Timothy, Titus*. New York: Abingdon, 1963.

Erdman, Charles R. *The Epistle of Paul to the Romans*. Philadelphia: Westminster, 1925.

Falconer, Robert. *The Pastoral Epistles*. Oxford: Clarendon, 1937.

Fee, Gordon D. *1 and 2 Timothy, Titus*. San Francisco: Harper and Row, 1984.

Finlayson, R. *I Timothy*. *The Pulpit Commentary*, Vol. 21. Grand Rapids: Eerdmans, 1950.

Frame, James Everett. *Epistles of St. Paul to the Thessalonians*. *International Critical Commentary*. Edinburgh: T. & T. Clark, 1912.

Geldenhuys, Norval. *Commentary on the Gospel of Luke*. Grand Rapids: Eerdmans, 1951.

Gore, Charles. *The Epistle to the Romans*, Vol. 2. London: John Murray, 1907.

Gromacki, Robert G. *Stand True to the Charge*. Grand Rapids: Baker, 1982.

Guthrie, Donald. *The Pastoral Epistles*. Tyndale New Testament Commentaries. London: Tyndale, 1957.

Hamilton, Floyd E. *The Epistle to the Romans*. Grand Rapids: Baker, 1958.

Hanson, Anthony Tyrrell. *The Pastoral Epistles*. *New Century Bible Commentary*. Grand Rapids: Eerdmans, 1982.

---. *The Pastoral Letters*. *Cambridge Bible Commentary*. Cambridge: University, 1966.

Harrison, Everett F. *Romans*. *The Expositor's Bible Commentary*. Grand Rapids: Zondervan, 1976.

Hawthorne, Gerald F. *Philippians*. *Word Biblical Commentary*, Vol. 43. Waco, TX: Word, 1983.

Hendriksen, William. *The Pastoral Epistles*. New Testament Commentary. Grand Rapids: Baker, 1957.

---. *Paul's Epistle to the Romans*. *New Testament Commentary*. Grand Rapids: Baker, 1981.

Henry, Matthew. *Commentary on the Whole Bible*, Vol. 6. Scottdale, PA: Herald.

Hervey, A. C. *I Timothy*. *The Pulpit Commentary*, Vol. 21. Grand Rapids: Eerdmans, 1950.

Hinson, E. Glenn. *I Timothy*. *The Broadman Bible Commentary*, Vol. 11. Nashville: Broadman, 1971.

Houlden, J. L. *The Pastoral Epistles*. New York: Penguin, 1976.

Hultgren, Arland J. *I & II Timothy, Titus*. *Augsburg Commentary on the New Testament*. Minneapolis: Augsburg, 1984.

Hunter, A. M. *Epistle to the Romans*. London: SCM, 1955.

Karris, Robert J. *The Pastoral Epistles*. *New Testament Message*, Vol. 17. Wilmington, DE: Michael Glazier, 1979.

Kasemann, Ernst. *Commentary on Romans*. Grand Rapids: Eerdmans, 1980.

Kelly, J. N. D. *The Pastoral Epistles*. *Black's New Testament Commentaries*. London: Adam & Charles Black, 1963.

Kent, Homer. *The Pastoral Epistles*. Chicago: Moody, 1958.

Kirk, K. E. *Romans*. *The Clarendon Bible*. Oxford: Clarendon, 1937.

Knox, John. *Romans*. *The Interpreter's Bible*, Vol. 9. New York: Abingdon, 1954.

Lenski, R. C. H. *The Interpretation of St. Paul's Epistle to the Romans*. Minneapolis: Augsburg, 1936.

---. *The Interpretation of St. Paul's Epistles to Timothy*. Minneapolis: Augsburg, 1937.

Lightfoot, Joseph B. *Saint Paul's Epistle to the Philippians*. London: MacMillan, 1903.

Lock, Walter. *The Pastoral Epistles*. *The International Critical Commentary*. Edinburgh: T. & T. Clark, 1924.

Maly, Eugene H. *Romans*. *New Testament Message*. Wilmington, DE: Michael Glazier, 1979.

Moody, Dale. *Romans*. *The Broadman Bible Commentary*. Nashville: Broadman, 1970.

Morris, Leon. *The First and Second Epistles to the Thessalonians*. *The New International Commentary on the New Testament*. Grand Rapids: Eerdmans, 1959.

Moule, Handley C. G. *The Epistle of St. Paul to the Romans*. *The Expositors' Bible*. Cincinnati: Jennings & Graham, 1893.

Murray, John. *Romans*. *The New International Commentary on the New Testament*. Grand Rapids: Eerdmans, 1968.

Newell, William R. *Romans*. Chicago: Grace, 1945.

Newman, Barclay M., and Eugene A. Nida. *A Translator's Handbook on Paul's Letter to the Romans*. London: United Bible Societies, 1973.

Nygren, Anders. *Romans*. Trans. Carl C. Rasmussen. London: SCM, 1952.

O'Neill, J. C. *Paul's Letter to the Romans*. London: Penguin, 1975.

Perowne, J. J. S., ed. *Romans*. *Cambridge Bible for Schools and Colleges*. Cambridge: University, 1899.

Plummer, Alfred. *The Pastoral Epistles*. *The Expositors' Bible*. Cincinnati: Jennings & Graham.

Rhys, Howard. *The Epistle to the Romans*. New York: MacMillan, 1961.

Robertson, Archibald Thomas. *Word Pictures in the New Testament*, Vol. 4. Nashville: Broadman, 1931.

Rolston, Holmes. *The First and Second Letters of Paul to Timothy*. *The Layman's Bible Commentary*, Vol. 23. Richmond, VA: Knox, 1963.

Sanday, William, and Arthur Headlam. *The Epistle to the Romans*. *The International Critical Commentary*. Edinburgh: T. & T. Clark, 1924.

Schelkle, Karl Hermann. The Epistle to the Romans. New York: Herder and Herder, 1964.

Simpson, E. K. *The Pastoral Epistles.* Grand Rapids: Eerdmans, 1954.

Thomas, Robert L. *1 & 2 Thessalonians. The Expositor's Bible Commentary,* Vol. 11. Grand Rapids: Zondervan, 1978.

Thomas, W. H. Griffith. *St. Paul's Epistle to the Romans.* Grand Rapids: Eerdmans, 1946.

Thomson, J. Radford. *Romans. The Pulpit Commentary,* Vol. 18. Grand Rapids: Eerdmans, 1950.

Trentham, Charles. *Studies in Timothy.* Nashville: Convention, 1959.

Vincent, Marvin R. *The Epistle to the Philippians and to Philemon. International Critical Commentary.* Edinburgh: T. & T. Clark, 1897.

---. *Word Studies in the New Testament.* Grand Rapids: Eerdmans, 1887.

Ward, Ronald A. *1 & 2 Timothy & Titus.* Waco, TX: Word, 1974.

Wiersbe, Warren W. *Be Faithful.* Wheaton, IL: Victor, 1981.

Wuest, Kenneth S. *The Pastoral Epistles in the Greek New Testament.* Grand Rapids: Eerdmans, 1956.

---. *Romans in the Greek New Testament.* Grand Rapids: Eerdmans, 1955.

F. Biblical Studies - Non-Disciples

Brooten, Bernadette J. *Women Leaders in the Ancient Synagogue.* Chico, CA: Scholars, 1982.

Cerling, C. E., Jr. "Women Ministers in the New Testament Church?" *Evangelical Theological Studies* Summer 1976: 209 + .

Conybeare, W. J., and J. S. Howson. *Life and Epistles of St. Paul.* London: Longmans, Green & Co., 1872.

Conzelmann, Hans. *The Theology of Luke.* Trans. Geoffrey Bushwell. London: Faber and Faber, 1960.

Elliott, John H. "Ministry and Church Order in the NT: A Tradio-Historical Analysis (1Pt 5:1-5 & plls.)." *Catholic Biblical Quarterly* July 1970: 367 + .

Ford, J. Massyngberde. "Biblical Material Relevant to the Ordination of Women." *Journal of Ecumenical Studies* Fall 1973: 669 + .

Frend, W. H. C. *The Rise of Christianity.* Philadelphia: Fortress, 1984.

Gibson, Margaret D. "Phoebe." *Expository Times* 1911-12: 281.

Glasscock, Ed. "'The Husband of One Wife' Requirement in 1 Timothy 3:2." *Bibliotheca Sacra* July-Sept. 1983: 244 + .

Hatch, Edwin. *The Organization of the Early Christian Church.* London: Rivington, 1882.

Hiebert, D. Edmond. "Behind the Word 'Deacon': A New Testament Study." *Bibliotheca Sacra* Apr.-June 1983: 151 + .

Howe, E. Margaret. *Women and Church Leadership*. Grand Rapids: Zondervan, 1982.

Lampe, Geoffrey William Hugo. "*Diakonia* in the Early Church." *Service in Christ: Essays Presented to Karl Barth on his 80th Birthday*. Ed. J. I. McCord and J. H. L. Parker. London: Epworth, 1966. 49 + .

Lewis, Robert M. "The 'Women' of 1 Timothy 3:11." *Bibliotheca Sacra* Apr.-June 1979: 167 + .

Lightfoot, Joseph B. *On a Fresh Revision of the English New Testament*. New York: 1871.

Kaploun, Uri, ed. *The Synagogue. JPS Popular Judaic Library*. Philadelphia: Jewish Pub. Soc. of America, 1973.

Metzger, Bruce M. *The Text of the New Testament*. New York: Oxford Univ., 1968.

Moule, C. F. D. "Deacons in the New Testament." *Theology* Nov. 1955: 405 + .

Schurer, Emil. *The History of the Jewish People in the Age of Jesus Christ*, Vol. 2. Edinburgh: T. & T. Clark, 1979.

Schweizer, Eduard. *Church Order in the New Testament. Studies in Biblical Theology No. 32*. Trans. Frank Clarke. London: SCM, 1961.

Skemp, J. B. "Service to the Needy in the Graeco-Roman World." *Service in Christ: Essays Presented to Karl Barth on his 80th Birthday*. Ed. J. I. McCord and J. H. L. Parker. London: Epworth, 1966. 17 + .

Verner, David C. *The Household of God*. Chico, CA: Scholars, 1983.

G. Patristic Studies

Balsamon. As quoted in *Nicene and Post-Nicene Fathers*, Vol. 14. Grand Rapids: Eerdmans, 1979. 130.

Bingham, Joseph. *The Antiquities of the Christian Church: The Works of Joseph Bingham*. London: Robert Knaplock, 1726.

Bligh, John. "Deacons in the Latin West." *Theology* November 1955: 421 + .

Davies, J. G. "Deacons, Deaconesses and the Minor Order in the Patristic Period." *Journal of Ecclesiastical History* 1963: 1 + .

Gillet, Lev. "Deacons in the Orthodox East." *Theology* Nov. 1955: 415 + .

Halton, Thomas. "The Kairos of the Mass and the Deacon in John Chrysostom." *Diakonia: Studies in Honor of Robert T. Meyer*. Ed. Thomas Halton and Joseph P. Williman. Washington: Catholic Univ. of America, 1986. 53 + .

Hardy, Edward Rochie. "Deacons in History and Practice." *The Diaconate Now.* Ed. R. T. Nolan. Washington: Corpus, 1968. 11+.

Hennessey, Lawrence R. "*Diakonia* and *Diakonoi* in the Pre-Nicene Church." *Diakonia: Studies in Honor of Robert T. Meyer.* Ed. Thomas Halton and Joseph P. Williman. Washington: Catholic Univ. of America, 1986. 60+.

Hunermann, Peter. "Conclusions Regarding the Female Diaconate." *Theological Studies* June 1975: 325+.

Reicke, Bo. "Deacons in the New Testament and in the Early Church." *The Ministry of Deacons.* Geneva: World Council of Churches, 1965, 8+.

Riddle, M. B. "Introductory Notice to Constitutions of the Holy Apostles." *The Ante-Nicene Fathers,* Vol. 7. Grand Rapids: Eerdmans, 1981. 387+.

Symonds, R. P. "Deacons in the Early Church." *Theology* Nov. 1955: 408+.

Turner, Cuthbert Hamilton. "Ministries of Women in the Primitive Church: Widow, Deaconess, and Virgin in the First Four Christian Centuries." *Catholic and Apostolic.* Ed. Herbert Newell Bate. London: A. R. Mowbray & Co., 1931. 316+. (This is a reprint of the same article from *Constructive Quarterly* Sept. 1919.

H. Diaconal Historical Reviews

Barnett, James M. *The Diaconate: A Full and Equal Order.* Minneapolis: Winston, 1981.

Cross, F. D. "Deacon." *The Oxford Dictionary of the Christian Church.* London: Oxford University, 1974. 379.

---. "Deaconess." *The Oxford Dictionary of the Christian Church.* London: Oxford University, 1974. 380.

Danielou, Jean. *The Ministry of Women in the Early Church.* Trans. Glyn Simon. Leighton Buzzard, England: Faith, 1974.

Davies, J. G. "Deaconess." *A Dictionary of Christian Theology.* Ed. Alan Richardson. Philadelphia: Westminster, 1969. 87+.

Echlin, Edward P. *The Deacon in the Church.* Staten Island: Alba House, 1971.

Gryson, Roger. *The Ministry of Women in the Early Church.* Trans. Jean Laporte and Mary Louise Hall. Collegeville, MN: Liturgical, 1976.

Martimort, Aime Georges. *Deaconesses: An Historical Study.* Trans. K. D. Whitehead. San Francisco: Ignatius, 1986.

Prohl, Russell C. *Woman in the Church.* Grand Rapids: Eerdmans, 1957.

Ryrie, Charles Caldwell. *The Role of Women in the Church.* Chicago: Moody, 1958.

Schaff, D. S. "Deaconess." *The New Schaff-Herzog Encyclopedia of Religious Knowledge,* Vol. 3. Grand Rapids: Baker, 1963. 374+.

Schaff, Philip. "Deacon." *The New Schaff-Herzog Religious Encyclopedia,* Vol. 3. Grand Rapids: Baker, 1963. 370.

Stam, J. "Deacon, Deaconess." *The Zondervan Pictorial Encyclopedia of the Bible,* Vol. 2. Grand Rapids: Zondervan, 1975.

I. Reformation and Denominational Development

Agar, Frederick A. *The Deacon at Work.* Valley Forge: Judson, 1923.

Atkinson, James. "*Diakonia* at the time of the Reformation: Luther." *Service in Christ: Essays Presented to Karl Barth on his 80th Birthday.* Ed. J. I. McCord and J. H. L. Parker. London: Epworth, 1966. 80 +.

Baptism, Eucharist and Ministry. Geneva: World Council of Churches, 1982.

Beasley-Murray, George R. "The Diaconate in Baptist Churches." *The Ministry of Deacons.* Geneva: World Council of Churches, 1965, 72 +.

Bishops' Committee on the Liturgy. *The Deacon, Minister of Word and Sacrament.* Washington, D.C.: United States Catholic Conference, 1979.

Bishops' Committee on the Permanent Diaconate. *Permanent Deacons in the United States:* Guidelines on their Formation and Ministry. Washington, D.C.: United States Catholic Conference, 1971.

---. *A National Study of the Permanent Diaconate in the United States.* Washington, D.C.: United States Catholic Conference, 1981.

Biskupek, Aloysius. *Deaconship.* St. Louis: Herder, 1944.

The Book of Discipline of the United Methodist Church - 1984. Nashville: United Methodist, 1984.

Bouman, Stephen Paul. "The Diaconate: A Gift We offer the New." *Lutheran Perspective* 26 Oct. 1987: 14 +.

Bridel, Claude. "Note on the Diaconal Ministry in the Reformed Churches." *The Ministry of Deacons.* Geneva: World Council of Churches, 1965. 58 +.

Bromiley, G. W. *Christian Ministry.* Grand Rapids: Eerdmans, 1959.

Burroughs, P. E. *Honoring the Deaconship.* Nashville: Sunday School Board of the Southern Baptist Convention, 1929.

Calvin, John. *Calvin: Institutes of the Christian Religion.* Ed. John T. McNeill, trans. Fordes Lewis Battles. *The Library of Christian Classics,* XXI. London: SCM, 1960.

The Constitution of the Presbyterian Church (U. S. A.): Part II, Book of Order. New York: Office of the General Assembly, 1987.

Dana, H. E. *A Manual of Ecclesiology.* Kansas City: Central Seminary, 1944.

Deweese, Charles W. "Deaconesses in Baptist History: A Preliminary Study." *Baptist History and Heritage* Jan. 1977: 52+.

---. *The Emerging Role of Deacons*. Nashville: Broadman, 1979.

Dougherty, Mary Agnes. "The Methodist Deaconess: A Case of Religious Feminism." *Methodist History* Jan. 1983: 90+.

Dowd, Dick. "Too Many Deacons? Or Not Enough?" *Deacon Digest* May 1986: 8.

Every, George. "The Diaconate in the Anglican Communion." *The Ministry of Deacons*. Geneva: World Council of Churches, 1965. 45+.

Forshee, Howard B. *The Ministry of the Deacon*. Nashville: Convention, 1968.

Gibble, June A. "Remembering How It Was: An Interview with John Lapp and Clarence Kulp." *Called to Caregiving*. Ed. June A. Gibble and Fred W. Swartz. Elgin, IL: Brethren, 1987. 39+.

Gore, Charles. *The Church and the Ministry*. London: SPCK, 1949.

Graves, Allen W. *A Church at Work: A Handbook of Church Polity*. Nashville: Convention, 1972.

Harmon, Nolan B. "Deacon." *The Encyclopedia of World Methodism*, Vol. 1. Nashville: United Methodist, 1974. 639.

Henderson, Robert. "Notes on the Diaconate in American Presbyterianism." *The Ministry of Deacons*. Geneva: World Council of Churches, 1965. 63+.

Hort, Fenton John Anthony. *The Christian Ecclesia*. London: MacMillan, 1897.

Howell, R. B. C. *The Deaconship*. Valley Forge: Judson, 1847.

Huffman, Cathy Simmons. "Deacon." *The Brethren Encyclopedia*, Vol. 1. Philadelphia: Brethren Encyclopedia, 1983. 368.

---. "Deaconess." *The Brethren Encyclopedia*, Vol. 1. Philadelphia: Brethren Encyclopedia, 1983. 369.

Joanna, Sister. "The Deaconess Community of St. Andrew." *Journal of Ecclesiastical History* 1961: 215+.

Kingdon, Robert M. "Social Welfare in Calvin's Geneva." *The American Historical Review* Feb. 1971: 52+.

Krimm, Herbert. "The Diaconate in the Lutheran Church." *The Ministry of Deacons*. Geneva: World Council of Churches, 1965. 54+.

Kung, Hans. *Structures of the Church*. New York: Nelson, 1964.

Luther, Martin. *Luther's Works*. Ed. Abdel Ross Wentz and Helmut T. Lehmann. Philadelphia: Muhlenberg, 1959.

Maring, Norman H. and Winthrop S. Hudson. *A Baptist Manual of Polity and Practice.* Valley Forge: Judson, 1963.

McMinn, J. B. "Deacon." *Encyclopedia of Southern Baptists,* Vol. 1. Nashville: Broadman, 1958. 352.

Naylor, Robert E. *The Baptist Deacon.* Nashville: Broadman, 1955.

Neff, Christian Weierhof. "Deaconess." *The Mennonite Encyclopedia,* Vol. 2. Scottdale, PA: Mennonite, 1956. 22.

Neff, Christian Weierhof, and H. S. Bender. "Deacon." *The Mennonite Encyclopedia,* Vol. 2. Scottdale, PA: Mennonite, 1956. 21.

Norpel, Mary Louise. *The Relevance of the Lutheran Deaconess Tradition in America for Post-Conciliar Religious Life among Roman Catholic Women.* Ph.D. Diss. Catholic Univ. of America, 1971.

Nowell, Robert. *The Ministry of Service: Deacons in the Contemporary Church.* New York: Herder and Herder, 1968.

O'Rourke, J. J. "Deacon." *New Catholic Encyclopedia,* Vol. 4. New York: McGraw-Hill, 1967. 667.

Rand, Laurence. "Ordination of Women to the Diaconate." *Communio* Winter 1981: 370 + .

Reid, J. K. S. "*Diakonia* in the Thought of Calvin." *Service in Christ: Essays Presented to Karl Barth on his 80th Birthday.* Ed. J. I. McCord and J. H. L. Parker. London: Epworth, 1966. 101 + .

Riley, T. J. "Deacon." *New Catholic Encyclopedia,* Vol. 4. New York: McGraw-Hill, 1967. 668.

Robinson, Cecilia. *The Ministry of Deaconesses.* London: Methuen, 1914.

Ross, J. M. "Deacons in Protestantism." *Theology* Nov. 1955: 429 + .

---. "A Reconsideration of the Diaconate." *Scottish Journal of Theology* June 1959: 151 + .

Smith, Lena Mae. "Deaconess." *The Mennonite Encyclopedia,* Vol. 2. Scottdale, PA: Mennonite, 1956. 22.

Smith, Michael A. "Baptist Deacons in the Nineteenth Century." *The Quarterly Review* Oct.-Dec. 1982: 67 + .

Thurston, Herbert. "Deacon." *The Catholic Encyclopedia,* Vol. 4. New York: Appleton, 1908. 647 + .

---. "Deaconesses." *The Catholic Encyclopedia,* Vol. 4. New York: Appleton, 1908. 651 + .

Truesdell, Mary P. "The Office of Deaconess." *The Diaconate Now.* Ed. R. T. Nolan. Washington: Corpus, 1968. 143 + .

Vischer, Lukas. *The Problem of the Diaconate. The Ministry of Deacons.* Geneva: World Council of Churches, 1965. 14 + .

Wakefield, Gordon S. "*Diakonia* in the Methodist Church Today." *Service in Christ: Essays Presented to Karl Barth on his 80th Birthday.* Ed. J. I. McCord and J. H. L. Parker. London: Epworth, 1966. 182 + .

Weiser, Frederick S. "The Origin of the Modern Diaconate for Women." *Servants of Christ: Deaconesses in Renewal.* Ed. Donald G. Bloesch. Minneapolis: Bethany Fellowship, 1971. 15 + .

Whitley, W. T. *The Works of John Smyth.* Cambridge: University, 1915.

Winter, Sister Mildred. "Deacon." *The Encyclopedia of the Lutheran Church*, Vol. 1. Minneapolis: Augsburg, 1965. 659.

---. "Deaconess." *The Encyclopedia of the Lutheran Church,* Vol. 1. Minneapolis: Augsburg, 1965. 659 + .

Yule, George. "The Puritans." *Service in Christ: Essays Presented to Karl Barth on his 80th Birthday.* Ed. J. I. McCord and J. H. L. Parker. London: Epworth, 1966. 122 + .

J. Restoration History

Bailey, Fred Arthur. Ph. D,. History Dept., A. C. U. Personal interview. 24 Feb., 1988.

---. *The Status of Women In the Disciples of Christ Movement, 1865 - 1900.* Ph.D. Diss. U. of Tenn., Knoxville, 1979.

---. "Woman's Superiority in Disciple Thought, 1865-1900." *Restoration Quarterly* 32:3 (1980): 151 + .

Brown, John T. *Churches of Christ.* Louisville: John P. Morton, 1904.

Garrett, Leroy. *The Stone-Campbell Movement.* Joplin, MO: College, 1981.

Harrell, David Edwin, Jr. "The Sectional Origins of the Churches of Christ." *Journal of Southern History* Aug. 1964: 261 + .

---. *The Social Sources of Division in the Disciples of Christ 1865-1900.* Atlanta: Publishing Systems, 1973.

Hughes, Richard T. "The Role of Theology in the Nineteenth Century Division of Disciples of Christ." *American Religion, 1974.* Tallahassee: Am. Acad. of Religion, 1974.

---. "Twenty-Five Years of Restoration Scholarship: The Churches of Christ - Part I." *Restoration Quarterly* 25:4 (1982): 233 + .

---. "Twenty-Five Years of Restoration Scholarship: The Churches of Christ - Part II." *Restoration Quarterly* 26:1 (1983): 39 + .

Humble, B. J. *The Story of the Restoration.* Austin, TX: Firm Foundation, 1969.

Stroop, J. Ridley. *Restoration Ideas on Church Organization*. Nashville: Stroop.

K. Nineteenth Century Culture and Feminism

Blauvelt, Martha Tomhave. "Women and Revivalism." *Women and Religion in America,* Ed. Rosemary Radford Ruether and Rosemary Skinner Keller. San Francisco: Harper & Row, 1981. 1:1+.

Boles, John B. History Dept., Rice Un. Personal interview Apr. 5, 1987.

Douglas, Ann. *The Feminization of American Culture*. New York: Knopf, 1977.

Friedman, Jean E. *The Enclosed Garden: Women and Community in the Evangelical South 1830-1900.* Chapel Hill, NC: Univ. of N. C., 1985.

James, Larry. Minister and Ph. D. candidate, Richardson, TX. Personal interview Apr. 1, 1988.

Keller, Rosemary Skinner. "Lay Women in the Protestant Tradition." *Women and Religion in America*, Ed. Rosemary Radford Ruether and Rosemary Skinner Keller. San Francisco: Harper & Row, 1981. 1:242+.

Lerner, Gerda. "The Lady and the Mill Girl." *A Heritage of Her Own,* Ed. Nancy F. Cott and Elizabeth H. Pleck. New York: Simon and Schuster, 1979. 182+.

Loveland, Anne C. *Southern Evangelicals and the Social Order 1800-1860.* Baton Rouge, LA: Louisiana State Univ., 1980.

Martin, Patricia Summerlin. *Hidden Work: Baptist Women in Texas, 1880-1920.* Ph.D. Diss. Rice Univ., Houston, 1982.

Niebuhr, H. Richard. *The Social Sources of Denominationalism*. New York: World, 1957.

Scott, Anne Firor. *The Southern Lady.* Chicago: Univ. of Chicago, 1970.

Welter, Barbara. "The Cult of True Womanhood: 1820-1860." *American Quarterly* Summer 1966: 151+.

L. General Periodicals - Disciples

Abernathy, W. N. "Should All Churches have Deacons?" *Gospel Advocate* 31 May 1923: 539.

Barnes, Justus M. "Deacons." *Gospel Advocate* 19 Jan. 1893: 43.

---. "To J. F. Love, M. L. Strong, and L. A. Dale." *Gospel Advocate* 16 May 1895: 311.

---. "To J. F. Love, M. L. Strong, and L. A. Dale." *Gospel Advocate* 23 May 1895: 323.

Beckholt, I. H. "Phoebe Was a Deaconess." *Christian Standard* 27 June 1936: 635.

Boles, H. Leo. "Can An Unmarried Man Be a Scriptural Elder?" *Gospel Advocate* 9 Dec. 1920.

---. "The Deacons." *Gospel Advocate* 27 Mar. 1941: 292 + .

---. "Deaconesses." *Gospel Advocate* 3 Apr. 1941: 317.

---. "Elders." *Gospel Advocate* 14 Oct. 1920: 1188.

---. "Some Important Questions." *Gospel Advocate* 6 Jan. 1944: 5.

Briney, J. B. "Several Questions Considered." *Christian Standard* 2 Apr. 1927: 318.

Burnett, Thomas R. "Our Budget." *Christian Evangelist* 28 July 1892: 472, as cited in Harrell "Sectional" 271.

C., S. [Unnamed]. "The Elder's Office." *The Millennial Harbinger* 7.6 (1857): 375 + .

Campbell, Alexander. "Church Order." *The Millennial Harbinger* 4.2 (1847): 93 + .

---. "Church Organization, No. 2." *The Millennial Harbinger* 3:4 (1853): 183 + .

---. "Church Organization, No. 3." *The Millennial Harbinger* 3:5 (1853): 241 + .

---. "Church Organization, No. 5." *The Millennial Harbinger* (1849): 459 + .

---. "Ministers' and Deacons' Children." *The Millennial Harbinger* 1.6 (1858): 336.

---. "Nature of the Christian Organization, No. 12." *The Millennial Harbinger* 7.3 (1843): 133 + .

---. "Order." *The Millennial Harbinger* 6.10 (1835).

---. "The Restoration of the Ancient Order of Things, No. XIV, The Bishop's Office - No. 3." *The Christian Baptist* 7 Aug. 1826: 2 + .

---. "The Restoration of the Ancient Order of Things, No. XIX, The Deacon's Office." *The Christian Baptist* 7 Aug. 1826: 77 + .

---. "The Restoration of the Ancient Order of Things, No. XXXII, Official Names and Titles." *The Christian Baptist* 3 Aug. 1829: 17 + .

Campbell, Thomas. "Queries by A. S. H." *The Millennial Harbinger* 2.5 (1845), 220 + .

Challen, James. "Chronicles: Deacon's Office." *The Millennial Harbinger* 37.2 (1866): 56 + .

Cuff, R. P. "The Qualifications and Duties of Deacons." *Gospel Advocate* 29 July 1948: 738 + .

Davis, Morrison M. "Deaconesses." *Christian Standard* 19 Feb. 1916: 711.

Dennis, Fred E. "Deacons and their Qualifications." *Gospel Advocate* 26 Aug. 1954: 671 + .

Durst, John S. "Deacons." *Gospel Advocate* 26 Sept. 1883: 612.

E., D. [Unnamed]. "Christian Order." *The Evangelist* 4.8 (1835): 186 + .

---. "Christian Order, No. 3." *The Evangelist* 4.11 (1835): 241 + .

Errett, Isaac. "Deaconesses." *Christian Standard* 7 June 1873: 180.

---. "Deaconesses." *Christian Standard* 14 June 1873: 188.

---. "The Gospel Advocate." *Christian Standard* 16 Feb. 1867: 52.

---. "Querists' Drawer." *Christian Standard* 28 Sept. 1867.

Fanning, Tolbert. Cited by J. Ridley Stroop, *Restoration Ideas on Church Organization*. Nashville: Stroop. 215.

---. "The Church of Christ in History No. 4." *The Religious Historian* Aug. 1873: 225+.

---. "The Church of Christ in History No. 6." *The Religious Historian* Oct. 1873: 289+.

---. "The Church of Christ in History No. 7." *The Religious Historian* Nov. 1873: 321+.

---. "The Church of Christ in History No. 8." *The Religious Historian* Dec. 1873: 353+.

---. "Church Officers, No. 3, Deacons." *Gospel Advocate* Feb. 1859: 83+.

---. "Ministers of Christ." *The Religious Historian* Feb. 1873: 55+.

---. "Officers of the Church and their Ordination, No. 3." *Gospel Advocate* 29 Aug. 1867: 681+.

---. "Official Service in the Church." *Gospel Advocate* 13 Nov. 1866: 724+.

Ferguson, Everett, Tom Olbricht, and R. L. Roberts, Jr. "The Journal of the Church of Christ in Kelton, Pennsylvania." *Restoration Quarterly* 13.4 (1970): 224+.

Fulford, Hugh. "Deacons: Their Work and Qualifications." *Gospel Advocate* 28 Feb. 1974: 135.

Gardner, E. Claude. "Deacons." *Gospel Advocate* 18 June 1959: 392. Reprinted 1 Feb. 1968: 70.

Hadwin, D. H. "The Duties of Deacons." *Gospel Advocate* 16 Sept. 1937: 743.

Hines, John T. "Queries." *Gospel Advocate* 31 Mar. 1932: 395.

"Items from Correspondents." *Christian Standard* 19 Sept. 1868: 301.

James, B. B. "Deacons - Their Rank and Work." *Gospel Advocate* 1 July 1965: 425.

Lanier, Roy H., Sr. "Are Deaconesses Scriptural?" *Firm Foundation* 8 Aug. 1967: 505.

Lard, Moses. "Should Woman Speak in the Church." *Apostolic Times* 9 Apr. 1874: 1.

Lipscomb, A. B. "The New Testament Deacon." *Gospel Advocate* 20 Jan. 1916: 58. (Reprinted 2 Sept. 1920: 849.)

Lipscomb, David. "Appointment of Elders and Deacons." *Gospel Advocate* 3 July 1902: 424.

---. "Duties of Elders and Deacons." *Gospel Advocate* 20 Jan. 1898: 36.

---. "Is a Deacon a Deacon for Life?" *Gospel Advocate* 27 July 1905: 468.

---. "Queries." *Gospel Advocate* 1883: 499.

---. "Queries." *Gospel Advocate* 1 Sept. 1898: 555.

---. "Race Prejudice." *Gospel Advocate* 21 Feb. 1878: 121.

---. "Should Women Preach Publicly?" *Gospel Advocate* 5 Aug. 1891: 486.

---. "The Truth of History." *Gospel Advocate* 14 July 1892: 436.

---. "Woman's Work." *Gospel Advocate* 26 Mar. 1874: 305.

---. "Woman's Work." *Gospel Advocate* 1 Dec. 1892: 756+.

---. "Women as Public Preachers." *Gospel Advocate* 28 June 1894: 398.

Mathews, Robert T. "The Office of Deaconess, Scriptural." *Christian Standard* 6 May 1897: 219.

McGarvey, John W. "Deaconesses." *Christian Standard* 22 Nov. 1902: 1616.

---. "Deaconesses." *Christian Standard* 3 Feb. 1906: 166.

McNicol, Allan. "A Hierarchy or Mere Functional Leadership: Is There another Model for the Ministry?" *Institute for Christian Studies Faculty Bulletin* Nov. 1986: 37+.

McQuiddy, J. C. "Query Department." *Gospel Advocate* 18 May 1916: 494.

---. "Query Department." *Gospel Advocate* 16 Aug. 1917: 795.

---. "Query Department." *Gospel Advocate* 4 Mar. 1920: 222.

---. "Query Department." *Gospel Advocate* 14 Oct. 1920: 999.

---. "Query Department." *Gospel Advocate* 4 Nov. 1920: 1079.

---. "Query Department." *Gospel Advocate* 27 Jan. 1921.

---. "Query Department." *Gospel Advocate* 9 June 1921: 550.

---. "Query Department." *Gospel Advocate* 6 July 1922: 634.

Miller, John C. "The Deacon's Office." *The Millennial Harbinger* 41.3 (1870): 136+.

---. "The Deacon's Office Again." *The Millennial Harbinger* 41.5 (1870): 250+.

Milligan, Robert. "The Permanent Orders of the Christian Ministry - Of Elders." *The Millennial Harbinger* 5.12 (1855): 685+.

---.   "The Permanent Orders of the Christian Ministry - Of Deacons." *The Millennial Harbinger* 5.11 (1855): 623+.

Nichol, C. R. "The Deacon." *Gospel Advocate* 19 Apr. 1928: 363.

Nichols, Gus. "Queries Answers." *Gospel Advocate* 16 Dec. 1971: 797.

Oliver, R. C. "The Deacon and the Mystery." *Gospel Advocate* 22 Apr. 1971: 244+.

Ottinger, Dan J. "Misread." *Christian Standard* 16 Jan. 1937: 23.

---.   "Readers' Forum." *Christian Standard* 30 May 1936: 531+.

Owen, Dan R. "Ministers, Servants, and Deacons." *Firm Foundation* 26 Jan. 1982: 54.

Pendleton, W. K. "The Church of the New Testament." *The Millennial Harbinger* 37.8 (1866): 371+.

---.   "Deacons - Should the Church have Them?" *The Millennial Harbinger* 41.1 (1870): 50+.

---.   "Discipline, No. 7." *The Millennial Harbinger* 5.5 (1848): 289+.

---.   "Reply." *The Millennial Harbinger* 41.3 (1870): 141+.

Richardson, Robert. "Order - No. 3." *Millennial Harbinger* 11.7 (1876): 516+.

Scott, Walter. "An Address." *The Evangelist* 6 Jan. 1834: 1+.

---.   "Letters." *The Evangelist* 1 Mar. 1840: 72.

---.   "Query." *The Evangelist* 7 Dec. 1835: 264+.

Sewell, Elisha G. "Appointment of Overseers and Deacons, and the How of it." *Gospel Advocate* 25 Mar. 1891: 182+.

---.   "The Apostolic Church, Work of the Deacon." *Gospel Advocate* 23 Feb. 1893: 121.

---.   "Deaconesses." *Gospel Advocate* 27 June 1912: 761.

---.   "Diakoneoo." *Gospel Advocate* 16 June 1892: 377.

---.   "Elders and Eeacons" [sic.]. *Gospel Advocate* 12 Nov. 1884: 724.

---.   "Ordination of Church Officers." *Gospel Advocate* 26 June 1882: 403.

---.   "The Seven at Jerusalem." *Gospel Advocate* 23 June 1892: 388+.

---.   "The Tract on Church Organization Again." *Gospel Advocate* 10 June 1897: 356.

---.   "What is the Duty of Deacons in the Congregations?" *Gospel Advocate* 25 May 1905: 328.

Sneed, A. B. "As to Deaconesses." *Christian Standard* 13 Sept. 1930: 891.

Thompson, James W. "Authority and Leadership in the New Testament." *Institute for Christian Studies Faculty Bulletin* Nov. 1986: 20 + .

Thornberry, James L. "The North East Iowa Christian Association." *Gospel Advocate* 8 Feb. 1883: 89.

Vaughan, J. Roy. "The Deacons." *Gospel Advocate* 20 Sept. 1951: 594.

Walk, David. "Deaconesses." *Christian Standard* 28 Nov. 1868: 379.

Wells, L. C. "Elders, Deacons, Evangelists." *Gospel Advocate* 19 Mar. 1884: 178 + .

Whiteside, R. L. "Deaconesses." *Gospel Advocate* 24 Aug. 1939: 799.

---.   "Queries and Answers Department." *Gospel Advocate* 16 June 1938: 564.

Woods, Guy N. "Biblical Criticism." *Gospel Advocate* 17 Feb. 1977: 103 +

---.   "Questions and Answers." *Gospel Advocate* 24 Jan. 1980: 35.

M. Commentaries - Disciples

Batey, Richard A. *The Letter of Paul to The Romans. The Living Word Commentary.* Austin, TX: Sweet, 1969.

Coffman, James Burton. *Commentary on 1 & 2 Thessalonians, 1 & 2 Timothy, Titus & Philemon.* Austin, TX: Firm Foundation, 1978.

---.   *Commentary on Romans.* Austin, TX: Firm Foundation, 1973.

DeWelt, Don. *Paul's Letters to Timothy and Titus.* Joplin, MO: College, 1961.

---.   *Romans Realized.* Joplin, MO: College, 1959.

Grubbs, Isaiah Boone. *Commentary on Paul's Epistle to the Romans.* Nashville: Gospel Advocate, 1913.

Haldane, Robert. *An Exposition of Romans.* MacDonald, 1958.

Lard, Moses E. *Commentary on Paul's Letter to Romans.* Delight, AR: Gospel Light, 1875.

Lipscomb, David, edited with additional notes by J. W. Shepherd. *A Commentary on the New Testament Epistles, I Timothy.* Nashville: Gospel Advocate, 1942.

McClish, Dub. "Greetings - Along with a Warning - To Those in Rome (Rom. 16:1-20)." *The Book of Romans.* Ed. Garland Elkins and Thomas B. Warren. Jonesboro, AR: National Christian, 1983.

McGarvey, John W., and Philip Y. Pendleton. *Thessalonians, Corinthians, Galatians, and Romans.* Cincinnati: Standard.

Roberts, J. W. *Letters to Timothy. The Living Word.* Austin, TX: Sweet, 1964.

Spain, Carl. *The Letters of Paul to Timothy and Titus.* Austin, TX: Sweet, 1970.

Thomas, J. D. *Romans. The Living Word.* Austin, TX: Sweet, 1965.

Whiteside, Robert L. *Paul's Letter to the Saints at Rome.* Clifton, TX: Nichol, 1945.

N. General Works - Disciples

Allen, C. Leonard, and Richard T. Hughes. *Discovering Our Roots: The Ancestry of Churches of Christ.* Abilene, TX: A. C. U., 1988.

Baird, James O. "Role for Women in the Church." *Introducing the Church of Christ.* Ft. Worth: Star Bible, 1981. 121 + .

Bales, James D. *The Deacon and His Work.* Shreveport, LA: Lambert, 1967.

Brewer, G. C. *The Model Church.* Nashville: Gospel Advocate, 1957.

Campbell, Alexander. *The Christian System.* Nashville: Gospel Advocate, 1964 (written 1835, 2nd ed. 1839).

Casey, Michael Wilson. *The Development of Necessary Inference in the Hermeneutics of the Disciples of Christ/Churches of Christ.* Ph.D Diss. U. of Pittsburg, 1986.

Caskey, Guy. *What Can a Christian Woman Do in the Church?* Arlington, TX: Mission.

Davis, Morrison M. *The Eldership.* Cincinnati: Standard, 1913.

Dehoff, George W. *Gospel Sermons.* Murfreesboro, TN: Dehoff, 1953.

Deveny, Albert Lewis. *The Church and It's Elders.* Austin, TX: Deveny, 1941.

Dicus, A. W. *Church Leadership.* Tampa, FL: Dicus.

Echols, Eldred. "Deaconesses in the Early Church." Unpublished study guide, Feb. 1987, and other correspondence.

Flatt, Ben S. "Deacons Serve the Church." *Introducing the Church of Christ.* Ft. Worth: Star Bible, 1981. 81 + .

Gibson, John Paul. *The Church at Work.* Kansas City: Old Paths, 1947.

Gray, H. H., Jr. *Church Organization and Government.* Dallas: Buchanan Supply, 1947.

Harding, R. C. *Handbook for Elders and Deacons.* Cincinnati: Standard, 1932.

Hayden, W. L. *Church Polity.* Chicago: Clarke, 1894. Reprinted Kansas City: Old Paths.

Hobbs, A. I. "Ecclesiastic Polity." *The Western Preacher.* Ed. Elder J. M. Mathes. St. Louis: Christian, 1888. 64 + .

Kendrick, Carroll. *Live Religious Issues of the Day.* Nashville: Gospel Advocate, 1890.

Lappin, S. S. *The Training of the Church*. Joplin, MO: College, reprint of 1911.

Lightfoot, Neil R. *The Role of Women*. Memphis: Student Association (Harding Graduate School of Religion), 1978.

Lipscomb, David and E. G. Sewell. *Queries and Answers*. Ed. M. C. Kurfees. Nashville: McQuiddy, 1921.

Lyles, Cleon. *Bigger Men for Better Churches*. Little Rock: Cleon Lyles, 1971.

McGarvey, John W. *A Treatise on The Eldership*. Murfreesboro, TN: Dehoff, 1950 (Reprint of 1870 edition).

Milligan, Robert. *The Scheme of Redemption*. Nashville: Gospel Advocate, 1868.

Munnell, Thomas. *The Care of all the Churches*. St. Louis: Christian, 1888.

Nichol, C. R. *God's Woman*. Clifton, TX: Nichol, 1938.

Nichol, C. R., and R. L. Whiteside. *Sound Doctrine*, Vol. 3. Clifton, TX: Nichol, 1923.

Payne, E. K *Women in the Early Church*. St. Louis: United Christian Missionary Society.

Sommer, Daniel. *Concerning Church Government*. Indianapolis: Octographic Review, 1910.

Stevenson, Dwight G. *Lexington Theological Seminary, 1865-1965*. St. Louis: 1964.

Stroop, J. Ridley. *The Church of the Bible*. Montgomery, AL: Bible and School Supply, 1962.

Tyler, Benjamin B. "Organization." *The Old Faith Restated*, Vol. 2. Ed. J. H. Garrison. St. Louis: Christian, 1891. 350+.

Wharton, Edward C. *The Church of Christ*. West Monroe, LA: Howard, 1970.

Whitfield, Thomas C. "Should We have Deaconesses Today?" *The Eldership*. Nashville: Williams, 1950. 180+.

Wilson, L. R. *Congregational Development.* Nashville: Gospel Advocate, 1959.

Winkler, Herbert E. *The Eldership*. Nashville: Williams, 1950.

O. Misc. Tapes and Interviews - Disciples

Ferguson, Everett, Ph. D. Bible Dept., A. C. U. Letter to author. Dec. 31, 1987.

Harper, E. R. "Elders." Printed sermon text, Broadway Church of Christ, Lubbock, TX, 20 Oct. 1950.

Howard, Oliver. "How Narrow is the Way?" 45th Annual Pepperdine Univ. Bible Lectureship. Malibu, CA: April 22, 1988.

Lewis, Jack P., Ph. D. Bible Dept., Harding Univ. "Deacons." Photocopy, sermon text. 1987.

Olbricht, Thomas, Ph. D. Chairman, Religion Division, Pepperdine University. Letters to author. 1987.

Osburn, Carroll, Ph. D. "When Ministry Gets Tough." 70th Annual Bible Lectureship, Abilene Christian University. Abilene, TX: 22 Feb. 1988.

Oster, Richard, Ph.D. Bible Dept., Harding Univ. Letter to author. April 8, 1987.

P. British Materials

Brown, Albert. "The Place of Women in the Ministry of the Church." *Conference of Churches of Christ [Great Britain]* 1919. 26+.

Day, Fred C. "The Church of Christ: Its Government." *The Bible and The Church. Hindley Bible School,* 1946. Hindley, Lancs., England: L. Morgan, 1946.

King, David. *Memoirs of David King.* Birmingham, England: W. E. Harris, circa. 1890.

King, David, ed. "Christ and the Church." *Old Paths* Apr. 1868: 325.

Nisbet, Joe. "Spreading the Kingdom in the United Kingdom." 70th Annual Bible Lectureship, Abilene Christian University. Abilene, TX: 22 Feb. 1988, personal interviews and letters.

Winstanley, Albert Edward. British Evangelist. Letter to author. Sept. 1987.

Worgan, Frank. British Evangelist. Personal interview. Feb. 1988.

Q. Collingswood, New Jersey

Fellowship. Newsletter of the Collingswood Church of Christ. 3 Nov. 1957.

Fellowship. Newsletter of the Collingswood Church of Christ. 10 Nov. 1957.

Finn, Mark. Minister, Collingswood, N. J. Letter to author. June 30, 1987.

Ficher, Heinz. Former elder, Collingswood, N.J. Letters to author. 1987.

Graham, Irene (Mrs. Ralph V.). Wife of former minister, Collingswood, N. J. Letters to author. 1987.

Graham, Ralph V. "Why I Left the Churches of Christ." *Voices of Concern.* Ed. Robert Meyers. St. Louis: Mission Messenger, 1966. 128+.

Milnamow, Louise. Former deaconess, Collingswood, N. J. Letters to author. 1987.

Power for Life. Order of Worship for Collingswood Church of Christ. 5 Jan. 1958.

Power for Life. Order of Worship for Collingswood Church of Christ. 12 Jan. 1958.